Heal Your Life

by Forgiving

Everything

Transcendence Toolbooks, vol 5

Heal Your Life *by* Forgiving Everything

KIM MICHAELS

Copyright © 2014 Kim Michaels. All rights reserved. No part of this book may be used, reproduced, translated, electronically stored or transmitted by any means except by written permission from the publisher. A reviewer may quote brief passages in a review.

MORE TO LIFE PUBLISHING

www.morepublish.com

For foreign and translation rights,

contact info@ morepublish.com

ISBN: 978-9949-518-49-4

Series ISBN: 978-9949-518-04-3

The information and insights in this book should not be considered as a form of therapy, advice, direction, diagnosis, and/or treatment of any kind. This information is not a substitute for medical, psychological, or other professional advice, counseling and care. All matters pertaining to your individual health should be supervised by a physician or appropriate health-care practitioner. No guarantee is made by the author or the publisher that the practices described in this book will yield successful results for anyone at any time. They are presented for informational purposes only, as the practice and proof rests with the individual.

For more information: *www.ascendedmasterlight.com* and *www.transcendencetoolbox.com*

CONTENTS

Introduction 7
1 | The Mindset That Leads to True Healing 11
2 | Invoking the Mindset of True Healing 17
3 | What Is True Healing? 33
4 | Invoking Healing Energy 41
5 | You Cannot Give Away What You Do not Own 59
6 | Invoking Freedom from Anger against God 73
7 | Invoking the Power of God in Me 91
8 | Reconnecting to Your Original Love 109
9 | Invoking My Original Love 119
10 | Total Forgiveness Leads to Total Freedom 137
11 | Invocation for Rising above Old Patterns 163
12 | Invocation for Accepting that I Am Alive 181
13 | Invocation for Raising My Life Experience 201
14 | Invocation for Accepting My True Identity 219
15 | Unconditional Forgiveness and Joy 237
16 | Invocation for Hearing the Inner Message 259
17 | Invocation for Letting the Past Go 277
18 | Invoking Freedom from Emotional Pain 295
19 | The Power of Unconditional Acceptance 313
20 | Invoking the Power of Unconditional Acceptance 325
21 | How to Rise above the Past 347
22 | Invoking Freedom from the Past 355

INTRODUCTION

The idea behind *Transcendence Toolbooks* is to give you effective tools for shifting your consciousness. This book contains spiritual teachings combined with techniques for invoking spiritual light. Both the teachings and the invocations are given by the universal spiritual teachers of humankind, also known as the ascended masters. The teachings will challenge your limiting beliefs about yourself and the exercises will help you transform the energies qualified through those beliefs. The combination of teachings and exercises has the potential to help you go through a real transformation that will bring you to a higher level of your personal path.

This book is designed to help you develop an entirely new and spiritually holistic approach to healing both physical and psychological problems. This approach is based on the fact that your physical body is the most dense part of a larger energy field. This energy field has four levels that form a hierarchical structure. At the highest level is your sense of identity. Then comes your thoughts, then your feelings and finally your physical body. The body is a product of the mental images and beliefs that you hold in the emotional, mental and identity levels. You subconsciously project these images through your mind and this produces your physical circumstances.

The key to healing any aspect of your life is to bring these subconscious images back to conscious awareness so you can dismiss those that do not get you where you want to go. This requires you to forgive other people, God and yourself. In this book you will find profound teachings and very effective exercises for applying this form of total forgiveness, thereby setting yourself free from all limiting images and beliefs from your past.

The teachings and tools in this book are given by representatives of the universal teachers of humankind, also known as the ascended masters. If you are not familiar with the ascended masters and their teachings, it is recommended that you read the book *The Power of Self*, which explains who the masters are, how they can help you and how you can follow the path to self-mastery offered by the masters. You can find more information on the website: *www.ascendedmasterlight.com*.

Using the tools in this book

Along with the teachings in this book, you will find a number of invocations. These invocations are meant to be read aloud by you. You can read them in a slow, meditative way or you can give them faster and with more power in your voice. There is no one right way to give the invocations, but they obviously cannot work unless you read them aloud. If you desire more detailed instructions for how to give invocations, please visit the website: *www.transcendencetoolbox.com*. You might also find it helpful to give the invocations along with a recording. You can purchase and download sound files of the invocations from the website: *www.morepublish.com*.

It is suggested that you study a chapter and then give the invocation or invocations that follow that chapter. It is

Introduction

recommended that you spend at least nine days using a particular invocation. You would therefore give a particular invocation once a day for nine days while studying the corresponding dictation. When there is more than one invocation following a chapter, give each invocation once a day for nine days before moving on to the next chapter.

It is recommended that you start by going through the dictations and invocations in the order they are listed. This would be a basic clearance that would give you an intuitive sense of which areas might need further clearance. You could then focus on one invocation and give it once a day for 33 consecutive days. You could also give a larger clearance by giving each invocation once a day for 33 days.

Another option is to give several invocations in a row. For example, you might give all invocations associated with a certain dictation. If you decide to do this, you do not have to give the opening prayer or the sealing with each invocation. You give an opening prayer when you start and the sealing after you finish the last invocation.

Feel free to be creative in the use of the tools included in this book. For example, you can give the matrix for another person or persons that you desire to see healed. You can even use the tools for clearing the planetary energy field or the energy field of your nation.

If you make the effort to overcome your initial resistance and build a momentum on giving the invocations, you will likely find that it is one of the most powerful and effective spiritual tools you have ever used. By combining this tool with a willingness to look into your own psyche and let go of limiting beliefs, you can turn your life into an upward spiral and heal both psychological and physical ailments. Truly, as the masters say, everything revolves around your free will. If you can accept that transcendence is possible for you, then the results *will* be manifest for you. Invoke, and ye shall receive. You will notice that some of the following chapters give only excerpts of a dictation. The reason is that this book is focused on the topic of healing through forgiveness and a dictation often talks about a broad range of topics. You can find the complete dictations at *www.ascendedmasterlight.com*. You can use the Search function to locate a particular dictation or you can use the master's name in combination with the date. The dictations in this book have been edited slightly in order to make them easier to read.

Please note that you will also find a set of powerful tools for healing in the book *The Song of Life Healing Matrix*, which is a good supplement to this book. Other books on healing are *Heal Yourself by Clearing the Chakras* and *Heal Your Life by Forgiving Everything*.

1 | THE MINDSET THAT LEADS TO TRUE HEALING

Excerpt from a dictation by Mother Mary, March 27, 2005.

People have taken on illness as a labor of love

I ask you to consider what it means to be healed. What is true healing? There is a difference between the outer will – the human will, the will of the ego – and the Will of God. How can you possibly understand healing unless you have attunement with the Will of God? How can you know what should be done to bring about healing, what type of healing should occur – or *if* healing should occur – if you are not attuned to the will of God?

For many thousands of years, the karma and the darkness on earth has been so heavy that many individual people have volunteered to take upon themselves a part of the weight of that karma. For many of them, it has manifested in the form of mental or physical illness. They have carried this in their bodies and in their minds, often for an entire lifetime. This is truly the story of those who are willing to sacrifice so that others may have an opportunity not to be so burdened by their karma and by the darkness that they could not possibly make any spiritual progress in that embodiment.

Even though Jesus has carried a large portion of the sins of the world for these 2,000 years, there have still been many individuals who have taken upon themselves a part of the darkness in order to give other people an opportunity of a lifetime where they were not so burdened in body and mind that they could not discover the spiritual side of life.

You must consider that for many people an illness, mental or physical, can be a labor of love. There is a possibility that the lifestream, at deeper levels, does not want to be healed of that illness or does not want to be healed just yet. Unless you are attuned to this in your own mind, how can you truly know? Thus, there is the possibility that you can seek to attain healing through unlawful means. This can be spiritually unlawful means whereby someone else takes upon themselves the karma that you have volunteered to bear. Or it can be unlawful material means whereby you use some form of modern medicine as a shortcut to either take away the pain or take away an illness that was meant to be borne.

Illness caused by other factors

There are other scenarios that come into play. For some people an illness is not caused by them carrying the karma of other people; it is caused by their own karma. Again, if they seek to pass it on to others, or if they seek to simply numb themselves to the pain, then *that* can be a form of dodging their responsibility.

Another common scenario is that an illness is actually created by the lower mind, by the ego. It is created in order to give the Conscious You an excuse for not taking command over its own destiny, for not taking responsibility for itself. The Conscious You reasons that "Because I have this or that illness, I cannot rise and become the Christ, I cannot fulfill my divine plan, I cannot challenge the darkness and take a stand for Light."

There are some instances where the person wants to be healed, but from a deeper level, the healing should not occur. There are some instances where the soul does not want to be healed, but the healing *should* occur because otherwise the Conscious You cannot grow.

The key to knowing is to tune in to the will of God. We have attempted to explain to you, from different perspectives, that the most important concept that you can know about the will of God is that the will of God is not outside of yourself, is not separate from your own will—the higher will of your conscious self and I AM Presence. You need to tune in to your own higher will and see what is God's will concerning any particular illness you have. If you feel in your heart that the healing *should* occur, then you can use appropriate means.

Taking on a certain state of consciousness

You also need to consider that any physical illness, any mental illness, is the expression of a particular state of consciousness. In some cases that state of consciousness is created by your own ego, and it is your responsibility to take care of it because truly it is something you have created from inside your own being. However, for many of you, who are open to the spiritual path, there is a different scenario that is very likely.

When you step back and look at planet earth from a higher perspective, you see that there are many different forms and states of consciousness on this planet that are expressions of the human consciousness, aspects of the human consciousness. Each of those states of consciousness is the outpicturing in form of a particular lie that springs from the mind of anti-christ, the anti-mind.

For each of these lies, there is a certain group of lifestreams who have bought into that lie. They have believed that lie and have absorbed it into their sense of identity. They believe that, because of this or that condition or expression, they cannot rise beyond a certain level, they cannot become the Christ in embodiment, they cannot be who they are in God here on earth. These lifestreams – once they accept this lie at the level of their identity bodies – have no way of freeing themselves by their own internal power.

The lifestream is trapped in the consciousness that Jesus called "Death." How is that lifestream to be saved? Well, it can be saved only when God is willing to send one of his sons or daughters into the world so that through *that* being the world might be saved.

How lifestreams can be saved

How is the world saved? It is saved when a true being of light descends to this earth and takes upon itself that particular state of consciousness. Then, by internalizing and expanding its connection to its spiritual self, while it is in a body and overshadowed by the outer mind, the lifestream carves a trail through the jungle of ego-illusions. It demonstrates that it is possible to take on a certain infirmity, a certain limitation, and rise above it through the mind of Christ and the mind of God.

When another lifestream, who is still trapped, sees that a person from the same background, a person who had the same problems, can rise above those limitations, then that lifestream will often be awakened and say: "If *he* can do it, maybe *I* can do it."

This is the principle of the Great White Brotherhood: "What one has done, all can do." Which really says that the only way to truly teach is to teach by example. *That* is why Jesus Christ took embodiment. That is why *I* took embodiment as his mother in that lifetime. That is why many other beings of light, spiritual beings, have taken physical embodiment on earth. They have done this in order to show that no matter what human condition or limitation a lifestream might be facing, it is possible to rise above it through the power of God within you.

2 | INVOKING THE MINDSET OF TRUE HEALING

In the name I AM THAT I AM, Jesus Christ, I call to all representatives of the Divine Mother, especially Mother Mary, to help me develop the mindset that will empower me to accept the healing of my body mind and soul. I call for you to help me overcome all illusions that stand in the way of my healing, especially…

[Make personal calls.]

1. I know God's will

1. I accept the mindset that leads to the true healing of physical illness, psychological conditions and my outer situation.

> O Blessed Mary's Song of Life,
> consuming every form of strife.
> As I attune to sound so fair,
> each cell is healthy, I declare.

**O Mother Mary, generate,
the song that does accelerate,
my mind into a peaceful state,
God's perfect love I radiate.**

2. I know the difference between the outer will – the human will, the will of the ego – and the Will of God.

As life's own song I ever hear,
it does consume all sense of fear.
In tune with Mother's symphony,
from all diseases I AM free.

**O Mother Mary, generate,
the song that does accelerate,
my mind into a peaceful state,
God's perfect love I radiate.**

3. I am in attunement with the Will of God.

In Mother's love I do transcend,
and all my struggles hereby end.
For when with Mother's eye I see,
no imperfection touches me.

**O Mother Mary, generate,
the song that does accelerate,
my mind into a peaceful state,
God's perfect love I radiate.**

4. I know what can be done to bring about healing, what type of healing can occur and when healing can occur.

I see that healing must begin
by finding Living Christ within.
For as I see with single eye,
each cell the light does amplify.

**O Mother Mary, generate,
the song that does accelerate,
my mind into a peaceful state,
God's perfect love I radiate.**

5. I know whether I have volunteered to take upon myself a part of the planetary karma and whether this has manifested in the form of mental or physical illness.

In Mother's music I am free,
from memories of a lesser me.
My vision in a perfect state,
that all my cells regenerate.

**O Mother Mary, generate,
the song that does accelerate,
my mind into a peaceful state,
God's perfect love I radiate.**

6. I know whether an illness, mental or physical, is a labor of love.

O Mother's Love, sweet melody,
from imperfections I AM free.
O Mother Mary, sound of sounds,
within my heart your love abounds.

> O Mother Mary, generate,
> the song that does accelerate,
> my mind into a peaceful state,
> God's perfect love I radiate.

7. I know if, at deeper levels, I do not want to be healed or do not want to be healed yet.

> Through Mother's beauty so sublime,
> transcending bounds of space and time.
> All cells beyond the mortal tomb,
> as they are whole in Mother's womb.
>
> **O Mother Mary, generate,
> the song that does accelerate,
> my mind into a peaceful state,
> God's perfect love I radiate.**

8. I have no need to seek healing by getting other people to take upon themselves the karma that I have volunteered to bear.

> In resonance with life's own song,
> in life's harmonics I belong.
> The blueprint of my perfect state
> does every cell reconsecrate.
>
> **O Mother Mary, generate,
> the song that does accelerate,
> my mind into a peaceful state,
> God's perfect love I radiate.**

9. I have no need to seek healing by using modern medicine as a shortcut to either take away the pain or take away an illness that is meant to be borne.

> The tuning fork in every cell
> is now attuned to Mother's bell.
> From curse of death I AM now free,
> I claim my immortality.

> **O Mother Mary, generate,**
> **the song that does accelerate,**
> **my mind into a peaceful state,**
> **God's perfect love I radiate.**

2. I attune to my higher will

1. I know whether a condition is caused by my own karma.

> O Blessed Mary's Song of Life,
> consuming every form of strife.
> As I attune to sound so fair,
> each cell is healthy, I declare.

> **O Mother Mary, generate,**
> **the song that does accelerate,**
> **my mind into a peaceful state,**
> **God's perfect love I radiate.**

2. I am invoking spiritual light in order to transmute the karma so that I do not have to bear the physical condition.

As life's own song I ever hear,
it does consume all sense of fear.
In tune with Mother's symphony,
from all diseases I AM free.

**O Mother Mary, generate,
the song that does accelerate,
my mind into a peaceful state,
God's perfect love I radiate.**

3. I know whether an illness is created by the ego in order to give the Conscious You an excuse for not taking command over my own destiny, for not taking responsibility for myself.

In Mother's love I do transcend,
and all my struggles hereby end.
For when with Mother's eye I see,
no imperfection touches me.

**O Mother Mary, generate,
the song that does accelerate,
my mind into a peaceful state,
God's perfect love I radiate.**

4. I am free from the ego-based reasoning that limits me because of an illness. I know I can rise and be the Christ, I can fulfill my divine plan, I can challenge the darkness and take a stand for Light.

I see that healing must begin
by finding Living Christ within.
For as I see with single eye,
each cell the light does amplify.

**O Mother Mary, generate,
the song that does accelerate,
my mind into a peaceful state,
God's perfect love I radiate.**

5. I know whether healing should or should not occur, and I will grow and fulfill my divine plan.

In Mother's music I am free,
from memories of a lesser me.
My vision in a perfect state,
that all my cells regenerate.

**O Mother Mary, generate,
the song that does accelerate,
my mind into a peaceful state,
God's perfect love I radiate.**

6. The will of God is not outside of myself, is not separate from my own will—the higher will of my conscious self and I AM Presence.

O Mother's Love, sweet melody,
from imperfections I AM free.
O Mother Mary, sound of sounds,
within my heart your love abounds.

**O Mother Mary, generate,
the song that does accelerate,
my mind into a peaceful state,
God's perfect love I radiate.**

7. I tune in to my own higher will and I know what is God's will concerning any particular illness I have or condition I face.

> Through Mother's beauty so sublime,
> transcending bounds of space and time.
> All cells beyond the mortal tomb,
> as they are whole in Mother's womb.
>
> **O Mother Mary, generate,**
> **the song that does accelerate,**
> **my mind into a peaceful state,**
> **God's perfect love I radiate.**

8. I feel in my heart if healing should occur, and I see the appropriate means for healing.

> In resonance with life's own song,
> in life's harmonics I belong.
> The blueprint of my perfect state
> does every cell reconsecrate.
>
> **O Mother Mary, generate,**
> **the song that does accelerate,**
> **my mind into a peaceful state,**
> **God's perfect love I radiate.**

9. I am invoking spiritual light that will transform any illness or condition I face.

> The tuning fork in every cell
> is now attuned to Mother's bell.
> From curse of death I AM now free,
> I claim my immortality.

**O Mother Mary, generate,
the song that does accelerate,
my mind into a peaceful state,
God's perfect love I radiate.**

3. I know my true origin

1. Any physical illness, any mental illness, is the expression of a particular state of consciousness.

> O Blessed Mary's Song of Life,
> consuming every form of strife.
> As I attune to sound so fair,
> each cell is healthy, I declare.

> **O Mother Mary, generate,
> the song that does accelerate,
> my mind into a peaceful state,
> God's perfect love I radiate.**

2. I know whether a certain state of consciousness is created by my own ego. It is my responsibility to take care of it because it is something I have created from inside my own being.

> As life's own song I ever hear,
> it does consume all sense of fear.
> In tune with Mother's symphony,
> from all diseases I AM free.

> O Mother Mary, generate,
> the song that does accelerate,
> my mind into a peaceful state,
> God's perfect love I radiate.

3. I see any aspect of the human consciousness that affects me or that I have absorbed into my sense of identity.

> In Mother's love I do transcend,
> and all my struggles hereby end.
> For when with Mother's eye I see,
> no imperfection touches me.

> O Mother Mary, generate,
> the song that does accelerate,
> my mind into a peaceful state,
> God's perfect love I radiate.

4. Any human state of consciousness is the outpicturing in form of a particular lie that springs from the mind of anti-christ, the anti-mind.

> I see that healing must begin
> by finding Living Christ within.
> For as I see with single eye,
> each cell the light does amplify.

> O Mother Mary, generate,
> the song that does accelerate,
> my mind into a peaceful state,
> God's perfect love I radiate.

2 | Invoking the Mindset of True Healing

5. I am free from these lies and I am rising beyond my present level. I am becoming the Christ in embodiment, I am being who I am in God here on earth.

> In Mother's music I am free,
> from memories of a lesser me.
> My vision in a perfect state,
> that all my cells regenerate.

> **O Mother Mary, generate,**
> **the song that does accelerate,**
> **my mind into a peaceful state,**
> **God's perfect love I radiate.**

6. I am free from the consciousness that Jesus called "Death."

> O Mother's Love, sweet melody,
> from imperfections I AM free.
> O Mother Mary, sound of sounds,
> within my heart your love abounds.

> **O Mother Mary, generate,**
> **the song that does accelerate,**
> **my mind into a peaceful state,**
> **God's perfect love I radiate.**

7. I am one of the sons or daughters of God, and I have come into the world so that through me the world might be saved.

> Through Mother's beauty so sublime,
> transcending bounds of space and time.
> All cells beyond the mortal tomb,
> as they are whole in Mother's womb.

**O Mother Mary, generate,
the song that does accelerate,
my mind into a peaceful state,
God's perfect love I radiate.**

8. I am one of the beings of light who have descended to this earth and have taken upon myself a particular state of consciousness.

In resonance with life's own song,
in life's harmonics I belong.
The blueprint of my perfect state
does every cell reconsecrate.

**O Mother Mary, generate,
the song that does accelerate,
my mind into a peaceful state,
God's perfect love I radiate.**

9. I am connected to my spiritual self while I am in a body. I am carving a trail through the jungle of ego-illusions.

The tuning fork in every cell
is now attuned to Mother's bell.
From curse of death I AM now free,
I claim my immortality.

**O Mother Mary, generate,
the song that does accelerate,
my mind into a peaceful state,
God's perfect love I radiate.**

4. I will do what I came for

1. I am demonstrating that it is possible to take on a certain infirmity, a certain limitation, and rise above it through the mind of Christ and the mind of God.

> O Blessed Mary's Song of Life,
> consuming every form of strife.
> As I attune to sound so fair,
> each cell is healthy, I declare.
>
> **O Mother Mary, generate,**
> **the song that does accelerate,**
> **my mind into a peaceful state,**
> **God's perfect love I radiate.**

2. I rise above my limitations so that others might be awakened and say: "If he or she can do it, I can do it."

> As life's own song I ever hear,
> it does consume all sense of fear.
> In tune with Mother's symphony,
> from all diseases I AM free.
>
> **O Mother Mary, generate,**
> **the song that does accelerate,**
> **my mind into a peaceful state,**
> **God's perfect love I radiate.**

3. I am attuned to the principle of the Great White Brotherhood: "What one has done, all can do."

In Mother's love I do transcend,
and all my struggles hereby end.
For when with Mother's eye I see,
no imperfection touches me.

**O Mother Mary, generate,
the song that does accelerate,
my mind into a peaceful state,
God's perfect love I radiate.**

4. It is indeed possible for me to heal any condition in my life.

I see that healing must begin
by finding Living Christ within.
For as I see with single eye,
each cell the light does amplify.

**O Mother Mary, generate,
the song that does accelerate,
my mind into a peaceful state,
God's perfect love I radiate.**

5. I have the vision of how I can teach through example.

In Mother's music I am free,
from memories of a lesser me.
My vision in a perfect state,
that all my cells regenerate.

**O Mother Mary, generate,
the song that does accelerate,
my mind into a peaceful state,
God's perfect love I radiate.**

2 | Invoking the Mindset of True Healing

6. I am demonstrating that no matter what human condition or limitation I am facing, it is possible to rise above it through the power of God within me.

> O Mother's Love, sweet melody,
> from imperfections I AM free.
> O Mother Mary, sound of sounds,
> within my heart your love abounds.
>
> **O Mother Mary, generate,**
> **the song that does accelerate,**
> **my mind into a peaceful state,**
> **God's perfect love I radiate.**

7. The power of God is indeed within me as it was in Jesus.

> Through Mother's beauty so sublime,
> transcending bounds of space and time.
> All cells beyond the mortal tomb,
> as they are whole in Mother's womb.
>
> **O Mother Mary, generate,**
> **the song that does accelerate,**
> **my mind into a peaceful state,**
> **God's perfect love I radiate.**

8. The power of God within me is transforming any condition I face here in the material realm, including any condition in my body and mind.

In resonance with life's own song,
in life's harmonics I belong.
The blueprint of my perfect state
does every cell reconsecrate.

O Mother Mary, generate,
the song that does accelerate,
my mind into a peaceful state,
God's perfect love I radiate.

9. I am letting the power of God within me flow into and transform the limitations I face. I serve to raise the whole.

The tuning fork in every cell
is now attuned to Mother's bell.
From curse of death I AM now free,
I claim my immortality.

O Mother Mary, generate,
the song that does accelerate,
my mind into a peaceful state,
God's perfect love I radiate.

Sealing

In the name of the Divine Mother, I call to Mother Mary for the sealing of myself and all people in the creative flow of the Divine Mother, the River of Life. I call for the multiplication of my calls by all representatives of the Divine Mother, so that we form the perfect figure-eight flow of "As Above, so below." Thus, I accept that this is fully manifest, because the mouth of the Lord, the Divine Mother that I AM, has spoken it. Amen.

3 | WHAT IS TRUE HEALING?

Excerpt from a dictation by Mother Mary, March 27, 2005.

My beloved hearts, I am your Mother Mary, and I come to give you a little more teaching about healing. There are those of you who might feel, at some level of your being, that you cannot move beyond a certain infirmity in your body or in your mind. I would ask you to reconsider, and perhaps reread your Bible about the healing miracles performed by Jesus. You will see that there are subtle hints in the scriptures that there were instances where Jesus came to a town and none were healed because of their unbelief.

You will also see, that there were instances where Jesus asked people: "Do you believe, that I have the power to heal you?" And if they said "Yes," they were healed. If they believed not, they were not healed. Truly, in order to be healed, you have to be willing to let go of the limitation, but you also have to be willing to let go of the very consciousness behind that limitation. That is why you will see that some who are healed by religious healers will actually fall back, and their disease will reappear after a short time. They have not separated themselves out from the consciousness behind the disease.

Healing requires surrender

I come to ask you to consider that before you can be healed, you must be willing to surrender, not only the outer illness, but you also have to be willing to surrender something in the mind. There are two things you have to surrender, there are two levels of surrender. First of all, when you have had an illness for some time, or even in many cases for a short period of time, your mind has built a certain mindset to deal with that illness. Your mind has become accustomed to viewing the illness in a certain way. Before you can be healed, you have to let go of that mindset.

One might say that there is a part of your mind who has come to believe that either the illness is necessary, or it is unavoidable, or it is in some way offering you something. As I said earlier, your ego can believe that the illness is actually an advantage for the soul because it gives the soul an excuse for not transcending itself. There can be many other subtle beliefs that the mind can create for why you need an illness or why it is advantageous for you to keep a certain limitation.

You must discover that mindset and let go of it. When you have done that – letting go of the personal mindset that you have created around this illness – you then need to go deeper and realize that the illness itself, be it physical or mental, is the outpicturing of a certain mindset in the collective consciousness. In order to be healed, you have to separate yourself from that mindset. It might indeed be a part of your divine plan that you came here to demonstrate that it is possible to have a certain illness in the physical body and yet to rise above it.

The belief in incurable diseases

If you will think back across history, you will see that from time to time many people have had the belief that a certain illness was incurable. Once you had contracted that illness, it was just a matter of time before you died. It was not very long ago that most people in the West looked at cancer in this way. Yet in the last decade or so, a shift has begun to occur.

Today, many people realize that even cancer can be dealt with and that many forms of cancer can be cured. This has created a shift in the collective consciousness, and thereby more and more people do not fall into despair and hopelessness when they have cancer in their bodies. Instead of falling into despair, they decide that they will do everything they *can* to fight it. Thereby, they carve a trail that helps humankind conquer the mindset that cancer is a limitation that is absolute.

The physical cures for cancer will never be able to cure every form of cancer, or to cure it completely, because behind cancer is a mindset, a consciousness. It is truly a consciousness of the anti-will and the anger against God's will, as something that is imposed upon you from without. This consciousness permeates the very cells of the physical body, until the cell itself feels that it is so restricted by outside forces that it no longer wants to live—so it destroys itself from within.

This is a mindset you will see in many other manifestations in society where people have allowed themselves to be separated from the will of God, which wants only that they experience love, light and freedom. They have submitted themselves to and identified themselves with the mind of the ego, the anti-mind or the forces of this world. Through that anti-mind, the soul has become so boxed-in that it says: "This life is not worth living." The soul has become so trapped in this consciousness that it cannot do what all of you have done. All of you have experienced that at some point – even though you had many difficulties, even though you had severe problems – you came to a point where instead of saying: "This life is not worth living" you said: "There must be a better way; there must be something more." In asking that question, you discovered something, and it is because of *that* you are alive today. Those souls who are trapped and cannot even ask the question: "There must be more to life, where is it?," those souls will eventually be so boxed-in by their own negativity and limitations that they no longer want to live. Many of them do not commit physical suicide, but they commit a slow suicide of engaging in all kinds of activities – such as addictions, war, terrorism, fights or conflicts – that eventually lead to the death of the body.

The consciousness behind illness

In order to truly be healed, you need to consider that any physical or mental illness is the expression of a certain state of consciousness. When you discover what that consciousness is, it is then your task to free yourself from it. How do you free yourself from it? By realizing that this is not a creation of the true you. Your I AM Presence and your soul did not create this consciousness.

It was created by your ego, the egos of other human beings and the consciousness of dark beings. They are so steeped in selfishness that they do not even have an ego anymore in the sense that human beings have an ego. They have no sense of individuality, they have just become a part of the mass mind or a particular perversion of God's consciousness. They have created this consciousness that has manifested as physical disease. *You* did not create it; the higher you, the real you, did not create it. *You took it on* because you wanted to show others that it is possible to rise above it. I say to you: when you connect to your divine plan, you will know when it is time to rise above that consciousness and thereby rise above the physical disease.

All healing is energy healing

Everything is energy. Energy cannot be created or destroyed, at least not in the material universe. Energy can be transformed; any form of energy can be transformed into any other form of energy. Darkness can be transformed into light, and the energy that makes up a particular disease can be transformed into purity and health. Yet in order to transform the energy, or rather to allow the light of God within you to transform the energy, you must free that energy from the matrix that has been put upon it through your mind and through the collective mind.

That is why all healing is energy healing. This is not necessarily in the sense that it is currently understood where you think you take one form of physical energy and move it around. It is in the sense that by invoking the light of God, and by affirming the purity and the perfection of God, you can transform the imperfect energy, the energy that has currently taken on an imperfect form.

Many of you have not come into embodiment to experience an instant healing that is miraculous to the human mind. When someone is healed through a miracle, other people will say: "Well, unless I experience that miracle by some grace of God, I can't be healed." What you are here to demonstrate is that you can allow God within you to heal you, and to heal you through a process whereby you rise above the limiting state of consciousness that created the disease. Thereby, you do not show people an instantaneous miracle that they cannot understand or accept for themselves. You show them a gradual, systematic path that leads them out of darkness and into light. Thereby, they suddenly can see that: "If *that* person can do it; *I* can do it." Suddenly, the healing process becomes believable.

All healing is faith healing

Unless you can have the faith that the healing is possible, how can you be healed? There were those who stood before Jesus and did not have the faith that Jesus had the power of God within him to heal their disease. Jesus could not violate their free will and let it be healed. You are here to demonstrate that when you have the faith – not in an outer miracle, but in the inner process of the Light of God consuming the imperfections – you *can* be healed.

When enough people demonstrate that path, you will see a shift in the collective consciousness. The challenge that faces humankind is to realize the connection between their consciousness and the conditions in their physical bodies and the conditions in the body of the Earth Mother. This is truly the great awakening that needs to happen on this planet. This is the true wisdom: When you realize that everything is created through the power of the mind. *That* is true wisdom in this realm of duality. *That* is when you will experience freedom from the dualistic mind, from the human ego and from all human limitations. *That* is what I desire to see happen in you and in the lives of all people.

I charge you with the joy, the enthusiasm and the love of freedom, freedom for your souls from all these limitations that have been put upon you from without. I desire that you will have that inner fire and drive to look the limitations straight in the eye and say: "But the emperor has nothing on. I am no longer his slave, I am no longer the subject of that lie. I am free in God, and I rise above it, and I let the consciousness of the lie pass into the Pillar of Fire of the Will of God. I see it consumed, and I see all of my brothers and sisters awakening to the reality that the kingdom of God is within them."

I seal you with the fire of the Mother of God below, forming a polarity to the fire of the Father Above. Therefore, I say to the four corners of the Earth: "Choose Life! Choose Life! Choose Life! Choose Life!" In the name of the Father, the Son, the Holy Spirit and the Divine Mother, it is sealed; it is finished.

4 | INVOKING HEALING ENERGY

In the name I AM THAT I AM, Jesus Christ, I call to all representatives of the Divine Mother, especially Mother Mary, to help me be filled with the healing energy that will heal my body mind and soul. I call for you to help me overcome all illusions that stand in the way of my healing, especially…

[Make personal calls.]

1. I surrender the mindset behind disease

1. I am moving beyond this particular infirmity in my body or mind and this particular limitation in my outer situation.

> O Blessed Mary's Song of Life,
> consuming every form of strife.
> As I attune to sound so fair,
> each cell is healthy, I declare.

**O Mother Mary, generate,
the song that does accelerate,
my cells into a higher state,
in perfect health they scintillate.**

2. I am accepting that I am healed, and therefore Jesus and Mother Mary can indeed heal me.

> As life's own song I ever hear,
> it does consume all sense of fear.
> In tune with Mother's symphony,
> from all diseases I AM free.

**O Mother Mary, generate,
the song that does accelerate,
my cells into a higher state,
in perfect health they scintillate.**

3. I am letting go of this limitation, and the consciousness behind the limitation.

> In Mother's love I do transcend,
> and all my struggles hereby end.
> For when with Mother's eye I see,
> no imperfection touches me.

**O Mother Mary, generate,
the song that does accelerate,
my cells into a higher state,
in perfect health they scintillate.**

4. I am separating myself from the consciousness behind this disease.

I see that healing must begin
by finding Living Christ within.
For as I see with single eye,
each cell the light does amplify.

O Mother Mary, generate,
the song that does accelerate,
my cells into a higher state,
in perfect health they scintillate.

5. I surrender not only the outer illness, but also the mindset that my mind has built in order to deal with that illness.

In Mother's music I am free,
from memories of a lesser me.
My vision in a perfect state,
that all my cells regenerate.

O Mother Mary, generate,
the song that does accelerate,
my cells into a higher state,
in perfect health they scintillate.

6. I am free from the mindset that causes my mind to view the illness a certain way.

O Mother's Love, sweet melody,
from imperfections I AM free.
O Mother Mary, sound of sounds,
within my heart your love abounds.

**O Mother Mary, generate,
the song that does accelerate,
my cells into a higher state,
in perfect health they scintillate.**

7. This illness is *not* necessary. This illness is *not* unavoidable. This illness is *not* offering me anything. I am surrendering this illness to Mother Mary.

Through Mother's beauty so sublime,
transcending bounds of space and time.
All cells beyond the mortal tomb,
as they are whole in Mother's womb.

**O Mother Mary, generate,
the song that does accelerate,
my cells into a higher state,
in perfect health they scintillate.**

8. The illness itself, be it physical or mental, is the outpicturing of a certain mindset in the collective consciousness.

In resonance with life's own song,
in life's harmonics I belong.
The blueprint of my perfect state
does every cell reconsecrate.

**O Mother Mary, generate,
the song that does accelerate,
my cells into a higher state,
in perfect health they scintillate.**

9. I am separating myself from that mindset. I am demonstrating that it is possible to have a certain illness in the physical body and rise above it.

> The tuning fork in every cell
> is now attuned to Mother's bell.
> From curse of death I AM now free,
> I claim my immortality.

> **O Mother Mary, generate,**
> **the song that does accelerate,**
> **my cells into a higher state,**
> **in perfect health they scintillate.**

2. I see the consciousness behind disease

1. I am surrendering the belief that a certain illness is incurable.

> O Blessed Mary's Song of Life,
> consuming every form of strife.
> As I attune to sound so fair,
> each cell is healthy, I declare.

> **O Mother Mary, generate,**
> **the song that does accelerate,**
> **my cells into a higher state,**
> **in perfect health they scintillate.**

2. I am transcending all despair and hopelessness concerning my condition. I am transcending my limitations and carving a trail that helps humankind conquer the mindset that some limitations are absolute.

As life's own song I ever hear,
it does consume all sense of fear.
In tune with Mother's symphony,
from all diseases I AM free.

**O Mother Mary, generate,
the song that does accelerate,
my cells into a higher state,
in perfect health they scintillate.**

3. I surrender the consciousness of anti-will and anger against God's will, as something that is imposed upon me from without.

In Mother's love I do transcend,
and all my struggles hereby end.
For when with Mother's eye I see,
no imperfection touches me.

**O Mother Mary, generate,
the song that does accelerate,
my cells into a higher state,
in perfect health they scintillate.**

4. I am transcending the separation from the will of God. I know God wants only that I experience love, light and freedom.

I see that healing must begin
by finding Living Christ within.
For as I see with single eye,
each cell the light does amplify.

**O Mother Mary, generate,
the song that does accelerate,
my cells into a higher state,
in perfect health they scintillate.**

5. I am transcending the mind of the ego, the anti-mind or the forces of this world. I feel that life is worth living.

In Mother's music I am free,
from memories of a lesser me.
My vision in a perfect state,
that all my cells regenerate.

**O Mother Mary, generate,
the song that does accelerate,
my cells into a higher state,
in perfect health they scintillate.**

6. I am deciding: "There is a better way; there is something more." I am seeing that more.

O Mother's Love, sweet melody,
from imperfections I AM free.
O Mother Mary, sound of sounds,
within my heart your love abounds.

**O Mother Mary, generate,
the song that does accelerate,
my cells into a higher state,
in perfect health they scintillate.**

7. I am discovering and transcending the state of consciousness behind all diseases and limitations.

Through Mother's beauty so sublime,
transcending bounds of space and time.
All cells beyond the mortal tomb,
as they are whole in Mother's womb.

**O Mother Mary, generate,
the song that does accelerate,
my cells into a higher state,
in perfect health they scintillate.**

8. I am realizing that this consciousness is not a creation of the true me. My I AM Presence and my conscious self did not create this consciousness.

In resonance with life's own song,
in life's harmonics I belong.
The blueprint of my perfect state
does every cell reconsecrate.

**O Mother Mary, generate,
the song that does accelerate,
my cells into a higher state,
in perfect health they scintillate.**

9. I am transcending the consciousness that was created by my ego, the egos of other human beings and the consciousness of dark beings.

The tuning fork in every cell
is now attuned to Mother's bell.
From curse of death I AM now free,
I claim my immortality.

> **O Mother Mary, generate,**
> **the song that does accelerate,**
> **my cells into a higher state,**
> **in perfect health they scintillate.**

3. I transform lower energies

1. The real me did not create the limiting consciousness. I took it on because I wanted to show others that it is possible to rise above it.

> O Blessed Mary's Song of Life,
> consuming every form of strife.
> As I attune to sound so fair,
> each cell is healthy, I declare.

> **O Mother Mary, generate,**
> **the song that does accelerate,**
> **my cells into a higher state,**
> **in perfect health they scintillate.**

2. I am connecting to my divine plan. I know when it is time to rise above the human consciousness and thereby rise above the physical disease.

> As life's own song I ever hear,
> it does consume all sense of fear.
> In tune with Mother's symphony,
> from all diseases I AM free.

**O Mother Mary, generate,
the song that does accelerate,
my cells into a higher state,
in perfect health they scintillate.**

3. Everything is energy and any form of energy can be transformed into any other form of energy.

In Mother's love I do transcend,
and all my struggles hereby end.
For when with Mother's eye I see,
no imperfection touches me.

**O Mother Mary, generate,
the song that does accelerate,
my cells into a higher state,
in perfect health they scintillate.**

4. Darkness can be transformed into light. The energy that makes up a particular disease can be transformed into purity and health.

I see that healing must begin
by finding Living Christ within.
For as I see with single eye,
each cell the light does amplify.

**O Mother Mary, generate,
the song that does accelerate,
my cells into a higher state,
in perfect health they scintillate.**

5. I am allowing the light of God within me to transform the energy. I am setting the energy free from the matrix that has been put upon it through my mind and through the collective mind.

> In Mother's music I am free,
> from memories of a lesser me.
> My vision in a perfect state,
> that all my cells regenerate.
>
> **O Mother Mary, generate,**
> **the song that does accelerate,**
> **my cells into a higher state,**
> **in perfect health they scintillate.**

6. All healing is energy healing.

> O Mother's Love, sweet melody,
> from imperfections I AM free.
> O Mother Mary, sound of sounds,
> within my heart your love abounds.
>
> **O Mother Mary, generate,**
> **the song that does accelerate,**
> **my cells into a higher state,**
> **in perfect health they scintillate.**

7. I am invoking the light of God. I am affirming the purity and the perfection of God. I am transforming all energy that has currently taken on an imperfect form.

Through Mother's beauty so sublime,
transcending bounds of space and time.
All cells beyond the mortal tomb,
as they are whole in Mother's womb.

**O Mother Mary, generate,
the song that does accelerate,
my cells into a higher state,
in perfect health they scintillate.**

8. I did not come into embodiment to experience an instant healing that is miraculous to the human mind.

In resonance with life's own song,
in life's harmonics I belong.
The blueprint of my perfect state
does every cell reconsecrate.

**O Mother Mary, generate,
the song that does accelerate,
my cells into a higher state,
in perfect health they scintillate.**

9. I am here to demonstrate that I can allow God within me to heal me through a process whereby I rise above the limiting state of consciousness that created the disease.

The tuning fork in every cell
is now attuned to Mother's bell.
From curse of death I AM now free,
I claim my immortality.

**O Mother Mary, generate,
the song that does accelerate,
my cells into a higher state,
in perfect health they scintillate.**

4. I am healed

1. I am showing people a gradual, systematic path that leads them out of darkness and into light. Thereby, they suddenly see that: "If that person can do it; I can do it."

> O Blessed Mary's Song of Life,
> consuming every form of strife.
> As I attune to sound so fair,
> each cell is healthy, I declare.

> **O Mother Mary, generate,
> the song that does accelerate,
> my cells into a higher state,
> in perfect health they scintillate.**

2. The healing process is believable and I am indeed healed.

> As life's own song I ever hear,
> it does consume all sense of fear.
> In tune with Mother's symphony,
> from all diseases I AM free.

> **O Mother Mary, generate,
> the song that does accelerate,
> my cells into a higher state,
> in perfect health they scintillate.**

3. I am here to demonstrate that I have faith in the inner process of the Light of God consuming the imperfections, whereby I am healed.

> In Mother's love I do transcend,
> and all my struggles hereby end.
> For when with Mother's eye I see,
> no imperfection touches me.

> **O Mother Mary, generate,**
> **the song that does accelerate,**
> **my cells into a higher state,**
> **in perfect health they scintillate.**

4. I am assisting others in realizing the connection between our consciousness and the conditions in our physical bodies, even the conditions in the body of the Earth Mother.

> I see that healing must begin
> by finding Living Christ within.
> For as I see with single eye,
> each cell the light does amplify.

> **O Mother Mary, generate,**
> **the song that does accelerate,**
> **my cells into a higher state,**
> **in perfect health they scintillate.**

5. I am finding my place in the great awakening that is happening on this planet. I am an open door for the true wisdom that everything is created through the power of the mind.

In Mother's music I am free,
from memories of a lesser me.
My vision in a perfect state,
that all my cells regenerate.

O Mother Mary, generate,
the song that does accelerate,
my cells into a higher state,
in perfect health they scintillate.

6. I am experiencing freedom from the dualistic mind, from the human ego and from all human limitations. I am bringing this into the lives of all people.

O Mother's Love, sweet melody,
from imperfections I AM free.
O Mother Mary, sound of sounds,
within my heart your love abounds.

O Mother Mary, generate,
the song that does accelerate,
my cells into a higher state,
in perfect health they scintillate.

7. I am filled with the joy, the enthusiasm and the love of freedom. I am free from all of the limitations that have been put upon me from without.

Through Mother's beauty so sublime,
transcending bounds of space and time.
All cells beyond the mortal tomb,
as they are whole in Mother's womb.

**O Mother Mary, generate,
the song that does accelerate,
my cells into a higher state,
in perfect health they scintillate.**

8. The emperor has nothing on. I am no longer his slave, I am no longer the subject of the lie. I am free in God, and I rise above it, and I let the consciousness of the lie pass into the Pillar of Fire of the Will of God. I see it consumed, and I see all of my brothers and sisters awakening to the reality that the kingdom of God is within them.

> In resonance with life's own song,
> in life's harmonics I belong.
> The blueprint of my perfect state
> does every cell reconsecrate.

**O Mother Mary, generate,
the song that does accelerate,
my cells into a higher state,
in perfect health they scintillate.**

9. I am sealed in the fire of the Mother of God below, forming a polarity to the fire of the Father Above. I say to the four corners of the Earth: "I choose Life! I choose Life! I choose Life! I choose Life!" In the name of the Father, the Son, the Holy Spirit and the Divine Mother, it is sealed; it is finished.

> The tuning fork in every cell
> is now attuned to Mother's bell.
> From curse of death I AM now free,
> I claim my immortality.

**O Mother Mary, generate,
the song that does accelerate,
my cells into a higher state,
in perfect health they scintillate.**

Sealing

In the name of the Divine Mother, I call to Mother Mary for the sealing of myself and all people in the creative flow of the Divine Mother, the River of Life. I call for the multiplication of my calls by all representatives of the Divine Mother, so that we form the perfect figure-eight flow of "As Above, so below." Thus, I accept that this is fully manifest, because the mouth of the Lord, the Divine Mother that I AM, has spoken it. Amen.

5 | YOU CANNOT GIVE AWAY WHAT YOU DO NOT OWN

Excerpt from a dictation by Jesus, March 28, 2005.

The psychological dynamic that blocks healing

I AM the Being that all people know as Jesus Christ. Although in the ongoingness of God, the constant self-transcendence of God, I have now become *more* than I was 2,000 years ago, I am ever happy and grateful for those who will listen to me in the form of Jesus Christ.

I am come to give you a teaching on healing, specifically why so many people cannot be healed. As you know from the scriptures, there were many people who met me 2,000 years ago and who were not healed. There were those who had healing, yet their condition reappeared. Why is it that so many cannot be healed?

In order to fully understand this, I would like you to consider what is the greatest threat, the greatest single threat, to your salvation. There are many answers that human beings would give, but very few human beings have discovered the real answer. The real answer is that the greatest single threat to the salvation of humankind is *religion*—an outer, fear-based religion that sets up and upholds the idol of the external God who resides outside of the inner kingdom.

This creates a schism in the psyche of every soul that has been exposed to this form of religion, especially if they were exposed to it from early childhood and were brought up in a fear-based environment. The schism is that the lifestream knows from within that it came from somewhere else, that it is not a product of the body, that it is not the product of one lifetime, but that it is ancient and that it came from a higher source. Yet the outer religion – be it a religion that claims to worship God or be it a religion that denies God, such as scientific materialism – tells the soul that God is outside, that God is separate and that you cannot reach God on your own.

Many religions furthermore set up an ideal for how the perfect human being should be, the perfect human being that is acceptable in the eyes of God—that is: according to *that* religion. They portray the image that only those human beings who live up to this outer definition will be allowed to enter the kingdom of heaven. What is the lifestream to do when it is presented with this approach to salvation?

The lifestream tries, with the outer mind, to mold itself after the ideal that has been put before it since childhood. The lifestream does not know that this ideal is an idol and a violation of the first two commandments. The lifestream tries its best, using its outer mind, its outer will, to mold itself after this idol of the perfect human being. Not only does the lifestream fail to understand that it is an idol, but it also fails to understand – because it has never been told – that it is an *impossible* idol, and that no human being could ever live up to this outer standard of perfection.

The reason is that this outer standard originated in the mind of anti-christ, the mind of the devil himself, who believes that there is a mechanical path to salvation. This leads the lifestream to perhaps spend an entire lifetime striving for the outer righteousness, the righteousness of the scribes and Pharisees that I denounced when I said: "Unless your righteousness exceeds the righteousness of the scribes and Pharisees, ye shall in no wise enter the kingdom." Why will you not enter the kingdom? Because the kingdom is within you, and until you unite with the consciousness of the kingdom, how can you *be* in the kingdom?

You cannot enter the kingdom of heaven

In reality, you cannot *enter* the kingdom of heaven. You can *be* in the kingdom of heaven or you can be outside in consciousness. Truly, God is omnipresent. God is already where you are. The illusion that you are separated from God's kingdom can only exist in the lower mind, the mind that has been trapped in duality.

When the Conscious You identifies itself with this mind, the self is in a catch-22. It knows from within that it is more than this outer mind. Yet it has come to believe that in order to be saved, it needs to live up to this outer ideal, and the outer ideal is a denial of the lifestream's true creativity and true being. The outer mind is trying to force the outer matrix upon the lifestream, and at subconscious levels the Conscious You knows that this will not lead to salvation. The Conscious You rebels against the outer discipline, and thus you become a house divided against yourself. *You become your own worst enemy.*

You see so many people who are trapped in this no-man's land where they are neither hot nor cold; they are lukewarm. The true inner meaning of being lukewarm is that you are trapped in a catch-22. Your outer mind – assisted by your religious upbringing – is trying to force something upon the Conscious You. The Conscious You, in the core of its being, is rebelling against this because it knows it is not God's will. As long as you are trapped in that duality, that catch-22, you cannot move forward on your own. You cannot be healed of the conditions that your mind has created out of that duality consciousness, be it mental illness, physical disease or outer problems. You cannot be healed until you get out of that impasse, you get out of that catch-22. What is the key to escaping from this condition of being neither this nor that, neither fully alive nor fully dead?

Ownership is the key

In order to explain this to you, let me ask you to consider an analogy. Imagine that you are walking down the street with a child that is dear to your heart. You pass a toy store, and in the window is a beautiful toy and the child falls in love with the toy and says: "Will you give me that toy?" Can you reach through the glass and take the toy and give it to the child? Can you go into the store and grab the toy and run out with it and give it to the child? Well, you *can* but there will be consequences. What will you have to do before you can give that toy to the child and thereby fulfill the desire of the child and your desire to give the child a gift?

What you will have to do is simple. You will have to go into the store and pay for the toy, and when you have paid for it, you can take ownership of it. When *you* own the toy – instead of the store owner – then *you* can give the toy to the child. The essence of the story is that *you cannot give away that which you do not own.*

Remember this sentence, "You cannot give away what you do not own." To give something away, you must first take possession of it. You must take ownership, and when it is fully yours, *then* you have the option to give it away. This is what you must do before you can be healed of any condition in body, mind or soul. You must take ownership of that condition, you must take possession, and when it is yours, *then* you have the option to give it away. It is in the giving away of the condition that you can be free of the condition; you can be healed.

Most people have anger against God

You see so many conditions in the earth that spring, not just from the duality consciousness, but from the fact that the soul has been programmed by an outer religion to believe that it should not be experiencing this or that condition. This comes in many disguises, but let me just bring up one example. So many Christians have been brought up to believe that in order to be good Christians, they should never be angry.

They experience situations in their lives that bring up the feeling of anger. Because they are "good Christians," they do not recognize the anger, they do not take ownership of it. What do they do? They deny it, they stuff it into the subconscious mind. Yet anger is a form of energy, anger is thought imbued with the power of feeling, and thus it will eventually cycle through the energy system of the material universe until it manifests as a physical condition in the body or a severe schism in the mind.

How can you be healed of a physical disease that is the product of anger? You cannot be healed fully through surgery or by taking a pill. You can be healed only by recognizing that the condition is the product of anger. Then, you must take an honest look at the anger, going all the way into it, until you discover the cause that made you feel that anger in the first place. The cause is often an expectation that is not in alignment with the reality of life or the higher will of your being. Until you own the anger – until you take possession of it and accept that *you* created it by making a choice, and until you discover the cause for why you made that choice – how can you ever give away the anger?

So many Christians have been brought up with a belief system that does not make sense, that does not answer their questions about life, that does not explain why they have personally encountered tragedy or why one child is born with immense handicaps and another child is born rich or gifted. They see the inequality in the world, and their only option is to reason that God must have created it that way. When you reason that way, it is inevitable that you will feel that God is unjust, and so there is anger against God.

So many Christians, in fact over 90 percent of all who call themselves Christians, have an unrecognized anger against God. Because they have been programmed with the need to be "good Christians" – if they are not good Christians they cannot enter the kingdom of heaven and be saved – they have only one option and it is to ignore, deny and suppress that anger.

The master key to healing

How could you possibly enter the kingdom of God when you feel anger against God? You do not want to come close to something that makes you feel anger or fear—you want to run away from it. How can you enter the inner kingdom until you have resolved your anger? How can you resolve the anger until you take ownership of that anger and see that it was something *you* created because you came to believe in one of the serpentine lies?

Now that you own it – now that you understand why – all of a sudden you can do something you could never do before. You can say: "This anger is mine. I take responsibility for it, and at this very moment, I own it fully."

Then you can say: "I also realize that although I created the anger, the 'I' that created the anger was the human ego, the human 'I.' I am *more* than that human ego. I am an immortal being, created by God in his image and likeness. It was not my Conscious You who created the anger, and thus I don't want the anger anymore, I don't want it to be part of my being and my life experience."

Once you realize that the anger is separate from yourself – it is a thing you own and not a part of yourself – at that moment, you have the option to give it away. Instead of giving your anger, or rather trying to give away your anger, by taking it out on other people, you can give it to the one Being who will gladly take your anger. *That* being is God, because God loves you and does not want to see you live a life burdened by anger or the effects of anger, such as mental, emotional and physical disease.

God wants you to be free of the anger, and God is an unlimited fire, an all-consuming fire, that can consume the anger in an instant. God will gladly take it from you, but God gave you free will and will not take your anger until you give it to God. You cannot give it to God until you take ownership, until you take possession, and you say: "This was created by a part of my being, and thus I accept accountability and responsibility. Yet it was created by a part of my being that is not my true self. Neither my ego nor the anger created by the ego is part of my Conscious You. I will no longer identify with the ego or with the anger. I will separate myself out from it. I will come apart and be a separate and chosen people, elect unto God because I have chosen to separate myself from the consciousness of death."

When you do this, *then* you can take the anger and you can turn to God – the God in the kingdom within you – and say: "Oh Lord, I offer this to you, please take it from me." If you can fully let go, it *will* be taken. As the cycles turn in the material universe, even a physical condition that is the result of anger will be taken from you.

Healing and your divine plan

As Mother Mary has explained, there are conditions where healing may not occur or may not occur instantly. The reason is that the Conscious You either has not fully learned the lesson it needs to learn from that condition, or it has not fully balanced the karma that it was meant to balance by carrying that condition in its body or mind. This can be personal karma, but for many spiritual people it truly is world karma that they are holding for others. Many of you chose to come down into embodiment in order to carry a certain portion of world karma. All of you who are on the spiritual path have volunteered to carry a burden, to carry a cross, so that others might not have to carry that burden and therefore have the opportunity to rise.

What often happens to such beautiful and loving lifestreams is that when they come down into embodiment, they get overwhelmed by the intensity, by the weight, of the energies on this planet—that are truly so heavy now that it can overwhelm almost any lifestream. They get influenced by the programming of the world, which says they shouldn't really be having that condition. Perhaps it is an unjust and angry God that put it upon them, or perhaps there is no God. The Conscious You who volunteered to come down to carry that condition, to carry that cross for others, now is tricked into entering the same catch-22 that I described earlier where the outer mind rebels against the condition that you have volunteered to take on. The outer mind is trying frantically to overcome that condition through outer means, through mechanical, physical means, by running to doctors or health care practitioners or healers of any kind. Yet deep within, the Conscious You knows that it volunteered to carry that condition. It does not want to let go of that condition until the purpose has been fulfilled and the lifestream has carried that burden long enough so that others might rise and make use of the opportunity they were given. The Conscious You rebels against its own divine plan and the decision it made while it was in the lighter energies of the spiritual realm. So many wonderful and loving lifestreams go through an entire lifetime of rebelling against that which is their own choice and which they chose out of love. They have negative feelings about their condition, be it fear, anger or resentment. Those feelings only make it so much harder for them to bear that condition. Unfortunately, the harder they make it for themselves, the easier it is for the Conscious You to begin to identify itself with the condition so that it thinks it is a part of its being that it cannot overcome.

There is a very subtle difference between identifying with a condition with the outer mind and stepping outside of that condition and taking ownership by realizing that you *did* create that condition or you *did* take it on, but the condition itself is the expression of a state of consciousness. That state of consciousness was not created by the Conscious You. It was created by your ego and by the forces of this world, including the egos of other people.

Jesus also suffered and had frustrations

Many lifestreams, who volunteered to take on a condition in order to balance a certain amount of world karma, will get stuck in carrying that condition far beyond the point that is necessary. They carry it far beyond the point where they have actually balanced that portion of world karma and are now free to focus on the positive aspects of their divine plan, which is to bring their gifts to this world.

A lifestream has two purposes for taking embodiment. One is to carry the cross, one is to bring its gift. Spiritual people often choose to take on the cross first, and once they have conquered that task, they are then free to be whole in bringing their gift. If they are tricked into rebelling against carrying their cross, and if they are not willing to let their human ego and their attachments die on that cross, then the lifestream will be stuck. This is what happened to Peter. He recognized the Christ, but he was not willing to fully identify with me, even to the point where he was willing to be crucified next to me if that was God's plan.

The key to moving out of this impasse is to learn from my example where you saw me in the Garden of Gethsemane the night before my trial and crucifixion. Again, the serpents of this world have created the false image of Jesus Christ that makes it impossible for most people to identify with me. They tend to gloss over the fact that, while I was in that garden, I was deeply disturbed and deeply distraught.

I cried tears of blood. I was suffering, as so many other people are suffering, by carrying the burden that I was carrying, by carrying my cross, and by the thought of what would happen next. I was so burdened by this that even though my Conscious You had volunteered to come into that situation, I still asked God to take that cup away from me. This will show you that Jesus Christ was indeed human like yourself and not some God and not some superhuman for whom the path was easy.

The path was not easy for me. I was as frustrated and distraught that evening as any human being has ever been frustrated. Yet the inspiration you can take away from this is that I eventually came to the point where I took ownership of my situation. I decided that I was willing to let God's will be done, and not the lower will of the outer mind. I surrendered myself to God and said: "Nevertheless Father, not my will but thine be done." I could not have surrendered myself to God unless I had taken ownership of my situation, unless I had taken ownership to the point where, if I had to keep the condition forever, I would have been at peace with that.

Be willing to carry your cross

If you have a condition in your life – be it an outer condition, be it a mental, emotional condition or be it a physical ailment – you need to come to the point of inner peace and surrender to the higher will of your own being, your own Conscious You and I AM Presence. You are willing to say: "God, if I have to carry this for the rest of my life, I will not only be at peace with that, but I will take the situation and make the best of it because I will love that condition. I will approach it with love so that even if I have to carry that condition, I will not use it as a reason to turn off the flow of God's love through me. I will let that love flow, come what may in this world."

When you come to that point of total ownership, at that point you can surrender yourself fully to God. At that point, you might indeed get an inner direction of how you can actually balance the karma you are carrying in a different way than through the limitation you are facing. It might be through invocations [See *www.transcendencetoolbox.com*], it might be through service, it might be through the resolution of psychology. Thereby, you not only resolve your own psychology, but help resolve the mass consciousness, the collective unconscious of humankind, making it easier for your brothers and sisters to overcome the same condition.

Once you come to that point of total surrender – that does not spring from fear or the desire to get away from the condition, but it springs from total acceptance of the condition that can only come from love – you are setting yourself free to flow with the will of God, the higher will of your I AM Presence and Conscious You, for your present embodiment. At that moment, you will no longer be at an impasse. You will be back in the flow of life, and you will feel like a burden has been lifted from your shoulders. Even if the condition remains, you will no longer be as burdened by it, you will be free to be the loving being that you are, to feel the fulfillment, even the fulfillment of carrying that condition because you know you are giving someone else the opportunity to rise higher and come closer to God.

The making of a saint

Suddenly, your life will open up, and you will no longer be in resentment or anger or disappointment or fear. You will be in the flow of love, and you will feel that love flowing through you. *That* is when you will see the transformation that leads to the condition called sainthood. You see so many people who have suffered a condition for many years, and for many years they were so focused on themselves and their own suffering, but suddenly a change occurred. They opened up, and now they were no longer focused on themselves, they were only focused on how they could help others who are going through that same situation, or even others who had worse conditions to deal with.

Suddenly, you have the making of a saint, the awakening of a lifestream because the Conscious You is now back in the flow. It is not at an impasse, it is flowing with the love of God out of which it sprang. The Conscious You knows that even though it might not be perfect in an outer sense, and even though it might have this or that human condition, it is on the road to salvation, and it knows that it is coming home.

You know how the old horse starts walking faster when it smells that the barn is near. *That* is how the Conscious You feels when it is awakened to the acceptance that it chose to come here for a positive reason, a reason that sprang out of love. When it reconnects to that love, all of a sudden the weight of the world falls off your shoulders and you can stand upright, no matter what conditions you are facing. You can say: "But these imperfections on earth don't matter because I now see the barn, I am coming home and I see my God standing in the doorway and next to him is my older brother, Jesus, and my older sister, Mary. They are greeting me, and they are beaming their love to me, making it easier for me to walk the last steps of the road home."

My beloved, ponder these teachings. Go within your heart, be willing to face any condition in your psychology, in your consciousness. Be willing to take ownership, to accept it in love, and then give it to God. If God takes it away, be content. If God does not take it away, be content. Because either way, you are going home when you are in the flow of love.

This is my teaching for this Easter, and I would that all human beings could understand this and get back into the flow of love. Truly, what is that flow of love but the true meaning of the resurrection. Even the physical body can be resurrected and made new from any condition, including the condition that human beings call death. There is nothing on earth that cannot be transcended through the power of God. But to unleash that power of God, you must first take ownership and then give away that which is not of God.

I seal you in the love of my heart, and in the name of the Father, the Mother, the Holy Spirit and the only begotten Son of God, which *is* the Christ consciousness. Amen.

6 | INVOKING FREEDOM FROM ANGER AGAINST GOD

In the name I AM THAT I AM, Jesus Christ, I call to all representatives of the Divine Mother, especially Jesus and Mother Mary, to help me uncover and transcend all anger against God, life or myself. I call for you to help me overcome all illusions that stand in the way of my healing, especially…

[Make personal calls.]

1. I see the fallacy of an outer standard

1. I am transcending outer, fear-based religions and the idol of the external God who resides outside the inner kingdom.

> O Jesus, blessed brother mine,
> I walk the path that you outline,
> a great example to us all,
> I follow now your inner call.

> **O Jesus, let the Fire of Joy,**
> **consume the devil's subtle ploy,**
> **transfigured is our planet earth,**
> **the golden age is given birth.**

2. I am transcending the schism in my psyche created by religion. I know from within that I came from somewhere else, that I am not a product of the body, that I am not the product of one lifetime, that I am ancient and that I came from a higher source.

> O Jesus, open inner sight,
> the ego wants to prove it's right,
> but this I will no longer do,
> I want to be all one with you.

> **O Jesus, let the Fire of Joy,**
> **consume the devil's subtle ploy,**
> **transfigured is our planet earth,**
> **the golden age is given birth.**

3. I know God is inside. I know God is one with me and that I can reach God on my own.

> O Jesus, I now clearly see,
> the Key of Knowledge given me,
> my Christ self I hereby embrace,
> as you fill up my inner space.

> **O Jesus, let the Fire of Joy,**
> **consume the devil's subtle ploy,**
> **transfigured is our planet earth,**
> **the golden age is given birth.**

4. I am transcending the ideal for how the perfect human being should be. I know I am acceptable in the eyes of God.

> O Jesus, show me serpent's lie,
> expose the beam in my own eye,
> as Christ discernment you me give,
> in oneness I forever live.

> **O Jesus, let the Fire of Joy,**
> **consume the devil's subtle ploy,**
> **transfigured is our planet earth,**
> **the golden age is given birth.**

5. I am transcending all sense that I must mold myself after the ideal that has been put before me since childhood.

> O Jesus, I am truly meek,
> and thus I turn the other cheek,
> when the accuser attacks me,
> I go within and merge with thee.

> **O Jesus, let the Fire of Joy,**
> **consume the devil's subtle ploy,**
> **transfigured is our planet earth,**
> **the golden age is given birth.**

6. This ideal is an idol and a violation of the first two commandments. It is an impossible idol because no human being could ever live up to this outer standard of perfection.

> O Jesus, ego I let die,
> surrender ev'ry earthly tie,
> the dead can bury what is dead,
> I choose to walk with you instead.
>
> **O Jesus, let the Fire of Joy,**
> **consume the devil's subtle ploy,**
> **transfigured is our planet earth,**
> **the golden age is given birth.**

7. The outer standard originated in the mind of anti-christ, the mind of the devil himself, who believes there is a mechanical path to salvation.

> O Jesus, help me rise above,
> the devil's test through higher love,
> show me separate self unreal,
> my formless self you do reveal.
>
> **O Jesus, let the Fire of Joy,**
> **consume the devil's subtle ploy,**
> **transfigured is our planet earth,**
> **the golden age is given birth.**

8. The kingdom is within me. I am uniting with the consciousness of the kingdom, and I am in the kingdom.

> O Jesus, what is that to me,
> I just let go and follow thee,
> with this I do pass ev'ry test,
> to find with you eternal rest.

> **O Jesus, let the Fire of Joy,**
> **consume the devil's subtle ploy,**
> **transfigured is our planet earth,**
> **the golden age is given birth.**

9. God is already where I am, for God is omnipresent. I am transcending the illusion that I am separated from God's kingdom. I am transcending the lower mind, the mind that has been trapped in duality.

> O Jesus, fiery master mine,
> my heart now melting into thine,
> I love with heart and mind and soul,
> the God who is my highest goal.

> **O Jesus, let the Fire of Joy,**
> **consume the devil's subtle ploy,**
> **transfigured is our planet earth,**
> **the golden age is given birth.**

2. I take ownership of my life

1. I know from within that I am more than the dualistic mind. I am transcending the outer ideal, and I am accepting my true creativity and true being.

> O Jesus, blessed brother mine,
> I walk the path that you outline,
> a great example to us all,
> I follow now your inner call.

**O Jesus, let the Fire of Joy,
consume the devil's subtle ploy,
transfigured is our planet earth,
the golden age is given birth.**

2. The outer mind is trying to force the outer matrix upon me. I am transcending the outer discipline, and I am no longer a house divided against myself.

O Jesus, open inner sight,
the ego wants to prove it's right,
but this I will no longer do,
I want to be all one with you.

**O Jesus, let the Fire of Joy,
consume the devil's subtle ploy,
transfigured is our planet earth,
the golden age is given birth.**

3. I am transcending the catch-22 of being lukewarm. I am healed of the conditions that my mind has created out of the duality consciousness, both mental illness, physical disease and outer problems.

O Jesus, I now clearly see,
the Key of Knowledge given me,
my Christ self I hereby embrace,
as you fill up my inner space.

**O Jesus, let the Fire of Joy,
consume the devil's subtle ploy,
transfigured is our planet earth,
the golden age is given birth.**

4. I cannot give away what I do not own. To give something away, I must first take possession of it. I must take ownership, and when it is fully mine, then I have the option to give it away.

> O Jesus, show me serpent's lie,
> expose the beam in my own eye,
> as Christ discernment you me give,
> in oneness I forever live.

> **O Jesus, let the Fire of Joy,**
> **consume the devil's subtle ploy,**
> **transfigured is our planet earth,**
> **the golden age is given birth.**

5. I hereby take ownership of this condition, I take possession.

> O Jesus, I am truly meek,
> and thus I turn the other cheek,
> when the accuser attacks me,
> I go within and merge with thee.

> **O Jesus, let the Fire of Joy,**
> **consume the devil's subtle ploy,**
> **transfigured is our planet earth,**
> **the golden age is given birth.**

6. The condition is mine, and I now give it away. I am free of the condition; I am healed.

> O Jesus, ego I let die,
> surrender ev'ry earthly tie,
> the dead can bury what is dead,
> I choose to walk with you instead.

**O Jesus, let the Fire of Joy,
consume the devil's subtle ploy,
transfigured is our planet earth,
the golden age is given birth.**

7. I am transcending the many conditions that spring from the programming that makes me believe I should not be experiencing this or that condition.

> O Jesus, help me rise above,
> the devil's test through higher love,
> show me separate self unreal,
> my formless self you do reveal.

**O Jesus, let the Fire of Joy,
consume the devil's subtle ploy,
transfigured is our planet earth,
the golden age is given birth.**

8. I am transcending the belief that in order to be a good spiritual person, I should never have certain feelings. I acknowledge my feelings and I bring them out of the subconscious mind.

> O Jesus, what is that to me,
> I just let go and follow thee,
> with this I do pass ev'ry test,
> to find with you eternal rest.

**O Jesus, let the Fire of Joy,
consume the devil's subtle ploy,
transfigured is our planet earth,
the golden age is given birth.**

9. Feelings are a form of energy, and they will eventually cycle through the energy system of the material universe until it manifests as a physical condition in the body or a severe schism in the mind.

> O Jesus, fiery master mine,
> my heart now melting into thine,
> I love with heart and mind and soul,
> the God who is my highest goal.
>
> **O Jesus, let the Fire of Joy,**
> **consume the devil's subtle ploy,**
> **transfigured is our planet earth,**
> **the golden age is given birth.**

3. I acknowledge anger against God

1. The only way I can be healed of a physical disease that is the product of certain feelings is by recognizing that the condition is produced by those feelings.

> O Jesus, blessed brother mine,
> I walk the path that you outline,
> a great example to us all,
> I follow now your inner call.
>
> **O Jesus, let the Fire of Joy,**
> **consume the devil's subtle ploy,**
> **transfigured is our planet earth,**
> **the golden age is given birth.**

2. I take an honest look at my feelings, going all the way into them until I discover the expectation that is not in alignment with the reality of life or the higher will of my being.

> O Jesus, open inner sight,
> the ego wants to prove it's right,
> but this I will no longer do,
> I want to be all one with you.
>
> **O Jesus, let the Fire of Joy,**
> **consume the devil's subtle ploy,**
> **transfigured is our planet earth,**
> **the golden age is given birth.**

3. I own the feelings, I take possession of them. I accept that I created them by making a choice, and I now choose to give away the feelings.

> O Jesus, I now clearly see,
> the Key of Knowledge given me,
> my Christ self I hereby embrace,
> as you fill up my inner space.
>
> **O Jesus, let the Fire of Joy,**
> **consume the devil's subtle ploy,**
> **transfigured is our planet earth,**
> **the golden age is given birth.**

4. I am transcending the belief system that does not explain why we have personally encountered tragedy, or why one child is born with immense handicaps and another child is born rich or gifted.

6 | Invoking Freedom from Anger against God

O Jesus, show me serpent's lie,
expose the beam in my own eye,
as Christ discernment you me give,
in oneness I forever live.

**O Jesus, let the Fire of Joy,
consume the devil's subtle ploy,
transfigured is our planet earth,
the golden age is given birth.**

5. The inequality in the world does not mean that God must have created it that way. I am transcending the feeling that God is unjust. I surrender my anger against God.

O Jesus, I am truly meek,
and thus I turn the other cheek,
when the accuser attacks me,
I go within and merge with thee.

**O Jesus, let the Fire of Joy,
consume the devil's subtle ploy,
transfigured is our planet earth,
the golden age is given birth.**

6. I uncover my unrecognized anger against God. I cannot enter the kingdom of God when I feel anger against God.

O Jesus, ego I let die,
surrender ev'ry earthly tie,
the dead can bury what is dead,
I choose to walk with you instead.

**O Jesus, let the Fire of Joy,
consume the devil's subtle ploy,
transfigured is our planet earth,
the golden age is given birth.**

7. I take ownership of my anger. I see that it was something I created because I came to believe in one of the serpentine lies.

O Jesus, help me rise above,
the devil's test through higher love,
show me separate self unreal,
my formless self you do reveal.

**O Jesus, let the Fire of Joy,
consume the devil's subtle ploy,
transfigured is our planet earth,
the golden age is given birth.**

8. This anger is mine. I take responsibility for it, and at this very moment, I own it fully.

O Jesus, what is that to me,
I just let go and follow thee,
with this I do pass ev'ry test,
to find with you eternal rest.

**O Jesus, let the Fire of Joy,
consume the devil's subtle ploy,
transfigured is our planet earth,
the golden age is given birth.**

9. Although I created the anger, the 'I' that created the anger was the human ego, the human 'I.' I am more than that human ego. I am an immortal being, created by God in his image and likeness. It was not my Conscious You who created the anger, and thus I don't want the anger anymore, I don't want it to be part of my being and my life experience.

> O Jesus, fiery master mine,
> my heart now melting into thine,
> I love with heart and mind and soul,
> the God who is my highest goal.
>
> **O Jesus, let the Fire of Joy,
> consume the devil's subtle ploy,
> transfigured is our planet earth,
> the golden age is given birth.**

4. I give my anger to God

1. The anger is separate from myself, it is a thing I own and not a part of myself. I give my anger to the one Being who will gladly take my anger, namely God.

> O Jesus, blessed brother mine,
> I walk the path that you outline,
> a great example to us all,
> I follow now your inner call.
>
> **O Jesus, let the Fire of Joy,
> consume the devil's subtle ploy,
> transfigured is our planet earth,
> the golden age is given birth.**

2. God loves me and does not want to see me live a life burdened by anger or the effects of anger, such as mental, emotional and physical disease.

> O Jesus, open inner sight,
> the ego wants to prove it's right,
> but this I will no longer do,
> I want to be all one with you.
>
> **O Jesus, let the Fire of Joy,**
> **consume the devil's subtle ploy,**
> **transfigured is our planet earth,**
> **the golden age is given birth.**

3. God wants me to be free of the anger. God is an unlimited fire, an all-consuming fire, that can consume the anger in an instant. God gladly takes it from me, as I now use my free will to give my anger to God.

> O Jesus, I now clearly see,
> the Key of Knowledge given me,
> my Christ self I hereby embrace,
> as you fill up my inner space.
>
> **O Jesus, let the Fire of Joy,**
> **consume the devil's subtle ploy,**
> **transfigured is our planet earth,**
> **the golden age is given birth.**

4. I cannot give my anger to God until I take ownership, until I take possession. The anger was created by a part of my being, and thus I accept accountability and responsibility.

O Jesus, show me serpent's lie,
expose the beam in my own eye,
as Christ discernment you me give,
in oneness I forever live.

**O Jesus, let the Fire of Joy,
consume the devil's subtle ploy,
transfigured is our planet earth,
the golden age is given birth.**

5. The anger was created by a part of my being that is not my true self. Neither my ego nor the anger created by the ego is part of my Conscious You.

O Jesus, I am truly meek,
and thus I turn the other cheek,
when the accuser attacks me,
I go within and merge with thee.

**O Jesus, let the Fire of Joy,
consume the devil's subtle ploy,
transfigured is our planet earth,
the golden age is given birth.**

6. I no longer identify with the ego or with the anger. I separate myself out from it. I come apart and I am a separate and chosen people, elect unto God because I have chosen to separate myself from the consciousness of death.

O Jesus, ego I let die,
surrender ev'ry earthly tie,
the dead can bury what is dead,
I choose to walk with you instead.

> **O Jesus, let the Fire of Joy,**
> **consume the devil's subtle ploy,**
> **transfigured is our planet earth,**
> **the golden age is given birth.**

7. I now take the anger and I turn to God – the God in the kingdom within me – and I say: "Oh Lord, I offer this to you, please take it from me." I fully let go, and I know it is taken.

> O Jesus, help me rise above,
> the devil's test through higher love,
> show me separate self unreal,
> my formless self you do reveal.

> **O Jesus, let the Fire of Joy,**
> **consume the devil's subtle ploy,**
> **transfigured is our planet earth,**
> **the golden age is given birth.**

8. The anger keeps me on my personal cross. I do what Jesus did on the cross. I give up the ghost of my anger and the false expectations that caused it.

> O Jesus, what is that to me,
> I just let go and follow thee,
> with this I do pass ev'ry test,
> to find with you eternal rest.

> **O Jesus, let the Fire of Joy,**
> **consume the devil's subtle ploy,**
> **transfigured is our planet earth,**
> **the golden age is given birth.**

9. I am willing to spiritually die on my cross in order to follow Jesus into the Fire of the Resurrection.

> O Jesus, fiery master mine,
> my heart now melting into thine,
> I love with heart and mind and soul,
> the God who is my highest goal.
>
> **O Jesus, let the Fire of Joy,**
> **consume the devil's subtle ploy,**
> **transfigured is our planet earth,**
> **the golden age is given birth.**

Sealing

In the name of the Divine Mother, I call to Jesus and Mother Mary for the sealing of myself and all people in the creative flow of the Divine Mother, the River of Life. I call for the multiplication of my calls by all representatives of the Divine Mother, so that we form the perfect figure-eight flow of "As Above, so below." Thus, I accept that this is fully manifest, because the mouth of the Lord, the Divine Mother that I AM, has spoken it. Amen.

7 | INVOKING THE POWER OF GOD IN ME

In the name I AM THAT I AM, Jesus Christ, I call to all representatives of the Divine Mother, especially Lord Maitreya and Mother Mary, to help me unlock the power of God to flow from within myself through my sense of identity, my thoughts, my feelings and my actions. I call for you to help me overcome all illusions that stand in the way of my healing, especially…

[Make personal calls.]

1. I do not rebel against my condition

1. I see where I have not fully learned the lesson I need to learn from a certain condition. I know where I have not fully balanced the karma that I was meant to balance by carrying that condition in my body or mind.

Maitreya, I am truly meek,
your counsel wise I humbly seek,
your vision I so want to see,
with you in Eden I will be.

**Maitreya, kindness is the cure,
in fires of kindness I am pure.
Maitreya, now release the fire,
that raises me forever higher.**

2. I know whether a condition is caused by personal karma or world karma that I have volunteered to carry, so that others might not have to carry that burden and therefore have the opportunity to rise.

Maitreya, help me to return,
to learn from you, I truly yearn,
as oneness is all I desire
I feel initiation's fire.

**Maitreya, kindness is the cure,
in fires of kindness I am pure.
Maitreya, now release the fire,
that raises me forever higher.**

3. I am transcending the intensity, the weight, of the energies on this planet, energies that are truly so heavy that it can overwhelm almost any lifestream. I am free.

Maitreya, I hereby decide,
from you I will no longer hide,
expose to me the very lie
that caused edenic self to die.

**Maitreya, kindness is the cure,
in fires of kindness I am pure.
Maitreya, now release the fire,
that raises me forever higher.**

4. I am transcending the programming of the world, which says I shouldn't be having a certain condition. I know God is just and has not put my condition upon me.

> Maitreya, blessed Guru mine,
> my heart of hearts forever thine,
> I vow that I will listen well,
> so we can break the serpent's spell.

**Maitreya, kindness is the cure,
in fires of kindness I am pure.
Maitreya, now release the fire,
that raises me forever higher.**

5. I know how I volunteered to carry a cross for others. I am transcending the catch-22 of rebellion, and I accept the condition I have taken on.

> Maitreya, help me see the lie
> whereby the serpent broke the tie,
> the serpent now has naught in me,
> in oneness I am truly free.

**Maitreya, kindness is the cure,
in fires of kindness I am pure.
Maitreya, now release the fire,
that raises me forever higher.**

6. I am transcending the pattern of my outer mind seeking to overcome a condition through mechanical, physical means, by running to doctors or health care practitioners or healers.

> Maitreya, truth does set me free
> from falsehoods of duality,
> the fruit of knowledge I let go,
> so your true spirit I do know.
>
> **Maitreya, kindness is the cure,**
> **in fires of kindness I am pure.**
> **Maitreya, now release the fire,**
> **that raises me forever higher.**

7. I see that deep within I do not want to let go of that condition until the purpose has been fulfilled, and I have carried that burden long enough, so that others might make use of the opportunity they were given.

> Maitreya, I submit to you,
> intentions pure, my heart is true,
> from ego I am truly free,
> as I am now all one with thee.
>
> **Maitreya, kindness is the cure,**
> **in fires of kindness I am pure.**
> **Maitreya, now release the fire,**
> **that raises me forever higher.**

8. I fully accept my own divine plan and the decision I made while I was in the lighter energies of the spiritual realm.

7 | Invoking the Power of God in Me

> Maitreya, kindness is the key,
> all shades of kindness teach to me,
> for I am now the open door,
> the Art of Kindness to restore.
>
> **Maitreya, kindness is the cure,**
> **in fires of kindness I am pure.**
> **Maitreya, now release the fire,**
> **that raises me forever higher.**

9. I surrender my negative feelings about my condition, be it fear, anger or resentment. They only make it so much harder for me to bear the condition. I transcend all identification with the condition. It is *not* part of my being and I *can* overcome it.

> Maitreya, oh sweet mystery,
> immersed in your reality,
> the myst'ry school will now return,
> for this, my heart does truly burn.
>
> **Maitreya, kindness is the cure,**
> **in fires of kindness I am pure.**
> **Maitreya, now release the fire,**
> **that raises me forever higher.**

2. I do not rebel against my cross

1. I do not identify with a condition with the outer mind. I step outside of that condition and take ownership.

> Maitreya, I am truly meek,
> your counsel wise I humbly seek,
> your vision I so want to see,
> with you in Eden I will be.
>
> **Maitreya, kindness is the cure,**
> **in fires of kindness I am pure.**
> **Maitreya, now release the fire,**
> **that raises me forever higher.**

2. I did create or take on the condition, but the condition itself is the expression of a state of consciousness.

> Maitreya, help me to return,
> to learn from you, I truly yearn,
> as oneness is all I desire
> I feel initiation's fire.
>
> **Maitreya, kindness is the cure,**
> **in fires of kindness I am pure.**
> **Maitreya, now release the fire,**
> **that raises me forever higher.**

3. This state of consciousness was not created by my Conscious You. It was created by my ego and by the forces of this world, including the egos of other people.

> Maitreya, I hereby decide,
> from you I will no longer hide,
> expose to me the very lie
> that caused edenic self to die.

> **Maitreya, kindness is the cure,**
> **in fires of kindness I am pure.**
> **Maitreya, now release the fire,**
> **that raises me forever higher.**

4. I will no longer carry a condition beyond the point where I have balanced that portion of world karma. I am now free to focus on the positive aspects of my divine plan.

> Maitreya, blessed Guru mine,
> my heart of hearts forever thine,
> I vow that I will listen well,
> so we can break the serpent's spell.

> **Maitreya, kindness is the cure,**
> **in fires of kindness I am pure.**
> **Maitreya, now release the fire,**
> **that raises me forever higher.**

5. I know whether I have chosen to take on my cross first, so that I can conquer that task quickly and be whole in bringing my gift.

> Maitreya, help me see the lie
> whereby the serpent broke the tie,
> the serpent now has naught in me,
> in oneness I am truly free.

> **Maitreya, kindness is the cure,**
> **in fires of kindness I am pure.**
> **Maitreya, now release the fire,**
> **that raises me forever higher.**

6. I will not be tricked into rebelling against carrying my cross. I am letting my human ego and my attachments die on that cross, and I am free.

> Maitreya, truth does set me free
> from falsehoods of duality,
> the fruit of knowledge I let go,
> so your true spirit I do know.
>
> **Maitreya, kindness is the cure,**
> **in fires of kindness I am pure.**
> **Maitreya, now release the fire,**
> **that raises me forever higher.**

7. I am moving out of my impasse by learning from Jesus' example in the Garden of Gethsemane. I know Jesus was human like myself and not some God or superhuman for whom the path was easy.

> Maitreya, I submit to you,
> intentions pure, my heart is true,
> from ego I am truly free,
> as I am now all one with thee.
>
> **Maitreya, kindness is the cure,**
> **in fires of kindness I am pure.**
> **Maitreya, now release the fire,**
> **that raises me forever higher.**

8. Based on Jesus' example, I decide that I am willing to let God's will be done, and not the lower will of the outer mind. I surrender myself to God and I say: "Nevertheless Father, not my will but thine be done."

Maitreya, kindness is the key,
all shades of kindness teach to me,
for I am now the open door,
the Art of Kindness to restore.

**Maitreya, kindness is the cure,
in fires of kindness I am pure.
Maitreya, now release the fire,
that raises me forever higher.**

9. God, if I have to carry this for the rest of my life, I will not only be at peace with that, but I will take the situation and make the best of it because I will love that condition. I will approach it with love and I will *not* use it as a reason to turn off the flow of God's love through me. I am letting love flow, come what may in this world.

Maitreya, oh sweet mystery,
immersed in your reality,
the myst'ry school will now return,
for this, my heart does truly burn.

**Maitreya, kindness is the cure,
in fires of kindness I am pure.
Maitreya, now release the fire,
that raises me forever higher.**

3. I accept transformation

1. I receive the inner direction for how I can balance the karma I am carrying in a different way than through the limitation I am facing. I see how I can do it through invocations, through service or through the resolution of psychology.

> Maitreya, I am truly meek,
> your counsel wise I humbly seek,
> your vision I so want to see,
> with you in Eden I will be.
>
> **Maitreya, kindness is the cure,**
> **in fires of kindness I am pure.**
> **Maitreya, now release the fire,**
> **that raises me forever higher.**

2. I see how to resolve my own psychology, and how to help resolve the mass consciousness, the collective unconscious of humankind, making it easier for my brothers and sisters to overcome the same condition.

> Maitreya, help me to return,
> to learn from you, I truly yearn,
> as oneness is all I desire
> I feel initiation's fire.
>
> **Maitreya, kindness is the cure,**
> **in fires of kindness I am pure.**
> **Maitreya, now release the fire,**
> **that raises me forever higher.**

3. I am at the point of total surrender that does not spring from fear but from love. I accept that I am free to flow with the will of God for my present embodiment.

> Maitreya, I hereby decide,
> from you I will no longer hide,
> expose to me the very lie
> that caused edenic self to die.

> **Maitreya, kindness is the cure,**
> **in fires of kindness I am pure.**
> **Maitreya, now release the fire,**
> **that raises me forever higher.**

4. I am transcending any impasse. I am back in the flow of life, and a burden has been lifted from my shoulders.

> Maitreya, blessed Guru mine,
> my heart of hearts forever thine,
> I vow that I will listen well,
> so we can break the serpent's spell.

> **Maitreya, kindness is the cure,**
> **in fires of kindness I am pure.**
> **Maitreya, now release the fire,**
> **that raises me forever higher.**

5. Even if a condition remains, I am free to be the loving being that I am. I feel the fulfillment of carrying that condition because I know I am giving someone else the opportunity to rise higher and come closer to God.

Maitreya, help me see the lie
whereby the serpent broke the tie,
the serpent now has naught in me,
in oneness I am truly free.

**Maitreya, kindness is the cure,
in fires of kindness I am pure.
Maitreya, now release the fire,
that raises me forever higher.**

6. My life is opening up, and I am no longer in resentment, or anger, or disappointment, or fear. I am in the flow of love, and I feel that love flowing through me.

Maitreya, truth does set me free
from falsehoods of duality,
the fruit of knowledge I let go,
so your true spirit I do know.

**Maitreya, kindness is the cure,
in fires of kindness I am pure.
Maitreya, now release the fire,
that raises me forever higher.**

7. I accept the transformation and I am no longer focused on myself. I am focused on how I can help others who are going through the same situation, or even others who have worse conditions to deal with.

Maitreya, I submit to you,
intentions pure, my heart is true,
from ego I am truly free,
as I am now all one with thee.

**Maitreya, kindness is the cure,
in fires of kindness I am pure.
Maitreya, now release the fire,
that raises me forever higher.**

8. Even though I might not be perfect in an outer sense, and even though I might have this or that human condition, I am on the road to salvation, and I know I am coming home.

Maitreya, kindness is the key,
all shades of kindness teach to me,
for I am now the open door,
the Art of Kindness to restore.

**Maitreya, kindness is the cure,
in fires of kindness I am pure.
Maitreya, now release the fire,
that raises me forever higher.**

9. I am awakened to the acceptance that I chose to come here for a positive reason, a reason that sprang out of love.

Maitreya, oh sweet mystery,
immersed in your reality,
the myst'ry school will now return,
for this, my heart does truly burn.

**Maitreya, kindness is the cure,
in fires of kindness I am pure.
Maitreya, now release the fire,
that raises me forever higher.**

4. I am the open door

1. I am reconnecting to my original love. The weight of the world falls off my shoulders and I stand upright, no matter what condition I am facing.

> Maitreya, I am truly meek,
> your counsel wise I humbly seek,
> your vision I so want to see,
> with you in Eden I will be.
>
> **Maitreya, kindness is the cure,**
> **in fires of kindness I am pure.**
> **Maitreya, now release the fire,**
> **that raises me forever higher.**

2. The imperfections on earth don't matter because I am coming home. I see my God standing in the doorway and next to him is my older brother, Jesus, and my older sister, Mary. They are greeting me, and they are beaming their love to me, making it easier for me to walk the last steps of the road home.

> Maitreya, help me to return,
> to learn from you, I truly yearn,
> as oneness is all I desire
> I feel initiation's fire.
>
> **Maitreya, kindness is the cure,**
> **in fires of kindness I am pure.**
> **Maitreya, now release the fire,**
> **that raises me forever higher.**

3. I am willing to go within my heart and to face any condition in my psychology, in my consciousness. I am willing to take ownership, to accept it in love, and then give it to God.

> Maitreya, I hereby decide,
> from you I will no longer hide,
> expose to me the very lie
> that caused edenic self to die.

> **Maitreya, kindness is the cure,**
> **in fires of kindness I am pure.**
> **Maitreya, now release the fire,**
> **that raises me forever higher.**

4. If God takes it away, I am content. If God does not take it away, I am content. Either way, I am going home because I am in the flow of love.

> Maitreya, blessed Guru mine,
> my heart of hearts forever thine,
> I vow that I will listen well,
> so we can break the serpent's spell.

> **Maitreya, kindness is the cure,**
> **in fires of kindness I am pure.**
> **Maitreya, now release the fire,**
> **that raises me forever higher.**

5. The flow of love is the true meaning of the resurrection. Even my physical body can be resurrected and made new from any condition, including the condition that human beings call death.

Maitreya, help me see the lie
whereby the serpent broke the tie,
the serpent now has naught in me,
in oneness I am truly free.

**Maitreya, kindness is the cure,
in fires of kindness I am pure.
Maitreya, now release the fire,
that raises me forever higher.**

6. I fully accept that there is nothing on earth that cannot be transcended through the power of God.

Maitreya, truth does set me free
from falsehoods of duality,
the fruit of knowledge I let go,
so your true spirit I do know.

**Maitreya, kindness is the cure,
in fires of kindness I am pure.
Maitreya, now release the fire,
that raises me forever higher.**

7. In order to unleash the power of God, I must first take ownership and then give away that which is not of God.

Maitreya, I submit to you,
intentions pure, my heart is true,
from ego I am truly free,
as I am now all one with thee.

**Maitreya, kindness is the cure,
in fires of kindness I am pure.
Maitreya, now release the fire,
that raises me forever higher.**

8. I take full ownership of my present condition. I accept that I took on the condition by taking on the consciousness behind it. I did this through a choice, which means I have the power to undo that choice.

Maitreya, kindness is the key,
all shades of kindness teach to me,
for I am now the open door,
the Art of Kindness to restore.

**Maitreya, kindness is the cure,
in fires of kindness I am pure.
Maitreya, now release the fire,
that raises me forever higher.**

9. I surrender the choice to shut off the power of God's love flowing through me. In oneness with Maitreya, I accept that I am the open door which no human can shut.

Maitreya, oh sweet mystery,
immersed in your reality,
the myst'ry school will now return,
for this, my heart does truly burn.

**Maitreya, kindness is the cure,
in fires of kindness I am pure.
Maitreya, now release the fire,
that raises me forever higher.**

Sealing

In the name of the Divine Mother, I call to Maitreya and Mother Mary for the sealing of myself and all people in the creative flow of the Divine Mother, the River of Life. I call for the multiplication of my calls by all representatives of the Divine Mother, so that we form the perfect figure-eight flow of "As Above, so below." Thus, I accept that this is fully manifest, because the mouth of the Lord, the Divine Mother that I AM, has spoken it. Amen.

8 | RECONNECTING TO YOUR ORIGINAL LOVE

A dictation by Mother Mary, April 7, 2007.

It is impossible to be in this world without being wounded, without being hurt, by those who are so trapped in anti-love that they actually feel threatened by anyone who expresses love. When they are exposed to those who express love, they feel they have to somehow silence them, beat them down, stop the flow of love through them, so that they can overcome the sense of panic that literally makes them believe they will die if they receive true love.

Earth is a planet with much anti-love

You should look upon this planet not the way you were brought up to look at it—whatever that might be. You should look upon it as a world that is designed specifically to give certain beings an opportunity to live in a world where they can deny God's Presence for as long as they like—or almost as long as they like.

You who are the spiritual people should realize that you have come here as a sacrifice. You came here because you desired to descend into this world, where so many beings had become trapped in anti-love, and you wanted to bring the sunlight of love in order to give them an opportunity to experience that there is something beyond anti-love. When you look at this, you can realize that you volunteered to come into a situation that you knew would be very difficult. You knew that your love would be rejected, you knew that you would be hurt and bruised.

I am not saying this to justify the hurt, to justify the abuse. I am saying it because when you accept the reality of this planet, you can overcome the very dysfunctional and non-productive attitude of feeling that you should not have been treated this way, that something is wrong, perhaps even feeling that: "God should not have allowed this to happen to me." When you go into that frame of mind – of feeling that some injustice has been done to you on earth, possibly even that God has been unjust towards you – then you inevitably become a victim of the consciousness of anti-love that you came here to eradicate.

You cut off the flow of God's love through your being. Now you feel that God has abandoned you, for you no longer experience that love. My beloved, it is not that God has abandoned you. It is that when you do not feel God's love flowing *through* you, you do not feel God's love *for* you. Love is not a static force, it cannot be captured, it cannot be controlled, it cannot be put in a mental box. It can be experienced only when you allow it to flow. When you allow yourself to become trapped in the consciousness of anti-love, then you shut off the flow and now you no longer experience unconditional love.

What is left? Only conditional love is left—the worldly form of love that even those who are trapped in anti-love need. Surely, there is not one being who can live without love. The problem is that so many beings cannot receive the true unconditional love, and they are on an impossible quest, a never-ending quest, to fill the desire for love. They are seeking to fill it with conditional love, thinking that the love they receive should live up to certain conditions and that they should seek to possess the love or the persons through whom that love is being expressed.

You came here to bring love

This becomes a catch-22. We who are your spiritual teachers face the dilemma of how to awaken you without shattering your self-esteem or even your sense of identity. The only way to escape the duality consciousness is by reconnecting to the love that is still there in the core of your being.

I realize you are in this world and you look at life and the universe from *inside* the mental box of this world. I tell you that you did not come here, you did not decide to descend here, with the limited perspective you have now. Even though you may have been bruised and hurt and have shut off the flow of God's love and feel abandoned by God, I can assure you that you came here out of love.

I realize that there are some of you who have come here from higher realms and who feel that you have been unjustly sent here by God. Nevertheless, you did not start in that higher realm. You started in an even higher realm. There was a point where your lifestream decided to first descend into the world of form, into the latest sphere in the world of form. That decision was based on love, the desire to express your true God quality, your true divine individuality, and bring that gift to the world in order to light up a world.

It is possible for you to go beyond the outer facade and reconnect to the core of that love in your being. When you do so, you will realize that you love something more than what you are experiencing right now. I tell you, my beloved, it is only when you recognize that you have a love for something more than what you have right now that you can overcome your current limitations. You can overcome your current limitations in only one way, namely, as we have explained many times, by letting the old sense of identity die. In order to be willing to let the old die, you must have a love for something *more*. This makes you realize that letting the old die does not mean a loss, for you will be reborn into a higher state of identity.

When you have a negative awakening – where you realize that you are a terrible person and you need to change, you are a miserable sinner – then your sense of self-esteem is shattered. You feel that in order to overcome the bad aspects of yourself, you have to destroy your sense of self. You think there is no sense of self beyond the ego.

Overcome selfishness without destroying the self

There are indeed people in this world, both in traditional religions and even in new spiritual movements, who believe that the way to spiritual growth is to destroy all sense of self, all sense of a separate self. You see, my beloved, this is coming from a negative. This is coming from wanting to eliminate a negative by creating another negative or by destroying the first negative which is another negative action. As two wrongs do not make a right, you cannot correct an imperfection by acting out another imperfection.

There is no way to destroy something. Deep within, you have a basic survival instinct that is even beyond the survival instinct of the body and the survival instinct of the ego. Your true divine individuality wants to survive, wants to grow and wants to express itself in this world. It wants to fulfill its original reason for being, its reason for coming here. If you try to destroy all sense of self, you end up working against yourself, seeking to destroy not only the false sense of self of the ego but also the true sense of self of your divine individuality.

This simply cannot be done. You may actually be able to destroy much of your sense of self but you will eventually come to a point where the inner conflict becomes so intense – so illogical, so contradictory – that you simply cannot stand it anymore. This is not the way. The way to salvation is not through self-denial or self-destruction. *It is through self-transcendence.*

You are not seeking to destroy the old self. You are simply seeking to transcend it and be reborn into a new self, a higher self, that replaces the old. The trick is – as Jesus demonstrated on the cross – you cannot be reborn into the new until you allow the old to die.

Here is where the scary part comes in. There will be a cosmic interval between the death of the old and the resurrection of the Conscious You into a higher sense of identity. When you let the old die, you will literally feel like you are plunging yourself into a vacuum. I say you will *feel* like it, because in reality you will not. Your conscious self will not lose consciousness. It will remain conscious. But as you face the moment of having to give up the old self, you will feel like there will be nothing after that old self. That is what Jesus experienced on the cross when he cried out: "My God, my God, why hast thou forsaken me?"

What was it that pulled Jesus beyond that state of fear and paralysis, that state of panic? It was that he had integrated into his being the higher love that brought him into this world. He had uncovered that love, and he knew in his conscious mind why he originally came here. Therefore, he did not feel like a victim of life. He did not feel that God had unjustly sent him into this world. Even though he had his trials and tribulations, deep within him, he knew that he had volunteered to come here and he knew what could happen to him.

Because Jesus had the conscious awareness of the deeper, innermost love of his being, he realized that he simply needed to give up the ghost of the last vestiges of the separate self. In his love for God he was willing to do that. What I am saying to you is that the essential key to everything is to reconnect to the deeper love of your being, the innermost love of your being, that originally caused you to volunteer to descend into the denser sphere in order to bring your light and your love. This is a topic you might meditate upon.

Reconnect to your original love

This is something you can take with you: the idea of seeking to reconnect to the original love of your being. My Course in Abundance is designed to help you reconnect to that inner love. I assure you that the course was designed to help a broad range of people, even those who for a very long time have been trapped in the consciousness of anti-love. No matter how far you might have descended into anti-love, if you will keep reading and re-reading and studying and absorbing my book while you give the invocations, then you will eventually break through.

I assure you that I am a capable spiritual teacher. I am capable of taking a child by the hand, even if it is an unruly child, and bringing that child to my heart—even if the child comes kicking and screaming. I have dealt with my share of unruly children, one of which bore the name of Jesus, who was by no means an easy child, as he well knows. We have often sat together and chuckled about some of his naughtiness, some of his stubbornness, some of his extreme sense that he was right.

When you are in a human body, you have certain human imperfections. But so what? They are all unreal, they can all be transcended, they can all be left behind. There is not one of you who cannot transcend your imperfections. But you can only transcend them by letting them go. You can only let them go when you know that there is going to be something to take their place, something that is more than the imperfection. You can only know *that* through love.

When you reconnect to the original love, you also reconnect to the source of that love. Therefore, you know that you came from that source. You know that you are infinitely more than your present sense of identity.

My beloved, think about images of distant galaxies and the vastness of this physical universe, and see how it gives you a different perspective. You realize how small the earth is compared to the vastness of the physical universe. When you reconnect to your original love, you take that broader perspective to an even higher level. You magnify it a billion, billion times.

God's love is infinitely greater than the vastness of the material universe, so you have an entirely different perspective. It is through *that* perspective that you can see how ridiculously insignificant are these things that you have held on to on this planet, and that other people hold on to. *That* is when you can let them go. *That* is when you can reconnect to your original purpose.

You can then pass the initiation when the angel of God appears to you within your heart – in the form of your Christ Self – to remind you that it is time to start some aspect of your own divine plan. Instead of rejecting it, instead of explaining it away, instead of finding some clever reasoning why you cannot possibly do this now – perhaps in 10,000 lifetimes but not today – you can simply come to that point of surrender and say: "Oh Lord, be it unto me according to thy will."

You realize that the Lord is not the remote being in the sky who is seeking to force his will upon you, the Lord truly is your own higher being. You are only being reminded of the higher choices you made when you had the broader perspective that has been lost as you entered the denseness of this world.

A special dispensation

My beloved, I am eternally grateful for your giving of my invocations. They have opened up your hearts to a point where I can give you a special dispensation, which is that I will give you the opportunity to surrender anything you want to surrender.

What I will do is that what you can surrender personally, I will multiply by a certain multiplication factor so that your personal surrender has a multiplied impact on the collective consciousness. For each limitation that you can surrender, thereby setting yourself free, you can also set free a substantial number of other people. Certainly, this is subject to their free will, but by your surrender, they will get a better opportunity to surrender themselves. This is how we have the figure-eight flow between us here Above and you below.

Your willingness to surrender becomes, as Jesus' willingness to surrender his physical life, the one thing that can be multiplied and therefore count for many. Truly, as they say, Jesus came to give his life as ransom for many (Matthew 20:28). The deeper meaning is that Jesus' willingness to surrender – instead of holding on – became the true sacrifice, the acceptable offering, that enabled the lifting of a certain amount of burden from humankind, thereby making it easier for others to follow in Jesus' footsteps and raise themselves above duality. My beloved, I will now give you this opportunity to surrender.

My beloved hearts, flow with the music, flow with the River of Life [Music was played as the dictation was originally given, but you can play meditative music while performing the meditation of surrender]. Allow yourself to feel how – in your heart, in your mind, in your being – you are letting go. Letting go of what you think you need to hold on to on the banks of the river that keeps you outside that flow of the River of Life.

Just feel how something within you lets go. You are letting go and flowing with the River of Life, the ocean of God's love, where there is no separation, no darkness, no fear, no anger. You are one with life itself. You are one in that River of Life where nothing can be separate, for all is light and no shadows remain. [You can perform this meditation for as long as you like while surrendering anything from which you want to be free.]

My beloved, with great gratitude for your willingness to participate in this interchange, I seal you in the love of my heart. I seal you against the forces of anti-love who would surely – if they could – disturb your newfound peace and surrender. I say to you: "Be sealed in the nurturing love of the Divine Mother. Remain sealed in the Eternal NOW that *is* the flow of that love." It is finished!

9 | INVOKING MY ORIGINAL LOVE

In the name I AM THAT I AM, Jesus Christ, I call to all representatives of the Divine Mother, especially Venus and Mother Mary, to help me reconnect to and unlock the love that caused me to make the decision to descend into the matter world. I call for you to help me overcome all illusions that stand in the way of my healing, especially…

[Make personal calls.]

1. I accept earth for what it is

1. It is impossible to be in this world without being hurt by those who are so trapped in anti-love that they feel threatened by anyone who expresses love.

> O Venus, show me how to serve,
> your cosmic beauty I observe.
> What love from Venus you now bring,
> our planets do in tandem sing.

> **O Venus, service so divine,**
> **you are for earth a cosmic sign.**
> **Your selfless service is now mine,**
> **a life in service I define.**

2. This planet is a world that is designed specifically to give certain beings an opportunity to live in a place where they can deny God's Presence.

> O Venus, your love is the key,
> the hardened hearts on earth are free.
> Embracing future bright and bold,
> our planet's story is retold.

> **O Venus, service so divine,**
> **you are for earth a cosmic sign.**
> **Your selfless service is now mine,**
> **a life in service I define.**

3. I have come here as a sacrifice. I came here because I desired to bring the sunlight of love in order to give people an opportunity to experience that there is something beyond anti-love.

> O Venus, loving Mother mine,
> my heart your love does now refine.
> I am the open door for love,
> descending like a Holy Dove.

> **O Venus, service so divine,**
> **you are for earth a cosmic sign.**
> **Your selfless service is now mine,**
> **a life in service I define.**

9 | *Invoking My Original Love*

4. I volunteered to come into a situation that I knew would be very difficult. I knew that my love would be rejected, I knew that I would be hurt and bruised.

> O Venus, play the secret note,
> that is for hatred antidote.
> All poisoned hearts you gently heal,
> as love's true story you reveal.

> **O Venus, service so divine,**
> **you are for earth a cosmic sign.**
> **Your selfless service is now mine,**
> **a life in service I define.**

5. I accept the reality of this planet. I transcend the attitude of feeling that I should not have been treated this way, that something is wrong, that: "God should not have allowed this to happen to me."

> O Venus, love fills every need,
> for truly, love is God's first seed.
> O let it blossom, let it grow,
> sweep earth into your loving flow.

> **O Venus, service so divine,**
> **you are for earth a cosmic sign.**
> **Your selfless service is now mine,**
> **a life in service I define.**

6. No injustice has been done to me. God has *not* been unjust towards me. I am transcending the consciousness of anti-love that I came here to eradicate.

O Venus, music of the spheres,
heard by those who God reveres.
Our voices now as one we raise,
singing in adoring praise.

**O Venus, service so divine,
you are for earth a cosmic sign.
Your selfless service is now mine,
a life in service I define.**

7. I am allowing the flow of God's love through my being. I am feeling that God is here with me, and I am experiencing God's love.

O Venus, we are joining ranks,
Sanat Kumara we give thanks.
Our planet has received new life,
to lift her out of war and strife.

**O Venus, service so divine,
you are for earth a cosmic sign.
Your selfless service is now mine,
a life in service I define.**

8. I am transcending the illusion that God has abandoned me. I feel God's love flowing *through* me, and I feel God's love *for* me.

O Venus, your sweet melody,
consumes veil of duality.
Absorbed in tones of Cosmic Love,
all conflict we now rise above.

**O Venus, service so divine,
you are for earth a cosmic sign.
Your selfless service is now mine,
a life in service I define.**

9. Love is not a static force, it cannot be captured, it cannot be controlled, it cannot be put in a mental box. It can be experienced only when I allow it to flow.

O Venus, shining Morning Star,
a cosmic herald, that you are.
The earth set free by sacred sound,
our planet is now heaven-bound.

**O Venus, service so divine,
you are for earth a cosmic sign.
Your selfless service is now mine,
a life in service I define.**

2. I discover my love for something more

1. I am transcending the consciousness of anti-love. I am opening the flow and I experience unconditional love.

O Venus, show me how to serve,
your cosmic beauty I observe.
What love from Venus you now bring,
our planets do in tandem sing.

> **O Venus, service so divine,**
> **you are for earth a cosmic sign.**
> **Your selfless service is now mine,**
> **a life in service I define.**

2. I am transcending the tendency to fill my desire for love through conditional love. I surrender the belief that the love I receive should live up to certain conditions and that I should seek to possess love or other people.

> O Venus, your love is the key,
> the hardened hearts on earth are free.
> Embracing future bright and bold,
> our planet's story is retold.

> **O Venus, service so divine,**
> **you are for earth a cosmic sign.**
> **Your selfless service is now mine,**
> **a life in service I define.**

3. I am awakening with my self-esteem and sense of identity intact. I am escaping the duality consciousness by reconnecting to the love in the core of my being.

> O Venus, loving Mother mine,
> my heart your love does now refine.
> I am the open door for love,
> descending like a Holy Dove.

> **O Venus, service so divine,**
> **you are for earth a cosmic sign.**
> **Your selfless service is now mine,**
> **a life in service I define.**

4. I see how my perspective on life and the universe is limited by the mental box of this world. I did not decide to descend here with the limited perspective I have now. I came here out of love.

> O Venus, play the secret note,
> that is for hatred antidote.
> All poisoned hearts you gently heal,
> as love's true story you reveal.

> **O Venus, service so divine,**
> **you are for earth a cosmic sign.**
> **Your selfless service is now mine,**
> **a life in service I define.**

5. I am reconnecting to the point where I decided to descend into the world of form. That decision was based on love, the desire to express my true God quality, my true divine individuality, and bring that gift to the world in order to light up the world.

> O Venus, love fills every need,
> for truly, love is God's first seed.
> O let it blossom, let it grow,
> sweep earth into your loving flow.

> **O Venus, service so divine,**
> **you are for earth a cosmic sign.**
> **Your selfless service is now mine,**
> **a life in service I define.**

6. I go beyond the outer facade and reconnect to the core of love in my being. I love something more than what I am experiencing right now.

O Venus, music of the spheres,
heard by those who God reveres.
Our voices now as one we raise,
singing in adoring praise.

**O Venus, service so divine,
you are for earth a cosmic sign.
Your selfless service is now mine,
a life in service I define.**

7. I have a love for something more than what I have right now. I can overcome my current limitations by letting the old sense of identity die.

O Venus, we are joining ranks,
Sanat Kumara we give thanks.
Our planet has received new life,
to lift her out of war and strife.

**O Venus, service so divine,
you are for earth a cosmic sign.
Your selfless service is now mine,
a life in service I define.**

8. I am willing to let the old die. I am discovering my love for something more. Letting the old die does not mean a loss, for I am reborn into a higher state of identity.

O Venus, your sweet melody,
consumes veil of duality.
Absorbed in tones of Cosmic Love,
all conflict we now rise above.

**O Venus, service so divine,
you are for earth a cosmic sign.
Your selfless service is now mine,
a life in service I define.**

9. I am willing to let the old sense of self die. Beloved Venus, show me the way.

O Venus, shining Morning Star,
a cosmic herald, that you are.
The earth set free by sacred sound,
our planet is now heaven-bound.

**O Venus, service so divine,
you are for earth a cosmic sign.
Your selfless service is now mine,
a life in service I define.**

3. I am reborn

1. I am transcending the illusion that in order to overcome the bad aspects of myself, I have to destroy my sense of self. I know there is a sense of self beyond the ego.

O Venus, show me how to serve,
your cosmic beauty I observe.
What love from Venus you now bring,
our planets do in tandem sing.

**O Venus, service so divine,
you are for earth a cosmic sign.
Your selfless service is now mine,
a life in service I define.**

2. I am transcending the illusion that the way to spiritual growth is to destroy all sense of self. One cannot eliminate a negative by creating another negative or by destroying the first negative. One cannot correct an imperfection by acting out another imperfection.

> O Venus, your love is the key,
> the hardened hearts on earth are free.
> Embracing future bright and bold,
> our planet's story is retold.

**O Venus, service so divine,
you are for earth a cosmic sign.
Your selfless service is now mine,
a life in service I define.**

3. There is no way to destroy something. Deep within, I have a basic survival instinct. My true divine individuality wants to survive, wants to grow and wants to express itself in this world. I want to fulfill my original reason for being, my reason for coming here.

> O Venus, loving Mother mine,
> my heart your love does now refine.
> I am the open door for love,
> descending like a Holy Dove.

**O Venus, service so divine,
you are for earth a cosmic sign.
Your selfless service is now mine,
a life in service I define.**

4. If I try to destroy all sense of self, I end up working against myself, seeking to destroy not only the false sense of self of the ego but also the true sense of self of my divine individuality. This simply cannot be done.

O Venus, play the secret note,
that is for hatred antidote.
All poisoned hearts you gently heal,
as love's true story you reveal.

**O Venus, service so divine,
you are for earth a cosmic sign.
Your selfless service is now mine,
a life in service I define.**

5. I may actually be able to destroy much of my sense of self, but I will eventually come to a point where the inner conflict becomes so intense, so illogical, so contradictory, that I simply cannot stand it anymore.

O Venus, love fills every need,
for truly, love is God's first seed.
O let it blossom, let it grow,
sweep earth into your loving flow.

> **O Venus, service so divine,**
> **you are for earth a cosmic sign.**
> **Your selfless service is now mine,**
> **a life in service I define.**

6. The way to salvation is not through self-denial or self-destruction. It is through self-transcendence. I am not seeking to destroy the old self. I am seeking to transcend it and be reborn into a new self that replaces the old.

> O Venus, music of the spheres,
> heard by those who God reveres.
> Our voices now as one we raise,
> singing in adoring praise.

> **O Venus, service so divine,**
> **you are for earth a cosmic sign.**
> **Your selfless service is now mine,**
> **a life in service I define.**

7. I cannot be reborn into the new until I allow the old to die. There will be a cosmic interval between the death of the old and the resurrection of the Conscious You into a higher sense of identity.

> O Venus, we are joining ranks,
> Sanat Kumara we give thanks.
> Our planet has received new life,
> to lift her out of war and strife.

**O Venus, service so divine,
you are for earth a cosmic sign.
Your selfless service is now mine,
a life in service I define.**

8. When I let the old die, I will feel like I am plunging myself into a vacuum. Yet my conscious self will not lose consciousness. It will remain conscious. I know God will not forsake me.

O Venus, your sweet melody,
consumes veil of duality.
Absorbed in tones of Cosmic Love,
all conflict we now rise above.

**O Venus, service so divine,
you are for earth a cosmic sign.
Your selfless service is now mine,
a life in service I define.**

9. I hereby choose to no longer feel like a victim of life. I accept that God has not unjustly sent me into this world. Even though I have had my trials and tribulations, I know that I volunteered to come here and I knew what could happen to me.

O Venus, shining Morning Star,
a cosmic herald, that you are.
The earth set free by sacred sound,
our planet is now heaven-bound.

**O Venus, service so divine,
you are for earth a cosmic sign.
Your selfless service is now mine,
a life in service I define.**

4. I let go of all unreality

1. The essential key to everything is to reconnect to the innermost love of my being that originally caused me to volunteer to descend into this denser sphere in order to bring my light and my love.

> O Venus, show me how to serve,
> your cosmic beauty I observe.
> What love from Venus you now bring,
> our planets do in tandem sing.
>
> **O Venus, service so divine,**
> **you are for earth a cosmic sign.**
> **Your selfless service is now mine,**
> **a life in service I define.**

2. I accept that when I am in a human body, I have certain human imperfections. They are all unreal and they can all be left behind. I transcend my imperfections by letting them go.

> O Venus, your love is the key,
> the hardened hearts on earth are free.
> Embracing future bright and bold,
> our planet's story is retold.
>
> **O Venus, service so divine,**
> **you are for earth a cosmic sign.**
> **Your selfless service is now mine,**
> **a life in service I define.**

3. I can only let imperfections go when I know that there is going to be something to take their place, something that is more than the imperfection. I can only know that through love.

> O Venus, loving Mother mine,
> my heart your love does now refine.
> I am the open door for love,
> descending like a Holy Dove.
>
> **O Venus, service so divine,**
> **you are for earth a cosmic sign.**
> **Your selfless service is now mine,**
> **a life in service I define.**

4. I am reconnecting to the original love and to the source of that love. I came from that source. I am infinitely more than my present sense of identity.

> O Venus, play the secret note,
> that is for hatred antidote.
> All poisoned hearts you gently heal,
> as love's true story you reveal.
>
> **O Venus, service so divine,**
> **you are for earth a cosmic sign.**
> **Your selfless service is now mine,**
> **a life in service I define.**

5. God's love is infinitely greater than anything in the material universe. How ridiculously insignificant are the things I have held on to on this planet. I now let them go. I now reconnect to my original purpose.

O Venus, love fills every need,
for truly, love is God's first seed.
O let it blossom, let it grow,
sweep earth into your loving flow.

**O Venus, service so divine,
you are for earth a cosmic sign.
Your selfless service is now mine,
a life in service I define.**

6. When my Christ Self reminds me that it is time to start some aspect of my divine plan, I will say: "Oh Lord, be it unto me according to thy will."

O Venus, music of the spheres,
heard by those who God reveres.
Our voices now as one we raise,
singing in adoring praise.

**O Venus, service so divine,
you are for earth a cosmic sign.
Your selfless service is now mine,
a life in service I define.**

7. The Lord is not the remote being in the sky who is seeking to force his will upon me. The Lord is my own higher being. I know the higher choices I made when I had the broader perspective that was lost when I entered the denseness of this world.

O Venus, we are joining ranks,
Sanat Kumara we give thanks.
Our planet has received new life,
to lift her out of war and strife.

9 | Invoking My Original Love

> **O Venus, service so divine,**
> **you are for earth a cosmic sign.**
> **Your selfless service is now mine,**
> **a life in service I define.**

8. I allow myself to feel how – in my heart, in my mind, in my being – I am letting go. I am letting go of what I think I need to hold on to on the banks of the river. I am immersed in the flow of the River of Life.

> O Venus, your sweet melody,
> consumes veil of duality.
> Absorbed in tones of Cosmic Love,
> all conflict we now rise above.

> **O Venus, service so divine,**
> **you are for earth a cosmic sign.**
> **Your selfless service is now mine,**
> **a life in service I define.**

9. I experience how something within me lets go. I am letting go and flowing with the River of Life, the ocean of God's love, where there is no separation, no darkness, no fear, no anger. I am one with life itself. I am one in that River of Life where nothing can be separate, for all is light and no shadows remain.

> O Venus, shining Morning Star,
> a cosmic herald, that you are.
> The earth set free by sacred sound,
> our planet is now heaven-bound.

**O Venus, service so divine,
you are for earth a cosmic sign.
Your selfless service is now mine,
a life in service I define.**

Sealing

In the name of the Divine Mother, I call to Venus and Mother Mary for the sealing of myself and all people in the creative flow of the Divine Mother, the River of Life. I call for the multiplication of my calls by all representatives of the Divine Mother, so that we form the perfect figure-eight flow of "As Above, so below." Thus, I accept that this is fully manifest, because the mouth of the Lord, the Divine Mother that I AM, has spoken it. Amen.

10 | TOTAL FORGIVENESS LEADS TO TOTAL FREEDOM

A dictation by Mother Mary, April 29, 2004.

My beloved hearts, I come to you on this joyous day, and I come to you in the Flame of Miracle Forgiveness because I truly am the Mother of Forgiveness. The Flame of Forgiveness is indeed the flame of spiritual freedom. It is only forgiveness that can set you free from the imperfections found in this world.

When will revenge end in the Middle East?

You have seen many examples of the force of non-forgiveness. While this force is not the cause of terrorism and war, it is indeed the force that keeps terrorism and war going strong on this planet. You have especially seen this in the Middle East where even the state of Israel has engaged in state-sponsored assassinations, which truly are acts of non-forgiveness that only breed more non-forgiveness from the other side. Thereby, these acts contribute to the downward spiral of violence and revenge for violence that has engulfed the Middle East for thousands upon thousands of years.

I tell you that even the ascended masters wonder if the people living in that region will ever have enough of this punch-counterpunch of revenge and revenge for revenge until it becomes revenge for the sake of revenge itself. Truly, there can no longer be any real meaning to these acts of revenge because the spiral of violence started so long ago that no one can remember why it started. They only remember that they must perpetuate it by getting even, by getting revenge.

Understanding the importance of forgiveness

I desire to give you a teaching so that you may understand why forgiveness is so important. To truly understand the importance of forgiveness, you need to realize the profound truth that my son Jesus has explained so many times, namely that the basic law of this universe is the Law of Free Will. You also need to understand that the very purpose of life, the very essence of life, is to grow, to move on, to self-transcend.

What is it that prevents you from growing, from moving on, from transcending your current state of consciousness, your current sense of identity? Well, it is the point of non-forgiveness. When there is something you have not forgiven, when there is something you are holding on to, when there is something you cannot let go of, in that point of emotional attachment to the things of this world, you are holding yourself back. You are holding yourself tied to a limited and imperfect sense of identity, and you are essentially worshiping an idol of your own making, or at least the making of your culture.

By not forgiving, you are taking away your own freedom to move on. When you do not move on, you will stagnate. If you stay too long in one place, you will become subject to the second law of thermodynamics, which means that a downward spiral, a negative vortex, of energy will begin forming around you. When that vortex becomes too strong, it will begin to overpower your feelings and your thoughts, until you begin to believe either that there is nothing outside the vortex or that you cannot escape the downward pull of the vortex.

No ultimate revenge

This is what causes so many people, especially in the Middle East, to believe that there is no other way to live than to be in opposition to the Jews or in opposition to the Arabs. It causes them to believe that there is no way to escape the cycle of violence, the cycle of revenge. They feel they simply must continue the cycle because they *must* have revenge, they *must* set things right by committing another act of violence to supposedly neutralize or make up for previous acts of violence.

Unfortunately, the intense energies of this negative vortex prevent people from asking the very logical question of when and how this could possibly end. Think about this, my beloved. Can there ever be an ultimate act of revenge? Can there ever be an ultimate act of revenge that will settle the score permanently and thereby bring about an end to violence?

Those of you who are not trapped by the relativity of the separate mind and by a downward vortex of non-forgiveness will be able to see the pure and simple logic behind these remarks. There can be no peace through revenge. It simply is not possible. There can be no act of revenge which stops the cycle of violence. If you avenge what has been done to you by doing something to another, you will inevitably create the desire for revenge in your opponent.

This should be obvious to anyone who knows elementary school physics and has learned about the law of action and reaction. For every action, there is an opposite reaction of equal strength. That is simply a law of the material universe. When you take revenge, you are reacting to what was done to you, but your reaction becomes a new action and it inevitably creates a reaction from your opponent, even from the universe itself. This cycle can literally go on forever—or at least it seems like forever.

There is indeed a very small minority of the people on this planet who do not want peace, who do not want resolution, who do not want an end to violence or an end to this spiral of revenge. These are the people who are completely trapped in the Luciferian state of consciousness. Those people are few, and the vast majority of the people who are caught in the spiral of revenge actually *do* want peace. This gives rise to the paradox that they say they want peace, but that they are not willing to stop the cycle of revenge.

While this can be almost impossible to understand for a person who is not caught in a negative spiral, your new understanding of energy and energy vortexes allows you to see the explanation. When people are caught in such a vortex of anger and revenge, they simply cannot see the fallacy of their thinking. They cannot think logically and rationally because they are so overpowered by the emotional energies that they do not even stop to think. This is why there is a need for something to break the spiral, to break the downward pull. That something is that someone must consume the energies created through revenge and non-forgiveness, the very energies that form a magnetic pull on people's emotions and overpower them so that they lose all logic and rationality. Those someone must be the balanced people who are not caught up in these negative momentums and vortexes. My beloved hearths, those someone are *you*.

The catch-22 of non-forgiveness

Before you can truly become an effective force in consuming the vortexes of non-forgiveness on this planet, you must free yourself from the point of non-forgiveness. You might say: "But Mother Mary, you just told us that we are not caught up in a vortex of non-forgiveness." And that is perfectly true. You are not caught in a vortex that is so intense that it overpowers your feelings and prevents you from thinking.

Yet many of you do not realize what is the true cause of non-forgiveness. You do not realize this because you were not brought up with a proper understanding. You were not brought up with a proper understanding because the beautiful teachings on forgiveness that my son gave 2,000 years ago have been obscured and distorted by the orthodox Christian churches.

The problem we have is that most people on earth simply do not see that non-forgiveness is based on a set of lies. They do not understand these lies, and therefore they cannot see the mindset behind those lies. If you cannot see through the lies of the devil, if you are not wise as a serpent, then you cannot completely free yourself from those lies that permeate every aspect of life on this planet. If you do not become wise as a serpent, how can you be harmless as a dove?

Let me now give you a teaching in an attempt to help you free yourself from the lies about non-forgiveness. As I said earlier, the basic law of this universe is the Law of Free Will. You have the right to experiment with your creative abilities. In fact, your lifestream was created with a drive, a desire, to experiment with God's laws and God's energies. Unfortunately, what has happened to most people on this planet is that they have lost their contact with their spiritual selves. Thereby, they have become enveloped in a lower state of consciousness that causes them to see themselves as being separated from their spiritual selves, even separated from God. Because of this sense of separation, you no longer realize the basic reality that God has never hurt you whatsoever.

God has not created the conditions on this planet that have caused your soul to be hurt and wounded. Those conditions were created by human beings trapped in the lower state of consciousness, in which they are easily controlled by dark forces, as I explained in my previous discourses [See *www.ascendedmasterlight.com*].

God has not created the conditions that caused you to be hurt, and God never wanted you to be wounded. Yet most people on this planet cannot fully understand and accept that the misery on earth was created by human beings and not created by God. Somewhere deep within their beings they have a sense that either God must have created their misery or God must have allowed it to be created. Therefore, most people blame God for certain conditions in their lives.

Many people blame God for various negative experiences they have had in this lifetime. But when you go deep within the subconscious mind, you see that many people actually blame God for what happened to them in the Garden of Eden. They blame God for the fact that they fell into a lower state of consciousness. After all, where did the serpent come from if it was not created by God? Where did the tree of the knowledge of good and evil come from if God did not put it in the Garden of Eden? If God had not put the tree in the garden and allowed the serpent to be in the garden, then their souls would not have fallen, and therefore it must be God's fault.

Stop blaming God!

My beloved, these beliefs are not your own. They have been carefully manufactured by Lucifer and his followers to trap you in a state of consciousness that makes it almost impossible for you to come back to God, to come back to a full realization and acceptance of who you are as a son or daughter of God. The dark forces have created such a web of interwoven lies that it is almost impossible for me to help you see through them, and it is certainly impossible for me to do it in one single discourse.

As I said in my last discourse, Lucifer fell because he truly believed that God made a mistake by giving people free will. He has created a lie, namely the lie that free will was a mistake because, after all, if people had not had free will, how could they have been tempted by the serpent and eaten of the forbidden fruit? This causes many people to blame God, not only for the fact that he gave them free will but even for the fact that he created them.

In reality, the serpent is a symbol for a state of consciousness, namely that of rebelling against God's laws. The potential to rebel is an inevitable result of giving you free will because if you could not rebel, you would not have *free* will. Nevertheless, you do not *need* to rebel in order to exercise your freedom of choice—that is simply a subtle lie promoted by those who chose to embody the serpentine consciousness. The serpentine consciousness simply follows free will, as the shadow follows your body. Nevertheless, God never wanted you to identify with your shadow or to be afraid of your own shadow. God wanted you to always face the light of your I AM Presence and keep the shadow behind you. What is the result of blaming God? The result is that you paralyze yourself, and you do this because, deep within, you have accepted the belief that you are not responsible for your situation. You have accepted the belief that you did not create your current situation, and because you did not create it, there is nothing you can do to uncreate it.

I hope you can see the very simple logic here. If you go outside without an umbrella and it suddenly starts raining, then obviously you did not create that rain and so there is nothing you can do to make the rain stop. This is the experience that causes many people to say that they have not created their current situation and they have not created the current misery on planet earth. They have not created the conditions that caused them to fall into a lower state of consciousness because they did not give themselves free will, they did not choose to be created, they did not choose to be born, they did not choose to come to this planet, they did not even choose to exist.

No mistake is permanent

Therefore, they can push aside all personal responsibility and accountability and feel that there is nothing they could do to change the situation for the better. Oh my beloved, I must tell you that this is the most insidious of all lies. The most insidious of all lies is the idea that you could possibly be in a situation in which there is nothing you could do to transcend that situation and come up higher. The most insidious of all lies is the idea that there could possibly be a prison in the matter universe from which there is no escape. It is the idea that you could possibly make one mistake that would make you doomed forever.

I wish you could see through my eyes as an ascended being and see how ridiculous this lie truly is. I chuckle as I say this because once you have ascended, you realize that everything in the matter universe is created from God's energy. God's energy is simply vibration. No matter how low that vibration is, no matter how dense the energy or the physical matter might seem, it is always possible to raise the vibration and bring it back into alignment with the purity and the perfection of God. My beloved hearts, please make an effort to understand this truth, this fundamental truth about the universe in which you live. There is nothing that you could do, or that any force could possibly do to you, which cannot be undone and purified by the light and the love of God.

The very idea that you could possibly do something that could not be undone is the most insidious lie created by the serpent and his seed. It is the most insidious misuse of the contracting force of the Mother, the very Mother of God. It is such a misuse because it is the contracting force of the Mother which gives you life, which gives you form, whether it be a physical body or a soul. Were it not for the contracting force of the Mother, you would have no individual consciousness, no individual sense of identity.

It has never been the intention of the Mother of God to trap you in a particular form. The very idea that the form created by the energies of the Mother of God could become a prison from which there is no escape is such an abomination, such an injustice against the Mother of God whose unconditional love is what gives you life and form.

How can you overcome this lie? Well, there is only one way to overcome the lie of the serpent, and that is to take full and complete responsibility for your current situation.

I am well aware that this will be a very provocative statement to many people, and they will find it extremely difficult to take responsibility for their situation. However, the reason for this difficulty is that many people have lost the true recognition of who they are. They have lost their true sense of identity, and they have been trapped, not only by the lie of a false identity, they have also been trapped in a negative vortex of energy that overpowers their feelings and their ability to think rationally. This vortex is not a vortex of revenge, but it is a vortex of energy that reinforces the false sense of identity, the idea that you are separated from God. Therefore, you think you are a victim of what God has created, and you have no responsibility for your situation because God set you up to fail.

My beloved son has given many teachings in an attempt to help you overcome your false sense of identity and realize that you were created as a spiritual being [See *The Mystical Teachings of Jesus*.]. While I do not in any way claim that I can do this better than Jesus, I would like to add the perspective of the Mother of God.

Nothing can hurt the real you

The problem we see on earth is that people think that because they have fallen into a lower state of consciousness, because they have made mistakes and because they have sinned, they have somehow been permanently stained. You need to see through this illusion and this lie, and you need to do so by realizing the reality of energy.

What I would like you to do to overcome this illusion is very simple. You can do this physically if you like, but I am sure that for most of you it will be enough just to imagine this exercise. Imagine that you go outside at night with a flashlight. You hang the flashlight in a tree so that the light beam is shining on the ground. Now imagine that you have a bucket of mud and you start throwing the mud at the light beam. Can you make that mud cling to the beam of light?

I am sure you can see that this is impossible but why is it impossible? As your scientists have told you, everything is created from energy. The mud is simply a different form of energy than the energy of the light beam. Both are forms of energy but the difference is that the mud has a much lower vibration than the light. Because it has a lower vibration, it cannot cling to and pollute the light beam.

Your true identity is not your soul, the soul that abides in a physical body in the material universe. Your true identity is the spiritual self, and that spiritual self resides in a higher realm, in a higher world, that is made entirely of higher vibrations. The very idea that the lifestream that descends into the material world could commit a sin that could permanently stain the spiritual self, residing in the spiritual world, is as ridiculous as the idea that mud can cling to a beam of light. Do you see my point?

Your true identity is a spiritual being, your I AM Presence. That spiritual self is, at this very moment, residing in the spiritual realm, and it is as perfect and as beautiful as when it was first created by God. Nothing you have ever done, and nothing you could possibly do, could pollute or destroy your spiritual self. You are as pure and you are as worthy of God's love as the day you were first created. Nothing you have done in this world has made you unworthy of God's love.

The forces of darkness want to make you think that because you have done this or that terrible thing, you are no longer worthy of God's love. When you subscribe to this lie, you begin to believe that you need to hide from God and that there is no point in trying to come home to God or even ask for forgiveness. You accept the lie that God is such an angry and judgmental God that he would not forgive you after all you have done. You do not even try to come back to God, you keep seeking to hide from God.

What keeps you trapped in your current state of consciousness, in your current set of limitations and even in your outer circumstances, is that you cannot accept God's forgiveness. Why can you not accept God's forgiveness? Well my beloved, the answer to that question lies in the Law of Free Will.

Taking responsibility for what you have created

According to the Law of Free Will, you have a right to create anything you want. If you create a false image of yourself, you can become trapped in that image, in that sense of identity. The only way you can overcome that limitation – the only way you can escape the prison that is truly created by your mind and exists only in your mind – is that you must decide that you no longer want to be that way. You do not want to be the limited person that you see yourself as being. You want to let go of those limitations and move on.

How can you let go of limitations? You can do so only by forgiving yourself for creating those limitations in the first place. How can you forgive yourself? You can do so only when you fully recognize and accept that it was *you* who created the limitations—and not God, and not even Lucifer or all of his henchmen.

This is what has put so many people in a catch-22 from which there seems to be no escape. They cannot improve their lives because they do not take responsibility for their situation and realize that they have created it. The reason they cannot take responsibility for the situation is because they believe that there is no forgiveness, there is no escape from the limitations. If they were to admit that they have created the limitations, they would condemn themselves for doing so. They would be permanently locked in experiencing suffering and limitation, and on top of that they would be blaming themselves for the situation. To the soul, this feels like adding insult to injury so in order to avoid condemning themselves, they avoid taking responsibility. What could possibly break this stalemate?

The only way out is to recognize that *you* have created the situation but that *God* does not condemn you for doing so. Therefore, there is no reason for condemning yourself. What you have done is simply to experiment with your free will and with the energy of God.

I am not trying to say here that everything you have created is what God wanted to see for you or that it is in alignment with God's laws. God never wanted you to create limitations that cause you suffering and pain. What I am saying is that when God made the decision to give you free will, God gave you the right to experiment. In so doing, God also set you free from all blame.

What God has done in creating you and giving you free will is that God has given you the opportunity to grow in awareness and identity until you can fully accept yourself as a son or daughter of God. Thereby, you become a co-creator with God who eventually becomes so powerful that you can create your own world. God has literally given you the opportunity to become all that God is and more. In creating you and giving you free will, God has no desire to blame you for doing what you were created to do in experimenting with your free will, or even for creating circumstances that cause you suffering.

God does not blame you

God does not want you to blame yourself and God does not want to blame you. God wants you to approach life as a scientist conducting experiments. Imagine that you were Thomas Edison trying to find the material that would make it possible to create the electric light bulb. As you might know, Edison tried dozens and dozens of different materials before he found one that worked. Imagine that Edison had blamed himself for being a failure or a sinner every time he tried a material that didn't work. He would soon have become so burdened and traumatized that he would have given up before he found the material that gave birth to the electric age. Instead, Thomas Edison simply discarded the material that didn't work and immediately went on to try another one. This is how God wants you to participate in the experiment of life.

When you become a spiritually aware person, you can begin to think rationally and logically about life. When you experience conditions that cause you suffering, the rational way of thinking is to say: "I do not want to experience these conditions any more. I have had enough of that experience so what can I do to change my experience? The first step I must take is to overcome the belief that I am the victim of circumstances beyond my control. As long as I feel like a victim, there is nothing I can do to change the circumstances that cause me suffering. I must take responsibility for my situation and recognize that I have either created these circumstances or I have attracted these circumstances to me because I have allowed myself to be in a lower state of consciousness than what is my highest potential. The very key to changing my circumstances is to change my state of consciousness. When I do change my state of consciousness, the first thing that will happen is that my experience of my circumstances will change and I will begin to suffer less, even if the outer circumstances do not change instantly. Yet if I keep raising my state of consciousness, I will eventually experience a change in the outer circumstances."

The material universe is created from energies that are quite dense. As Jesus and I have attempted to explain, there are levels in the material world. Everything that is created in the matter universe started as an idea in the etheric realm. It was then solidified as a thought in the mental realm. It received energy and motion in the emotional realm, before it finally broke through in the material realm. That is why a spiritually aware person cannot expect that outer circumstances, material circumstances, will change overnight. It will take some time to change the circumstances, and the reason for that is simple. In order to change the circumstances in the material universe, you need to go to the source. You need to begin by changing the images in the etheric realm, which will then change the thought and change the feelings, and finally cycle through to the material realm. However, because the energies in the material realm are the densest, it will take some time before you will see a change in the visible world. That is one reason Jesus told you that in your patience you will posses your souls.

Jesus has used the image that the material world is like a movie projected upon a screen. The driving force behind the movie is the white light coming from the light bulb in the film projector, and that light receives form as it passes through the filmstrip. What I am telling you here is that there are three filmstrips in your subconscious mind. One is your sense of identity, which abides in the etheric realm. The other is your mental image of yourself and the world, which abides in the mental realm. And the third is your feelings about yourself and the world, which abides in the emotional realm. Your outer circumstances are simply projections upon the screen of life, as the light of God passes through your consciousness and is colored and given shape by the images you hold in your etheric, mental and emotional bodies.

God did not create your soul

In order to change your *outer* circumstances, you must begin by changing your *inner* circumstances, your state of consciousness. That is why you need to realize that your outer circumstances are created by your consciousness, they are a reflection of the images in your consciousness. Those images were created by *you*. I am aware that these images are the products of a complicated process that has been going on for many lifetimes. This process has been affected by your culture and by the lies promoted by dark forces. Nevertheless, the images were created by you, and this brings me to the central truth that all spiritual people need to understand.

In order to explain that truth, let us begin with the spiritual self. Your lifestream was created by your spiritual parents and it is a spiritual being. It is as pure and perfect as when it was first created. I can assure you that your lifestream, your I AM Presence, is in constant, conscious contact with God. It constantly feels the infinite and unconditional love of God, and there is absolutely no point in your I AM Presence that has any negative feelings about being created or about having free will. Your I AM Presence feels only infinite joy and gratitude for the opportunity to exist and to be part of God's magnificent and wonderful creation. In other words, none of the negative feelings that affect so many souls on earth exist at the level of your I AM Presence.

My point for telling you this is to help you realize that the very idea that you are created by God is a truth with modifications. Your *I AM Presence* was created by God but your *soul* was not created by God. Your soul was created by the Conscious You as a vehicle for experiencing the material universe and for expressing its creativity in the material universe. [NOTE: The teaching about the Conscious You was given after this dictation, but it has been incorporated here. The important point is that the Conscious You is not made from the energies of this world and thus cannot be harmed by anything in this world. The soul is made from the energies of this world because it is a vehicle for expressing yourself in this world. The soul can be affected by the energies of this world.]

It simply is not logical and rational, nor is it true, to blame God for the fact that your soul exists. God did not create the soul that descended into the material universe and fell into a lower state of consciousness. Your I AM Presence created the

Conscious You and the Conscious You created the soul, but the Conscious You is *you*. *You* created your soul because you made the choice to create that soul, and you made that choice because you wanted to experience the material universe and you wanted to help co-create this universe as the kingdom of God.

You now see that even though you presently might experience yourself as a victim of circumstances beyond your control, the Conscious You is not a victim. Your soul is the result of a choice that you, meaning your true identity as a spiritual being, made. You made that choice because you wanted to descend into the material realm and have a positive experience that would lead to your growth, to a growth in your sense of identity as a co-creator with God. When you realize this truth, you can see that there is no point in blaming God and there is no point in blaming yourself.

Stop the blame game!

If you are currently experiencing circumstances that cause you suffering, then instead of blaming God, blaming other people, blaming dark forces or even blaming yourself, you simply need to stop the blame game. You need to forgive yourself and say: "I conducted an experiment that did not work out as I intended. I am going to leave that experiment behind and come up higher in consciousness." You need to decide that if your current situation does not give you the positive experience that you desire, then you will take the necessary steps to change your experience and use your present circumstances as a springboard for creating a positive experience for yourself.

In order to fully make the decision to simply leave behind that which is imperfect, you need to recognize the profound truth that no matter what the outer appearances might be in this world, nobody ever did anything to you. Let me say that again:

"*Nobody ever did anything to you.* No human being ever did anything to you and God never did anything to you."

The only force that ever did anything to you was yourself. The meaning behind that statement is that even though the Conscious You is in the material universe, it is not made from the energies of the material universe. The Conscious You is truly a light beam that is shining from your I AM Presence. The energies of the material universe cannot cling to the Conscious You, they cannot damage the Conscious You. However, what *is* the Conscious You?

The Conscious You is a state of consciousness, a sense of being, a sense of identity. It is a being that has imagination and free will. The Conscious You creates its own sense of identity, and it recreates that sense of identity every moment. The point here is this. If someone comes to you and slaps you on one cheek, that person has done something to your body but that person has done nothing to the Conscious You. Yet *you* have the ability, through your imagination and free will, to let the action performed by the other person affect your sense of identity. In so doing, you are doing something to yourself, to your soul. Another person cannot change your sense of identity—only *you* can do that. In order to change your sense of identity, *you must make a choice.*

I clearly realize that there are forces in this world who use very aggressive means in order to manipulate people into accepting an imperfect and false sense of identity. Those forces are very insidious, and they are very persuasive in the lies they use to make you believe that you are a sinner and a mortal human being who has done something so bad that you can never be free of it. I am not saying that it is *easy* for you to escape the clutches of these liars and their lies. What I am saying is that it is *possible* for you to escape all the lies in this world. To do so, you must come to a full acceptance of the fact that they cannot harm you, that

10 | Total Forgiveness Leads to Total Freedom

none of the forces of this world can harm the Conscious You; they can only harm your soul.

What can harm your soul is that you allow the forces of this world to cause you to change your sense of identity. *That* is what will harm you, but that harm can come about only through the decisions you make. The wonderful thing about this realization is that anything that has been done to your soul through a choice that you made, can be undone by you making a better choice. The key to being free of all imperfections of the past is that you must make a choice to let those imperfections go, to leave them behind, and you do so by forgiving yourself for making those choices.

Once again, we are back to the paradox that if you recognize that anything that ever happened to you was the result of decisions you made, you have been programmed by the forces of this world – and you have accepted their lies – that you need to blame yourself for making wrong choices. Well my beloved, as I have tried to explain to you, there is no need to blame yourself for making wrong choices. If you blame yourself for making the wrong choice, you will bind yourself to that choice because in blaming yourself, you are reinforcing that choice. You are reinforcing it by the energy that streams through your mind and attention. You are feeding the wrong choice, and as you keep feeding energy into it, you will build a vortex that will overpower your thoughts and feelings until you can no longer see beyond it.

Think back to my thought experiment about the light beam from your flashlight. You cannot throw mud at the light beam and make it stick to the light. However, you can make bricks out of mud and build a wall around the light until it is no longer visible. That is what most people have done to their souls. They have made wrong choices, and instead of simply forgiving themselves and moving on, they have reinforced those wrong choices. By feeding energy into these imperfect images, they have built a wall around their souls so that they no longer realize that they are beings of light. They think they are sinners and imperfect human beings who have all kinds of problems and errors that make them unworthy of God's forgiveness, unworthy to forgive themselves.

Ultimately, those walls are not real because the imperfect energies have no permanent reality in God. Yet as long as the Conscious You is in this world, the wall will affect your sense of identity, and that is why you need to break it down systematically. You need to break down one brick at a time and throw them into the spiritual fire to be consumed. Thereby, you gradually uncover the original beauty and perfection of the Conscious You.

The only thing that can break the negative spiral is that you make the decision that you will no longer feed the vortex, that you will no longer feed the wrong decision and that you will no longer blame yourself for making the wrong choice. You will accept the fact that God gave you the right to experiment. In so doing, God gave you the right to learn from a failed experiment and decide to simply leave it behind.

When Thomas Edison tried copper as the filament of a light bulb and it didn't work, he simply threw the copper away never to use it again. He left behind the idea that copper would ever produce light. He did not insist on keeping the materials from his failed experiments cluttering up his laboratory until he could barely move around. He simply threw away what didn't work and moved on, trying something new until he found something that worked.

Unmasking the lie that God caused you to fall

My beloved hearts, we now come to another insidious lie promoted by dark forces. The very essence of life is that the world of form is created by the expanding force of the Father acting upon the contracting force of the Mother. The very nature of the expanding force of the Father is to experiment. It is the force of the Father that causes your I AM Presence and Conscious You to have the desire to experiment, the curiosity to experience something new.

Here comes the subtle point. It is very true that it was the desire to experiment that made it possible for you to fall into a lower state of consciousness. You conducted certain experiments that gradually caused your consciousness to fall in vibration, until you forgot your spiritual origin. I have tried to explain to you that many people on this earth were misled and manipulated by dark forces into falling, into making the wrong decisions that caused them to fall. This should not be difficult to understand. Obviously, *you* made the choice to accept the lies of the serpent but nevertheless those lies were there and they were directed at you.

After you had fallen into a lower state of consciousness, the serpents kicked in phase two of their plot. They now told you that it was precisely your desire to experiment, it was precisely the fact that you have free will, that caused you to fall. Therefore, the only way to salvation is that you stop experimenting, that you stop exercising your free will and that you allow Lucifer, or some of the other serpents, to control you so that they can save you. They want to make you believe that God's way of doing things, meaning the gift of free will and imagination, has put your soul in danger because there is no guarantee that you will be saved. They also want you to believe that if you follow them and allow them to control you, your salvation will be guaranteed.

My beloved hearts, this is precisely the lie that permeates this world and has given rise to numerous claims that an outer organization or institution, be it a church, a dictator or a political ideology can save people or can save the world. You should not try to experiment, you should not think that you can know truth on your own. You should simply follow the leaders who know best. This is the lie that has trapped more people than any other lie. Yes, it was your drive to experiment that made it possible for you to fall, but at the same time it is only your drive to experiment that can help you rise back to the Christ consciousness.

Do you see what is actually happening here? It is true that you could fall only because you have free will and a desire to experiment. Yet it was not the desire to experiment that caused you to fall; it was the serpentine lies that caused you to fall. It was perfectly possible to experiment with your free will without falling. The fall was caused by the fact that you made the choice to accept some of the lies produced by the serpents. In reality, it was not God but the serpents who caused you to fall.

Here is the essential truth. The serpents used their lies to manipulate people into creating the current misery on this planet, and they have also attempted to set themselves up as the true saviors, as the *only* saviors, who can save you from the problem that they created. Their plot is to create so much suffering that you are willing to follow them blindly in order to escape the suffering. They create a problem and then try to sell you the "only" solution to the problem.

In reality, the serpents will never save you and the reason is simple. Salvation means that you reestablish your true identity as a son or daughter of God, as being one with God. The serpents have chosen to leave that sense of identity behind, and they identify themselves as being in opposition to God. As long as you see yourself in opposition to God, you cannot possibly obtain union with God, and therefore you cannot possibly be saved. Please take note that the true Savior, my beloved son Jesus, always affirmed his oneness with God. He came to show all people that they have the potential to attain oneness with God.

The serpents have perverted the original teachings of Jesus so that no one dare follow in his footsteps, lest they be accused of blasphemy by those who embody the serpentine consciousness.

What is it that gives you the opportunity to reestablish your union with God? It is your free will and your desire to experiment. Do you see the essential point? It was your ability to experiment that led to your fall, but it is this very ability that can lead you back to the Christ consciousness. It is precisely the plot of the serpents to use every subtle lie they can think of to prevent you from using your drive to experiment in order to come back to union with God. They want to stop you from experimenting so that you don't even dare to attempt reestablishing your union with God.

Do you see the very simple truth I am trying to explain? Your soul is a vehicle created by the Conscious You for experiencing the world. The Conscious You experiences the world through imagination and free will. Through those faculties it can add on to its sense of identity. What causes the Conscious You to become trapped in the material world is a limited sense of identity. That limited sense of identity is the result of an experiment with undesirable consequences. The only thing that can help the Conscious You escape the prison of the material world, the only thing that can "save the soul," is to continue experimenting until you find the higher identity of the Christ mind. The Conscious You must come back to a state of grace in which it accepts that it is worthy in the eyes of God because it identifies itself as a son or daughter of God.

The only way to get back to that true sense of identity is that the Conscious You must recreate its sense of identity as a Christed being; it must experiment with a higher state of consciousness. The Conscious You must dare to look for a higher understanding of truth than what it has found in the serpentine lies that permeate the world.

Jesus gave a very profound discourse on the fact that human beings can create their own god [See *www.ascendedmasteranswers.com*.] I must tell you that there is indeed an angry and judgmental god, as envisioned by many people on this planet. Yet it is an absolute truth that the angry god is a false god created by human beings and dark forces. The true God is a God of unconditional love. In fact, God's love is so unconditional that you have no need to even ask for God's forgiveness. The moment you forsake the state of consciousness that caused you to accept an imperfect sense of identity, at that very moment you are forgiven by God.

The key to your freedom is to turn the other cheek

I have given you many thoughts to ponder, and I know these are difficult concepts. I know that when you have been programmed for many lifetimes to accept the very subtle lies of the serpents, then you cannot in an instance, cannot as the result of reading one discourse, overcome those lies and leave them behind. There are those who claim to be spiritual teachers who tell people that they could change their minds in an instant, but it is not true.

A Conscious You is a being of energy, of spiritual energy. Over many lifetimes, the Conscious You can clothe itself in many layers of lower vibrations that form the soul. It is those layers that give the Conscious You a mortal sense of identity. The Conscious You cannot simply in an instant throw off the false sense of identity because it would be left with *no* sense of identity. The Conscious You must gradually replace the false sense of identity with a true sense of identity. It must, as Paul said, die daily. It must put *off* the old man and put *on* the new man. This will take time. You can greatly reduce the time it takes to build a new sense of identity by contemplating the fact that the key to true spiritual freedom is to forgive yourself, to forgive every part of life and to forgive God for anything that you think has ever been done to you. You must forgive what has been done both in this lifetime and in other lifetimes, going all the way back to when the Conscious You first descended into the material universe, and even beyond to the Garden of Eden.

The key to freedom from your current limitations is to forgive all who played a role in creating those limitations. My beloved hearts, those who seek revenge against other people, even those who engage in a battle against dark forces, are simply reinforcing the prison walls around their souls. You might recall that the Bible says: "Vengeance is mine; I will repay, saith the Lord." The truth behind that statement is that God has created an impersonal law, the law of karma, which makes sure that no being will ever escape the consequences of its uses and misuses of God's energy. Therefore, you do not need to become angry at those who harm you. You do not need to seek revenge because in so doing you misqualify God's energy and thereby you reinforce the prison around your own soul, your own mind.

That is why my son Jesus gave the wonderful teachings to forgive your enemies, to forgive those who harm you and to always turn the other cheek. When someone harms you and you turn the other cheek, you set yourself free from any negative influence of their actions. You avoid creating or reinforcing a negative sense of identity. You reaffirm that you are a spiritual being who is above and beyond any influence from the lower vibrations in the material world. Therefore, you will not let anything done to you in this world limit your sense of identity.

This is choosing God over mammon, and it is precisely what Jesus came to show all human beings. He came to show them that when you reunite with your Christ self and become a Christed being, the forces of this world might harm your body and do all kinds of things to you, including nailing you to a cross.

But no matter what they do to you, they cannot harm the Conscious You; they can only harm your soul. They cannot harm your true identity because you will rise above it all. You will rise above all of the limitations, all of the chains, that they use to bind you. You rise above it because you realize that they are simply throwing mud at the light beam of the Conscious You, and that mud has no power to cling to the true light that you are.

My beloved hearts, this has been a very long discourse, and I commend those of you who have endured to the end. There is so much more to say, but your cup is full and runneth over. Therefore, I seal you now in the infinite and unconditional love of God. I charge those who are willing with the infinite power of Forgiveness' Flame, the spiritual flame of forgiveness that conquers and consumes all sin, all mistakes, all imperfections and all limitations. I say: "Be free in the infinite forgiveness of God. Follow your highest love and come up higher. Be free of the shackles of mortality and sin and accept God's forgiveness of all imperfections that you have encountered during your journey in the lower vibrations of the material world."

You will be free of these imperfections only when you fully accept that you are free, only when you fully forgive yourself and accept your true identity as a spiritual being who has never been touched by anything in this world. In reality, you are who you are, namely a spiritual being. However, at the level of your soul, you are who you think you are. Stop thinking that you are an imperfect being and accept your true identity as a spiritual being. Be ye therefore perfect, even as your Father in heaven is perfect.

In the name of the Mother of Miracle Forgiveness, it is finished, and it is sealed in Spirit and in matter, as Above so below, now and forever. Amen.

11 | INVOCATION FOR RISING ABOVE OLD PATTERNS

In the name I AM THAT I AM, Jesus Christ, I call to all representatives of the Divine Mother, especially Maraytaii and Mother Mary, to help me fully accept that my own past choices have led to my current state of consciousness, and that my outer situation is a reflection of my state of mind. I call for you to help me overcome all illusions that stand in the way of my healing, especially…

[Make personal calls.]

1. I will stop the cycle of revenge

1. I understand the importance of forgiveness. The basic law of this universe is the Law of Free Will. The purpose of life is to grow, to move on, to self-transcend.

O Cosmic Mother, sound the gong,
that calls me home where I belong.
I know you love me tenderly,
and in that knowing I am free.

**Maraytaii, I resonate
with song that opens cosmic gate.
Your melody makes me vibrate
my sense of self I recreate.**

2. I am transcending the point of non-forgiveness. I am growing, I am moving on, I am transcending my current state of consciousness, my current sense of identity.

O Cosmic Mother, hold me tight,
I resonate with your own light.
Your music purifies my heart,
your love to all I do impart.

**Maraytaii, I resonate
with song that opens cosmic gate.
Your melody makes me vibrate
my sense of self I recreate.**

3. I am forgiving everything. I am holding on to nothing. I am letting go of any point of emotional attachment to the things of this world. I am not holding myself back; I am setting myself free.

O Cosmic Mother, we are one,
your heart is like a blazing sun.
My being can but amplify,
the sacred sound you magnify.

11 | Invocation for Rising above Old Patterns

**Maraytaii, I resonate
with song that opens cosmic gate.
Your melody makes me vibrate
my sense of self I recreate.**

4. I am free from any imperfect sense of identity. I am free from any idol of my own making or the making of my culture.

> O Cosmic Mother, I now hear,
> the subtle sound of Sacred Sphere.
> As I attune to Cosmic Hum,
> the lesser self I overcome.

**Maraytaii, I resonate
with song that opens cosmic gate.
Your melody makes me vibrate
my sense of self I recreate.**

5. I am forgiving, and I have the freedom to move on. I will move on instead of stagnating. I am transcending the second law of thermodynamics and any downward spiral, any negative vortex of energy, around me.

> O Cosmic Mother, take me home,
> I am in sync with Sacred OM,
> The sound of sounds will raise me up,
> so only light is in my cup.

**Maraytaii, I resonate
with song that opens cosmic gate.
Your melody makes me vibrate
my sense of self I recreate.**

6. I am invoking light to consume any vortex, and I am setting free my feelings and my thoughts. I know there is something outside the vortex, and I am free from the downward pull of the vortex.

> O Cosmic Mother, I will be,
> a part of cosmic symphony.
> All that I AM, an instrument,
> for sound that is from heaven sent.

> **Maraytaii, I resonate**
> **with song that opens cosmic gate.**
> **Your melody makes me vibrate**
> **my sense of self I recreate.**

7. There is a better way to live than to be in opposition to someone else. There is indeed a way to escape the cycle of violence, the cycle of revenge.

> O Cosmic Mother, I now call,
> to enter sacred music hall.
> I will be part of life's ascent,
> towards the starry firmament.

> **Maraytaii, I resonate**
> **with song that opens cosmic gate.**
> **Your melody makes me vibrate**
> **my sense of self I recreate.**

8. It is simple logic that there can be no ultimate act of revenge that ends the cycle of violence. There can be no peace through revenge because of action and reaction.

11 | Invocation for Rising above Old Patterns

O Cosmic Mother, tune my strings,
my total being with you sings.
Your song I now reverberate,
as cosmic love I celebrate.

**Maraytaii, I resonate
with song that opens cosmic gate.
Your melody makes me vibrate
my sense of self I recreate.**

9. I am transcending the pattern of seeking revenge, of reacting to what was done to me, whereby my reaction becomes a new action. This cycle will no longer consume my energy and attention because I am forgiving now.

O Cosmic Mother, I love you,
your love song keeps me ever true.
You fill me with your sacred tone,
and thus I never feel alone.

**Maraytaii, I resonate
with song that opens cosmic gate.
Your melody makes me vibrate
my sense of self I recreate.**

2. I will serve to stop non-forgiveness

1. I am separating myself from the Luciferian state of consciousness. I do want peace, I do want resolution, I do want an end to violence and an end to the spiral of revenge.

O Cosmic Mother, sound the gong,
that calls me home where I belong.
I know you love me tenderly,
and in that knowing I am free.

**Maraytaii, I resonate
with song that opens cosmic gate.
Your melody makes me vibrate
my sense of self I recreate.**

2. I am separating myself from the people who say they want peace, but they are not willing to stop the cycle of revenge.

O Cosmic Mother, hold me tight,
I resonate with your own light.
Your music purifies my heart,
your love to all I do impart.

**Maraytaii, I resonate
with song that opens cosmic gate.
Your melody makes me vibrate
my sense of self I recreate.**

3. I am free from any vortex of negative energy. I am willing to see the fallacy of my thinking. I think logically and rationally because I am no longer overpowered by emotional energies. I do indeed stop to think.

O Cosmic Mother, we are one,
your heart is like a blazing sun.
My being can but amplify,
the sacred sound you magnify.

11 | Invocation for Rising above Old Patterns

**Maraytaii, I resonate
with song that opens cosmic gate.
Your melody makes me vibrate
my sense of self I recreate.**

4. I am one of the balanced people. I am serving to consume the energies created through revenge and non-forgiveness, the very energies that form a magnetic pull on people's emotions and overpower them so that they lose all logic and rationality.

> O Cosmic Mother, I now hear,
> the subtle sound of Sacred Sphere.
> As I attune to Cosmic Hum,
> the lesser self I overcome.

**Maraytaii, I resonate
with song that opens cosmic gate.
Your melody makes me vibrate
my sense of self I recreate.**

5. I am an effective force in consuming the vortexes of non-forgiveness on this planet. I am indeed willing to free myself from the point of non-forgiveness.

> O Cosmic Mother, take me home,
> I am in sync with Sacred OM,
> The sound of sounds will raise me up,
> so only light is in my cup.

**Maraytaii, I resonate
with song that opens cosmic gate.
Your melody makes me vibrate
my sense of self I recreate.**

6. I see the true cause of non-forgiveness. Non-forgiveness is based on a set of lies. I understand these lies and see the mindset behind them.

> O Cosmic Mother, I will be,
> a part of cosmic symphony.
> All that I AM, an instrument,
> for sound that is from heaven sent.
>
> **Maraytaii, I resonate**
> **with song that opens cosmic gate.**
> **Your melody makes me vibrate**
> **my sense of self I recreate.**

7. I see through the lies of the devil. I am wise as a serpent, I am harmless as a dove.

> O Cosmic Mother, I now call,
> to enter sacred music hall.
> I will be part of life's ascent,
> towards the starry firmament.
>
> **Maraytaii, I resonate**
> **with song that opens cosmic gate.**
> **Your melody makes me vibrate**
> **my sense of self I recreate.**

8. The basic law of this universe is the Law of Free Will. I have the right to experiment with my creative abilities. My lifestream was created with a drive, a desire, to experiment with God's laws and God's energies.

11 | Invocation for Rising above Old Patterns

O Cosmic Mother, tune my strings,
my total being with you sings.
Your song I now reverberate,
as cosmic love I celebrate.

**Maraytaii, I resonate
with song that opens cosmic gate.
Your melody makes me vibrate
my sense of self I recreate.**

9. I am regaining the direct, inner contact with my spiritual self. I am transcending the lower state of consciousness of seeing myself as being separated from my spiritual self, even separated from God.

O Cosmic Mother, I love you,
your love song keeps me ever true.
You fill me with your sacred tone,
and thus I never feel alone.

**Maraytaii, I resonate
with song that opens cosmic gate.
Your melody makes me vibrate
my sense of self I recreate.**

3. I surrender my blame towards God

1. I am transcending the sense of separation, and I realize that God has never hurt me. God has not created the conditions on this planet. Those conditions were created by human beings trapped in the lower state of consciousness, in which they are easily controlled by dark forces.

> O Cosmic Mother, sound the gong,
> that calls me home where I belong.
> I know you love me tenderly,
> and in that knowing I am free.
>
> **Maraytaii, I resonate**
> **with song that opens cosmic gate.**
> **Your melody makes me vibrate**
> **my sense of self I recreate.**

2. I fully understand and accept that the misery on earth was created by human beings and not created by God. I surrender the sense that either God must have created my misery or God must have allowed it to be created.

> O Cosmic Mother, hold me tight,
> I resonate with your own light.
> Your music purifies my heart,
> your love to all I do impart.
>
> **Maraytaii, I resonate**
> **with song that opens cosmic gate.**
> **Your melody makes me vibrate**
> **my sense of self I recreate.**

3. I surrender all tendency to blame God for the conditions in my life, for the negative experiences I have had in this lifetime. I surrender the tendency to blame God for what happened to me in the Garden of Eden.

O Cosmic Mother, we are one,
your heart is like a blazing sun.
My being can but amplify,
the sacred sound you magnify.

**Maraytaii, I resonate
with song that opens cosmic gate.
Your melody makes me vibrate
my sense of self I recreate.**

4. I surrender the tendency to blame God for the fact that I fell into a lower state of consciousness. I surrender the lie that if God had not put the tree in the garden and allowed the serpent to be in the garden, then my soul would not have fallen. I surrender the sense that it must be God's fault.

O Cosmic Mother, I now hear,
the subtle sound of Sacred Sphere.
As I attune to Cosmic Hum,
the lesser self I overcome.

**Maraytaii, I resonate
with song that opens cosmic gate.
Your melody makes me vibrate
my sense of self I recreate.**

5. These beliefs are not my own. They have been manufactured by Lucifer and his followers in order to trap me in a state of consciousness that makes it almost impossible for me to come back to God, to come back to a full realization and acceptance of who I am as a son or daughter of God.

O Cosmic Mother, take me home,
I am in sync with Sacred OM,
The sound of sounds will raise me up,
so only light is in my cup.

**Maraytaii, I resonate
with song that opens cosmic gate.
Your melody makes me vibrate
my sense of self I recreate.**

6. I experience the fallacy of the luciferian lie that God made a mistake by giving people free will. I surrender all desire to blame God for the fact that he gave me free will and even for the fact that God created me.

O Cosmic Mother, I will be,
a part of cosmic symphony.
All that I AM, an instrument,
for sound that is from heaven sent.

**Maraytaii, I resonate
with song that opens cosmic gate.
Your melody makes me vibrate
my sense of self I recreate.**

7. The serpent is a symbol for a state of consciousness, namely that of rebelling against God's laws. The potential to rebel is an inevitable result of giving me free will because if I could not rebel, I would not have *free* will.

11 | Invocation for Rising above Old Patterns

O Cosmic Mother, I now call,
to enter sacred music hall.
I will be part of life's ascent,
towards the starry firmament.

**Maraytaii, I resonate
with song that opens cosmic gate.
Your melody makes me vibrate
my sense of self I recreate.**

8. I do not *need* to rebel in order to exercise my freedom of choice. God never wanted me to identify with my shadow or to be afraid of my own shadow. God wanted me to always face the light of my I AM Presence and keep the shadow behind me.

O Cosmic Mother, tune my strings,
my total being with you sings.
Your song I now reverberate,
as cosmic love I celebrate.

**Maraytaii, I resonate
with song that opens cosmic gate.
Your melody makes me vibrate
my sense of self I recreate.**

9. I am transcending the tendency to paralyze myself by blaming God. I am transcending the belief that I am not responsible for my situation. I accept that I did create my current situation, and therefore I can also uncreate it.

O Cosmic Mother, I love you,
your love song keeps me ever true.
You fill me with your sacred tone,
and thus I never feel alone.

**Maraytaii, I resonate
with song that opens cosmic gate.
Your melody makes me vibrate
my sense of self I recreate.**

4. I accept the Mother of God

1. I am transcending the illusion that I did not create the conditions that caused me to fall into a lower state of consciousness. I surrender the sense that I did not give myself free will, I did not choose to be created, I did not choose to be born, I did not choose to come to this planet, I did not even choose to exist.

O Cosmic Mother, sound the gong,
that calls me home where I belong.
I know you love me tenderly,
and in that knowing I am free.

**Maraytaii, I resonate
with song that opens cosmic gate.
Your melody makes me vibrate
my sense of self I recreate.**

2. I hereby accept personal responsibility and accountability. I fully accept that in any situation there is something I can do to transcend that situation and come up higher.

11 | Invocation for Rising above Old Patterns

O Cosmic Mother, hold me tight,
I resonate with your own light.
Your music purifies my heart,
your love to all I do impart.

**Maraytaii, I resonate
with song that opens cosmic gate.
Your melody makes me vibrate
my sense of self I recreate.**

3. It is possible for me to escape any prison in the matter universe. No matter what mistake I could possibly make, I cannot be doomed forever.

O Cosmic Mother, we are one,
your heart is like a blazing sun.
My being can but amplify,
the sacred sound you magnify.

**Maraytaii, I resonate
with song that opens cosmic gate.
Your melody makes me vibrate
my sense of self I recreate.**

4. I am seeing through the eyes of an ascended being, and I see how ridiculous are the serpentine lies. Everything in the matter universe is created from God's energy. God's energy is vibration, and it is always possible to raise the vibration and bring it back into alignment with the purity and the perfection of God.

O Cosmic Mother, I now hear,
the subtle sound of Sacred Sphere.
As I attune to Cosmic Hum,
the lesser self I overcome.

**Maraytaii, I resonate
with song that opens cosmic gate.
Your melody makes me vibrate
my sense of self I recreate.**

5. The idea that I could possibly do something that could not be undone is a misuse of the contracting force of the Mother, the very Mother of God. It is the contracting force of the Mother which gives me life, which gives me individual consciousness, individual sense of identity.

O Cosmic Mother, take me home,
I am in sync with Sacred OM,
The sound of sounds will raise me up,
so only light is in my cup.

**Maraytaii, I resonate
with song that opens cosmic gate.
Your melody makes me vibrate
my sense of self I recreate.**

6. It has never been the intention of the Mother of God to trap me in a particular form. The form created by the energies of the Mother of God could never become a prison from which there is no escape. The unconditional love of the Mother of God is what gives me life and form.

11 | Invocation for Rising above Old Patterns

O Cosmic Mother, I will be,
a part of cosmic symphony.
All that I AM, an instrument,
for sound that is from heaven sent.

**Maraytaii, I resonate
with song that opens cosmic gate.
Your melody makes me vibrate
my sense of self I recreate.**

7. I am reclaiming the true recognition of who I am. I am free from the lie of a false identity. I am free from any negative vortex of energy, setting free my feelings and my ability to think rationally.

O Cosmic Mother, I now call,
to enter sacred music hall.
I will be part of life's ascent,
towards the starry firmament.

**Maraytaii, I resonate
with song that opens cosmic gate.
Your melody makes me vibrate
my sense of self I recreate.**

8. I now consciously decide that I am transcending the lie of the serpent. I am taking full and complete responsibility for my current situation.

O Cosmic Mother, tune my strings,
my total being with you sings.
Your song I now reverberate,
as cosmic love I celebrate.

**Maraytaii, I resonate
with song that opens cosmic gate.
Your melody makes me vibrate
my sense of self I recreate.**

9. I fully and finally surrender the belief that I am a victim of what God has created, and I have no responsibility for my situation because God set me up to fail. I fully accept that God gave me everything needed for my victory. I hereby decide that I will use my free will to claim my victory in Christ.

O Cosmic Mother, I love you,
your love song keeps me ever true.
You fill me with your sacred tone,
and thus I never feel alone.

**Maraytaii, I resonate
with song that opens cosmic gate.
Your melody makes me vibrate
my sense of self I recreate.**

Sealing

In the name of the Divine Mother, I call to Maraytaii and Mother Mary for the sealing of myself and all people in the creative flow of the Divine Mother, the River of Life. I call for the multiplication of my calls by all representatives of the Divine Mother, so that we form the perfect figure-eight flow of "As Above, so below." Thus, I accept that this is fully manifest, because the mouth of the Lord, the Divine Mother that I AM, has spoken it. Amen.

12 | INVOCATION FOR ACCEPTING THAT I AM ALIVE

In the name I AM THAT I AM, Jesus Christ, I call to all representatives of the Divine Mother, especially Nada and Mother Mary, to help me truly accept that life is a gift and a wondrous opportunity. I call for you to help me overcome all illusions that stand in the way of my healing, especially…

[Make personal calls.]

1. I stop rejecting God's forgiveness

1. I fully accept that even though I have fallen into a lower state of consciousness, even though I have made mistakes and have sinned, I have *not* been permanently stained.

O Nada, blessed cosmic grace,
filling up my inner space.
Your song is like a sacred balm,
my mind a sea of perfect calm.

**With Nada's secret melody,
my mind remains forever free.
Conducting Nada's symphony,
eternal peace I do decree.**

2. My true identity is not my soul, the soul that abides in a physical body in the material universe. My true identity is the spiritual self, which resides in a realm that is made entirely of higher vibrations.

O Nada, in your Buddhic mind,
my inner peace I truly find.
As I your song reverberate,
your love I do assimilate.

**With Nada's secret melody,
my mind remains forever free.
Conducting Nada's symphony,
eternal peace I do decree.**

3. My I AM Presence is as perfect and as beautiful as when it was first created by God. I am as pure and as worthy of God's love as the day I was first created. Nothing I have done in this world has made me unworthy of God's love.

12 | *Invocation for Accepting that I Am Alive*

O Nada, beauty so sublime,
I follow you beyond all time.
In soundless sound we do immerse,
to recreate the universe.

**With Nada's secret melody,
my mind remains forever free.
Conducting Nada's symphony,
eternal peace I do decree.**

4. I am transcending the lie that I am no longer worthy of God's love. I surrender the illusion that I need to hide from God and that there is no point in trying to come home to God or even ask for forgiveness.

O Nada, future we predict
where nothing Christhood can restrict.
With Buddhic mind we do perceive,
a better future we conceive.

**With Nada's secret melody,
my mind remains forever free.
Conducting Nada's symphony,
eternal peace I do decree.**

5. What keeps me trapped in my current state of consciousness, in my current set of limitations and even in my outer circumstances, is that I cannot accept God's forgiveness.

O Nada, future we rewrite,
where might is never, ever right.
Instead, the mind of Christ is king,
we see the Christ in every thing.

> **With Nada's secret melody,**
> **my mind remains forever free.**
> **Conducting Nada's symphony,**
> **eternal peace I do decree.**

6. When I create a false image of myself, I become trapped in that sense of identity. The prison is created by my mind and exists only in my mind. I now decide that I no longer want to be that way. I do not want to be the limited person that I see myself as being. I am letting go of those limitations and I am moving on.

> O Nada, peace is now the norm,
> my Spirit is beyond all form.
> To form I will no more adapt,
> I use potential yet untapped.

> **With Nada's secret melody,**
> **my mind remains forever free.**
> **Conducting Nada's symphony,**
> **eternal peace I do decree.**

7. I can let go of limitations only by forgiving myself for creating those limitations in the first place. I can forgive myself only when I fully recognize and accept that it was me who created the limitations and not God or Lucifer.

> O Nada, such resplendent joy,
> my life I truly can enjoy.
> I am allowed to have some fun,
> my solar plexus like a sun.

**With Nada's secret melody,
my mind remains forever free.
Conducting Nada's symphony,
eternal peace I do decree.**

8. I am transcending the catch-22 in which I cannot improve my life because I do not take responsibility for my situation. I am taking responsibility because I know there *is* forgiveness.

> O Nada, service is the key,
> to living in reality.
> For I see now that life is one,
> my highest service has begun.

**With Nada's secret melody,
my mind remains forever free.
Conducting Nada's symphony,
eternal peace I do decree.**

9. I am transcending this lie and I accept that the angry God is a luciferian creation. The real God constantly offers me unconditional forgiveness. I now accept that forgiveness, and I forgive myself.

> O Nada, we do now decree,
> that life on earth shall be carefree.
> With Jesus we complete the quest,
> God's kingdom is now manifest.

**With Nada's secret melody,
my mind remains forever free.
Conducting Nada's symphony,
eternal peace I do decree.**

2. I will transcend all blame

1. If I believe there is no escape from limitations, I cannot admit that I have created the limitations because I would condemn myself for doing so. I am not permanently locked in experiencing suffering and limitation. I am no longer blaming myself for the situation.

> O Nada, blessed cosmic grace,
> filling up my inner space.
> Your song is like a sacred balm,
> my mind a sea of perfect calm.
>
> **With Nada's secret melody,**
> **my mind remains forever free.**
> **Conducting Nada's symphony,**
> **eternal peace I do decree.**

2. I have created my situation, but God does not condemn me for doing so. There is no reason for condemning myself. What I have done is to experiment with my free will and with the energy of God.

> O Nada, in your Buddhic mind,
> my inner peace I truly find.
> As I your song reverberate,
> your love I do assimilate.
>
> **With Nada's secret melody,**
> **my mind remains forever free.**
> **Conducting Nada's symphony,**
> **eternal peace I do decree.**

3. God never wanted me to create limitations that cause me suffering and pain. When God made the decision to give me free will, God gave me the right to experiment. In so doing, God also set me free from all blame.

> O Nada, beauty so sublime,
> I follow you beyond all time.
> In soundless sound we do immerse,
> to recreate the universe.

> **With Nada's secret melody,**
> **my mind remains forever free.**
> **Conducting Nada's symphony,**
> **eternal peace I do decree.**

4. By creating me and giving me free will, God has given me the opportunity to grow in awareness until I can fully accept myself as a son or daughter of God. Thereby, I become a co-creator with God.

> O Nada, future we predict
> where nothing Christhood can restrict.
> With Buddhic mind we do perceive,
> a better future we conceive.

> **With Nada's secret melody,**
> **my mind remains forever free.**
> **Conducting Nada's symphony,**
> **eternal peace I do decree.**

5. God has given me the opportunity to become all that God is and more. In creating me and giving me free will, God has no desire to blame me for doing what I was created to do in experimenting with free will, or even for creating circumstances that cause me suffering.

> O Nada, future we rewrite,
> where might is never, ever right.
> Instead, the mind of Christ is king,
> we see the Christ in every thing.

> **With Nada's secret melody,**
> **my mind remains forever free.**
> **Conducting Nada's symphony,**
> **eternal peace I do decree.**

6. God does not want me to blame myself and God does not want to blame me. God wants me to approach life as a scientist conducting experiments. God wants me to participate in the experiment of life.

> O Nada, peace is now the norm,
> my Spirit is beyond all form.
> To form I will no more adapt,
> I use potential yet untapped.

> **With Nada's secret melody,**
> **my mind remains forever free.**
> **Conducting Nada's symphony,**
> **eternal peace I do decree.**

7. I am thinking rationally and logically about life. When I experience conditions that cause me suffering, I say: "I do not want to experience these conditions any more. I have had enough of that experience, so what can I do to change my experience?"

> O Nada, such resplendent joy,
> my life I truly can enjoy.
> I am allowed to have some fun,
> my solar plexus like a sun.
>
> **With Nada's secret melody,**
> **my mind remains forever free.**
> **Conducting Nada's symphony,**
> **eternal peace I do decree.**

8. The first step I must take is to overcome the belief that I am the victim of circumstances beyond my control. As long as I feel like a victim, there is nothing I can do to change the circumstances that cause me suffering.

> O Nada, service is the key,
> to living in reality.
> For I see now that life is one,
> my highest service has begun.
>
> **With Nada's secret melody,**
> **my mind remains forever free.**
> **Conducting Nada's symphony,**
> **eternal peace I do decree.**

9. I take responsibility for my situation and recognize that I have either created these circumstances or I have attracted these circumstances to me. I did this by allowing myself to be in a lower state of consciousness than what is my highest potential. The very key to changing my circumstances is to change my state of consciousness.

> O Nada, we do now decree,
> that life on earth shall be carefree.
> With Jesus we complete the quest,
> God's kingdom is now manifest.
>
> **With Nada's secret melody,**
> **my mind remains forever free.**
> **Conducting Nada's symphony,**
> **eternal peace I do decree.**

3. I am changing my consciousness

1. When I change my state of consciousness, my experience of my circumstances will change and I will begin to suffer less, even if the outer circumstances do not change instantly.

> O Nada, blessed cosmic grace,
> filling up my inner space.
> Your song is like a sacred balm,
> my mind a sea of perfect calm.
>
> **With Nada's secret melody,**
> **my mind remains forever free.**
> **Conducting Nada's symphony,**
> **eternal peace I do decree.**

2. I will continue to raise my state of consciousness until I experience a change in the outer circumstances.

> O Nada, in your Buddhic mind,
> my inner peace I truly find.
> As I your song reverberate,
> your love I do assimilate.
>
> **With Nada's secret melody,**
> **my mind remains forever free.**
> **Conducting Nada's symphony,**
> **eternal peace I do decree.**

3. Everything in the matter universe started as an idea in the etheric realm. It was solidified as a thought in the mental realm. It received energy and motion in the emotional realm, before it finally broke through in the material realm.

> O Nada, beauty so sublime,
> I follow you beyond all time.
> In soundless sound we do immerse,
> to recreate the universe.
>
> **With Nada's secret melody,**
> **my mind remains forever free.**
> **Conducting Nada's symphony,**
> **eternal peace I do decree.**

4. As a spiritually aware person, I do not expect that outer, material circumstances will change overnight. It will take some time to change the circumstances, and the reason is that I need to go to the source.

O Nada, future we predict
where nothing Christhood can restrict.
With Buddhic mind we do perceive,
a better future we conceive.

**With Nada's secret melody,
my mind remains forever free.
Conducting Nada's symphony,
eternal peace I do decree.**

5. I need to begin by changing the images in the etheric realm, which will then change the thought and change the feelings, and then cycle through to the material realm. Because the energies in the material realm are the densest, it will take some time before I will see a change in the visible world. In my patience I will posses my soul.

O Nada, future we rewrite,
where might is never, ever right.
Instead, the mind of Christ is king,
we see the Christ in every thing.

**With Nada's secret melody,
my mind remains forever free.
Conducting Nada's symphony,
eternal peace I do decree.**

6. The material world is like a movie projected upon a screen. I have three filmstrips in my subconscious mind. One is my sense of identity, the other is my mental image of myself and the world, and the third is my feelings about myself and the world.

12 | Invocation for Accepting that I Am Alive

O Nada, peace is now the norm,
my Spirit is beyond all form.
To form I will no more adapt,
I use potential yet untapped.

**With Nada's secret melody,
my mind remains forever free.
Conducting Nada's symphony,
eternal peace I do decree.**

7. My outer circumstances are projections upon the screen of life, as the light of God passes through my consciousness and is colored and given shape by the images I hold in my etheric, mental and emotional bodies.

O Nada, such resplendent joy,
my life I truly can enjoy.
I am allowed to have some fun,
my solar plexus like a sun.

**With Nada's secret melody,
my mind remains forever free.
Conducting Nada's symphony,
eternal peace I do decree.**

8. In order to change my outer circumstances, I will begin by changing my inner circumstances, my state of consciousness.

O Nada, service is the key,
to living in reality.
For I see now that life is one,
my highest service has begun.

**With Nada's secret melody,
my mind remains forever free.
Conducting Nada's symphony,
eternal peace I do decree.**

9. My outer circumstances are created by my consciousness, they are a reflection of the images in my consciousness. Those images were created by me.

> O Nada, we do now decree,
> that life on earth shall be carefree.
> With Jesus we complete the quest,
> God's kingdom is now manifest.

**With Nada's secret melody,
my mind remains forever free.
Conducting Nada's symphony,
eternal peace I do decree.**

4. I stop the blame game

1. I see and accept the central truth that all spiritual people need to understand.

> O Nada, blessed cosmic grace,
> filling up my inner space.
> Your song is like a sacred balm,
> my mind a sea of perfect calm.

**With Nada's secret melody,
my mind remains forever free.
Conducting Nada's symphony,
eternal peace I do decree.**

2. My I AM Presence is in constant, conscious contact with God. It constantly feels the infinite and unconditional love of God. There is no point in my I AM Presence that has any negative feelings about being created or about having free will.

O Nada, in your Buddhic mind,
my inner peace I truly find.
As I your song reverberate,
your love I do assimilate.

**With Nada's secret melody,
my mind remains forever free.
Conducting Nada's symphony,
eternal peace I do decree.**

3. My I AM Presence feels only infinite joy and gratitude for the opportunity to exist and to be part of God's magnificent and wonderful creation. None of the negative feelings that affect so many people on earth exist at the level of my I AM Presence.

O Nada, beauty so sublime,
I follow you beyond all time.
In soundless sound we do immerse,
to recreate the universe.

**With Nada's secret melody,
my mind remains forever free.
Conducting Nada's symphony,
eternal peace I do decree.**

4. My I AM Presence was created by God but my soul was not created by God. My soul was created by the Conscious You as a vehicle for experiencing the material universe and for expressing my creativity in the material universe.

> O Nada, future we predict
> where nothing Christhood can restrict.
> With Buddhic mind we do perceive,
> a better future we conceive.

**With Nada's secret melody,
my mind remains forever free.
Conducting Nada's symphony,
eternal peace I do decree.**

5. It is not logical and rational, nor is it true, to blame God for the fact that my soul exists. God did not create the soul that descended into the material universe and fell into a lower state of consciousness. My I AM Presence created the Conscious You and the Conscious You created the soul, but the Conscious You is *me*.

> O Nada, future we rewrite,
> where might is never, ever right.
> Instead, the mind of Christ is king,
> we see the Christ in every thing.

**With Nada's secret melody,
my mind remains forever free.
Conducting Nada's symphony,
eternal peace I do decree.**

6. I created my soul because I made the choice to create that soul. I made that choice because I wanted to experience the material universe and I wanted to help co-create this universe as the kingdom of God.

> O Nada, peace is now the norm,
> my Spirit is beyond all form.
> To form I will no more adapt,
> I use potential yet untapped.

**With Nada's secret melody,
my mind remains forever free.
Conducting Nada's symphony,
eternal peace I do decree.**

7. Even though I presently experience myself as a victim of circumstances beyond my control, the Conscious You is not a victim. My soul is the result of a choice made by me, meaning my true identity as a spiritual being.

> O Nada, such resplendent joy,
> my life I truly can enjoy.
> I am allowed to have some fun,
> my solar plexus like a sun.

**With Nada's secret melody,
my mind remains forever free.
Conducting Nada's symphony,
eternal peace I do decree.**

8. I made that choice because I wanted to descend into the material realm and have a positive experience that would lead to my growth, to a growth in my sense of identity as a co-creator with God.

> O Nada, service is the key,
> to living in reality.
> For I see now that life is one,
> my highest service has begun.

**With Nada's secret melody,
my mind remains forever free.
Conducting Nada's symphony,
eternal peace I do decree.**

9. I am surrendering all tendency to blame God or blame myself. I give up blaming God, blaming other people, blaming dark forces or even blaming myself. I am stopping the blame game. I forgive myself and I say: "I conducted an experiment that did not work out as I intended. I am leaving that experiment behind and coming up higher in consciousness."

> O Nada, we do now decree,
> that life on earth shall be carefree.
> With Jesus we complete the quest,
> God's kingdom is now manifest.

**With Nada's secret melody,
my mind remains forever free.
Conducting Nada's symphony,
eternal peace I do decree.**

Sealing

In the name of the Divine Mother, I call to Nada and Mother Mary for the sealing of myself and all people in the creative flow of the Divine Mother, the River of Life. I call for the multiplication of my calls by all representatives of the Divine Mother, so that we form the perfect figure-eight flow of "As Above, so below." Thus, I accept that this is fully manifest, because the mouth of the Lord, the Divine Mother that I AM, has spoken it. Amen.

13 | INVOCATION FOR RAISING MY LIFE EXPERIENCE

In the name I AM THAT I AM, Jesus Christ, I call to all representatives of the Divine Mother, especially Kuan Yin and Mother Mary, to help me know how to consciously raise my life experience. I call for you to help me overcome all illusions that stand in the way of my healing, especially…

[Make personal calls.]

1. I am the only one who can change myself

1. I am determined to take the necessary steps to change my Life experience. I am using my present circumstances as a springboard for creating a positive experience for myself.

O Kuan Yin, what sacred name,
fill me now with Mercy's Flame.
In giving mercy I am free,
forgiving all is magic key.

**In Kuan Yin's sweet melody,
I am set free my Self to be.
In Kuan Yin's vitality,
I claim my immortality.**

2. No matter what the outer appearances might be in this world, nobody ever did anything to me. No human being ever did anything to me and God never did anything to me.

O Kuan Yin, I now let go,
of all attachments here below.
All pent-up feelings I release,
free from emotional disease.

**In Kuan Yin's sweet melody,
I am set free my Self to be.
In Kuan Yin's vitality,
I claim my immortality.**

3. The only force that ever did anything to me was myself.

O Kuan Yin, why must I feel,
that life falls short of my ideal?
All expectations I give up,
my mind is now an empty cup.

13 | Invocation for Raising My Life Experience

**In Kuan Yin's sweet melody,
I am set free my Self to be.
In Kuan Yin's vitality,
I claim my immortality.**

4. Even though the Conscious You is in the material universe, it is not made from the energies of the material universe. The Conscious You is truly a light beam that is shining from my I AM Presence.

O Kuan Yin, transcend the past,
as all resentment gone at last.
From future nothing I expect,
eternal now I won't reject.

**In Kuan Yin's sweet melody,
I am set free my Self to be.
In Kuan Yin's vitality,
I claim my immortality.**

5. The energies of the material universe cannot cling to the Conscious You, they cannot damage the real me.

O Kuan Yin, uplifting me,
beyond Samsara's raging sea.
All safe inside your Prajna boat,
the farther shore no more remote.

**In Kuan Yin's sweet melody,
I am set free my Self to be.
In Kuan Yin's vitality,
I claim my immortality.**

6. The Conscious You is a state of consciousness, a sense of being, a sense of identity. It is a being that has imagination and free will.

> O Kuan Yin, your alchemy,
> with miracles you set me free.
> As I forgive, I am forgiven,
> by guilt I am no longer driven.
>
> **In Kuan Yin's sweet melody,**
> **I am set free my Self to be.**
> **In Kuan Yin's vitality,**
> **I claim my immortality.**

7. The Conscious You creates its own sense of identity, and it recreates that sense of identity every moment.

> O Kuan Yin, all worries gone,
> with nothing done, no thing undone.
> Through separate self I will not do,
> and thus I rest, all one with you.
>
> **In Kuan Yin's sweet melody,**
> **I am set free my Self to be.**
> **In Kuan Yin's vitality,**
> **I claim my immortality.**

8. If someone comes to me and slaps me on one cheek, that person has done something to my body, but that person has done nothing to the Conscious You.

13 | Invocation for Raising My Life Experience

> O Kuan Yin, your sanity,
> now sets me free from vanity.
> For truly, what is that to me;
> I just let go and follow thee.
>
> **In Kuan Yin's sweet melody,**
> **I am set free my Self to be.**
> **In Kuan Yin's vitality,**
> **I claim my immortality.**

9. I am the only person who has the ability, through my imagination and free will, to let the action performed by another person affect my sense of identity. In so doing, I am doing something to myself, to my soul.

> O Kuan Yin, so sweet the sound,
> that emanates from holy ground.
> As I let go of ego's chore,
> I find myself on farther shore.
>
> **In Kuan Yin's sweet melody,**
> **I am set free my Self to be.**
> **In Kuan Yin's vitality,**
> **I claim my immortality.**

2. I stop harming myself

1. Another person cannot change my sense of identity—only *I* can do that. In order to change my sense of identity, I must make a choice.

O Kuan Yin, what sacred name,
fill me now with Mercy's Flame.
In giving mercy I am free,
forgiving all is magic key.

In Kuan Yin's sweet melody,
I am set free my Self to be.
In Kuan Yin's vitality,
I claim my immortality.

2. There are forces in this world who use very aggressive means in order to manipulate people into accepting an imperfect and false sense of identity. Those forces are very insidious, and they are very persuasive in the lies they use. I know I am more than a sinner, more than a mortal human being. Whatever I have done here on earth, I can rise above it.

O Kuan Yin, I now let go,
of all attachments here below.
All pent-up feelings I release,
free from emotional disease.

In Kuan Yin's sweet melody,
I am set free my Self to be.
In Kuan Yin's vitality,
I claim my immortality.

3. While it is not easy to escape the clutches of these liars and their lies, it is indeed possible for me to escape all the lies in this world. None of the forces of this world can harm the Conscious You; they can only harm my soul.

13 | *Invocation for Raising My Life Experience*

O Kuan Yin, why must I feel,
that life falls short of my ideal?
All expectations I give up,
my mind is now an empty cup

**In Kuan Yin's sweet melody,
I am set free my Self to be.
In Kuan Yin's vitality,
I claim my immortality.**

4. What can harm my soul is that I allow the forces of this world to cause me to change my sense of identity. That is what will harm me, but that harm can come about only through the decisions I make.

O Kuan Yin, transcend the past,
as all resentment gone at last.
From future nothing I expect,
eternal now I won't reject.

**In Kuan Yin's sweet melody,
I am set free my Self to be.
In Kuan Yin's vitality,
I claim my immortality.**

5. Anything that has been done to my soul through a choice that I made can be undone by me making a better choice.

O Kuan Yin, uplifting me,
beyond Samsara's raging sea.
All safe inside your Prajna boat,
the farther shore no more remote.

> **In Kuan Yin's sweet melody,**
> **I am set free my Self to be.**
> **In Kuan Yin's vitality,**
> **I claim my immortality.**

6. The key to being free of all imperfections of the past is that I make a choice to let those imperfections go, to leave them behind. I do so by forgiving myself for making those choices.

> O Kuan Yin, your alchemy,
> with miracles you set me free.
> As I forgive, I am forgiven,
> by guilt I am no longer driven.

> **In Kuan Yin's sweet melody,**
> **I am set free my Self to be.**
> **In Kuan Yin's vitality,**
> **I claim my immortality.**

7. I am transcending the programming by the forces of this world. I can accept that anything that ever happened to me was the result of decisions I made without having to blame myself for making wrong choices.

> O Kuan Yin, all worries gone,
> with nothing done, no thing undone.
> Through separate self I will not do,
> and thus I rest, all one with you.

> **In Kuan Yin's sweet melody,**
> **I am set free my Self to be.**
> **In Kuan Yin's vitality,**
> **I claim my immortality.**

8. There is no need to blame myself for making wrong choices. If I blame myself for making the wrong choice, I will bind myself to that choice because in blaming myself, I am reinforcing that choice.

> O Kuan Yin, your sanity,
> now sets me free from vanity.
> For truly, what is that to me;
> I just let go and follow thee.
>
> **In Kuan Yin's sweet melody,**
> **I am set free my Self to be.**
> **In Kuan Yin's vitality,**
> **I claim my immortality.**

9. I am transcending the tendency to reinforce past choices by the energy that streams through my mind and attention. I am freeing the energy created through old choices. I am consuming the vortexes that used to overpower my thoughts and feelings. I am free to see beyond the past.

> O Kuan Yin, so sweet the sound,
> that emanates from holy ground.
> As I let go of ego's chore,
> I find myself on farther shore.
>
> **In Kuan Yin's sweet melody,**
> **I am set free my Self to be.**
> **In Kuan Yin's vitality,**
> **I claim my immortality.**

3. I leave behind my failed experiments

1. I see how I have made wrong choices, and instead of forgiving myself and moving on, I reinforced those wrong choices. I am no longer feeding energy into these imperfect images. I am tearing down the wall around my soul, and I realize that I am a being of light.

> O Kuan Yin, what sacred name,
> fill me now with Mercy's Flame.
> In giving mercy I am free,
> forgiving all is magic key.
>
> **In Kuan Yin's sweet melody,**
> **I am set free my Self to be.**
> **In Kuan Yin's vitality,**
> **I claim my immortality.**

2. I surrender the belief that I am a sinner and an imperfect human being who has all kinds of problems and errors. I am indeed worthy of God's forgiveness, I am worthy to forgive myself.

> O Kuan Yin, I now let go,
> of all attachments here below.
> All pent-up feelings I release,
> free from emotional disease.
>
> **In Kuan Yin's sweet melody,**
> **I am set free my Self to be.**
> **In Kuan Yin's vitality,**
> **I claim my immortality.**

13 | Invocation for Raising My Life Experience

3. The walls around my soul are not real because the imperfect energies have no permanent reality in God. As long as the Conscious You is in this world, the wall will affect my sense of identity, and that is why I will break it down systematically.

> O Kuan Yin, why must I feel,
> that life falls short of my ideal?
> All expectations I give up,
> my mind is now an empty cup.

> **In Kuan Yin's sweet melody,**
> **I am set free my Self to be.**
> **In Kuan Yin's vitality,**
> **I claim my immortality.**

4. I am breaking down one brick at a time, and I throw them into the spiritual fire to be consumed. I am gradually uncovering the original beauty and perfection of the Conscious You.

> O Kuan Yin, transcend the past,
> as all resentment gone at last.
> From future nothing I expect,
> eternal now I won't reject.

> **In Kuan Yin's sweet melody,**
> **I am set free my Self to be.**
> **In Kuan Yin's vitality,**
> **I claim my immortality.**

5. I am breaking the negative spiral by making the decision that I will no longer feed the vortex, I will no longer feed the wrong decision and I will no longer blame myself for making that choice.

O Kuan Yin, uplifting me,
beyond Samsara's raging sea.
All safe inside your Prajna boat,
the farther shore no more remote.

In Kuan Yin's sweet melody,
I am set free my Self to be.
In Kuan Yin's vitality,
I claim my immortality.

6. God gave me the right to experiment. In so doing, God gave me the right to learn from a failed experiment and decide to simply leave it behind.

O Kuan Yin, your alchemy,
with miracles you set me free.
As I forgive, I am forgiven,
by guilt I am no longer driven.

In Kuan Yin's sweet melody,
I am set free my Self to be.
In Kuan Yin's vitality,
I claim my immortality.

7. The very essence of life is that the world of form is created by the expanding force of the Father, acting upon the contracting force of the Mother.

O Kuan Yin, all worries gone,
with nothing done, no thing undone.
Through separate self I will not do,
and thus I rest, all one with you.

**In Kuan Yin's sweet melody,
I am set free my Self to be.
In Kuan Yin's vitality,
I claim my immortality.**

8. The very nature of the expanding force of the Father is to experiment. It is the force of the Father that causes my I AM Presence and Conscious You to have the desire to experiment, the curiosity to experience something new.

> O Kuan Yin, your sanity,
> now sets me free from vanity.
> For truly, what is that to me;
> I just let go and follow thee.

**In Kuan Yin's sweet melody,
I am set free my Self to be.
In Kuan Yin's vitality,
I claim my immortality.**

9. It was the desire to experiment that made it possible for me to fall into a lower state of consciousness. I conducted certain experiments that gradually caused my consciousness to fall in vibration, until I forgot my spiritual origin.

> O Kuan Yin, so sweet the sound,
> that emanates from holy ground.
> As I let go of ego's chore,
> I find myself on farther shore.

**In Kuan Yin's sweet melody,
I am set free my Self to be.
In Kuan Yin's vitality,
I claim my immortality.**

4. I claim my right to experiment

1. I was misled and manipulated by dark forces into falling, into making the wrong decisions that caused me to fall. I made the choice to accept the lies of the serpent, but nevertheless those lies were there and they were directed at me.

> O Kuan Yin, what sacred name,
> fill me now with Mercy's Flame.
> In giving mercy I am free,
> forgiving all is magic key.

**In Kuan Yin's sweet melody,
I am set free my Self to be.
In Kuan Yin's vitality,
I claim my immortality.**

2. After I had fallen into a lower state of consciousness, the serpents kicked in phase two of their plot. They now told me that it was precisely my desire to experiment, it was precisely the fact that I have free will, that caused me to fall.

> O Kuan Yin, I now let go,
> of all attachments here below.
> All pent-up feelings I release,
> free from emotional disease.

13 | Invocation for Raising My Life Experience

> **In Kuan Yin's sweet melody,**
> **I am set free my Self to be.**
> **In Kuan Yin's vitality,**
> **I claim my immortality.**

3. The serpents told me that the only way to salvation is that I stop experimenting, that I stop exercising my free will and that I allow Lucifer, or some of the other serpents, to control me so that they can save me.

> O Kuan Yin, why must I feel,
> that life falls short of my ideal?
> All expectations I give up,
> my mind is now an empty cup.

> **In Kuan Yin's sweet melody,**
> **I am set free my Self to be.**
> **In Kuan Yin's vitality,**
> **I claim my immortality.**

4. The serpents want to make me believe that God's way of doing things, meaning the gift of free will and imagination, has put my soul in danger because there is no guarantee that I will be saved. They also want me to believe that if I follow them and allow them to control me, my salvation will be guaranteed.

> O Kuan Yin, transcend the past,
> as all resentment gone at last.
> From future nothing I expect,
> eternal now I won't reject.

**In Kuan Yin's sweet melody,
I am set free my Self to be.
In Kuan Yin's vitality,
I claim my immortality.**

5. This lie permeates this world and has given rise to numerous claims that an outer organization or institution, be it a church, a dictator or a political ideology, can save people or can save the world.

O Kuan Yin, uplifting me,
beyond Samsara's raging sea.
All safe inside your Prajna boat,
the farther shore no more remote.

**In Kuan Yin's sweet melody,
I am set free my Self to be.
In Kuan Yin's vitality,
I claim my immortality.**

6. The serpents are spreading the lie that I should not try to experiment, I should not think that I can know truth on my own. I should simply follow the leaders who know best.

O Kuan Yin, your alchemy,
with miracles you set me free.
As I forgive, I am forgiven,
by guilt I am no longer driven.

**In Kuan Yin's sweet melody,
I am set free my Self to be.
In Kuan Yin's vitality,
I claim my immortality.**

7. While it was my drive to experiment that made it possible for me to fall, at the same time it is *only* my drive to experiment that can help me rise back to the Christ consciousness.

> O Kuan Yin, all worries gone,
> with nothing done, no thing undone.
> Through separate self I will not do,
> and thus I rest, all one with you.

> **In Kuan Yin's sweet melody,**
> **I am set free my Self to be.**
> **In Kuan Yin's vitality,**
> **I claim my immortality.**

8. I could fall only because I have free will and a desire to experiment. Yet it was not the desire to experiment that caused me to fall; it was the serpentine lies that caused me to fall.

> O Kuan Yin, your sanity,
> now sets me free from vanity.
> For truly, what is that to me;
> I just let go and follow thee.

> **In Kuan Yin's sweet melody,**
> **I am set free my Self to be.**
> **In Kuan Yin's vitality,**
> **I claim my immortality.**

9. It was perfectly possible to experiment with my free will without falling. It is perfectly possible to use my free will to undo all choices that caused me to fall. I hereby decide that I am willing to use my free will to experiment. I once again join the River of Life.

O Kuan Yin, so sweet the sound,
that emanates from holy ground.
As I let go of ego's chore,
I find myself on farther shore.

In Kuan Yin's sweet melody,
I am set free my Self to be.
In Kuan Yin's vitality,
I claim my immortality.

Sealing

In the name of the Divine Mother, I call to Kuan Yin and Mother Mary for the sealing of myself and all people in the creative flow of the Divine Mother, the River of Life. I call for the multiplication of my calls by all representatives of the Divine Mother, so that we form the perfect figure-eight flow of "As Above, so below." Thus, I accept that this is fully manifest, because the mouth of the Lord, the Divine Mother that I AM, has spoken it. Amen.

14 | INVOCATION FOR ACCEPTING MY TRUE IDENTITY

In the name I AM THAT I AM, Jesus Christ, I call to all representatives of the Divine Mother, especially Lord Maitreya and Mother Mary, to help me accept that I am a co-creator with God. Help me return to the innocence of the Garden of Eden. I call for you to help me overcome all illusions that stand in the way of my healing, especially…

[Make personal calls.]

1. I transcend the serpentine plot

1. The serpents used their lies to manipulate people into creating the current misery on this planet. Then they tried to set themselves up as the only saviors who can save us from the problem that they created.

Maitreya, I am truly meek,
your counsel wise I humbly seek,
your vision I so want to see,
with you in Eden I will be.

**Maitreya, kindness is the cure,
in fires of kindness I am pure.
Maitreya, now release the fire,
that raises me forever higher.**

2. The serpentine plot is to create so much suffering that we are willing to follow them blindly in order to escape the suffering. The serpents create a problem and then try to sell us the "only" solution to the problem.

Maitreya, help me to return,
to learn from you, I truly yearn,
as oneness is all I desire
I feel initiation's fire.

**Maitreya, kindness is the cure,
in fires of kindness I am pure.
Maitreya, now release the fire,
that raises me forever higher.**

3. The serpents will never save me because salvation means that I reestablish my true identity as a son or daughter of God, as being one with God.

Maitreya, I hereby decide,
from you I will no longer hide,
expose to me the very lie
that caused edenic self to die.

14 | Invocation for Accepting My True Identity

**Maitreya, kindness is the cure,
in fires of kindness I am pure.
Maitreya, now release the fire,
that raises me forever higher.**

4. The serpents have chosen to leave that sense of identity behind, and they identify themselves as being in opposition to God. As long as I see myself in opposition to God, I cannot possibly obtain union with God, and therefore I cannot possibly be saved.

Maitreya, blessed Guru mine,
my heart of hearts forever thine,
I vow that I will listen well,
so we can break the serpent's spell.

**Maitreya, kindness is the cure,
in fires of kindness I am pure.
Maitreya, now release the fire,
that raises me forever higher.**

5. The true Savior, Jesus, always affirmed his oneness with God. He came to show me that I have the potential to attain oneness with God.

Maitreya, help me see the lie
whereby the serpent broke the tie,
the serpent now has naught in me,
in oneness I am truly free.

**Maitreya, kindness is the cure,
in fires of kindness I am pure.
Maitreya, now release the fire,
that raises me forever higher.**

6. The serpents have perverted the original teachings of Jesus so that I think I cannot follow in his footsteps without being accused of blasphemy by those who embody the serpentine consciousness.

Maitreya, truth does set me free
from falsehoods of duality,
the fruit of knowledge I let go,
so your true spirit I do know.

**Maitreya, kindness is the cure,
in fires of kindness I am pure.
Maitreya, now release the fire,
that raises me forever higher.**

7. What gives me the opportunity to reestablish my union with God is my free will and my desire to experiment.

Maitreya, I submit to you,
intentions pure, my heart is true,
from ego I am truly free,
as I am now all one with thee.

**Maitreya, kindness is the cure,
in fires of kindness I am pure.
Maitreya, now release the fire,
that raises me forever higher.**

8. It was my ability to experiment that led to my fall, but it is this very ability that can lead me back to the Christ consciousness.

> Maitreya, kindness is the key,
> all shades of kindness teach to me,
> for I am now the open door,
> the Art of Kindness to restore.
>
> **Maitreya, kindness is the cure,**
> **in fires of kindness I am pure.**
> **Maitreya, now release the fire,**
> **that raises me forever higher.**

9. I hereby decide that I will rise above the plot of the serpents and their subtle lies. I am using my drive to experiment in order to come back to union with God. I am experimenting and I am reestablishing my union with God.

> Maitreya, oh sweet mystery,
> immersed in your reality,
> the myst'ry school will now return,
> for this, my heart does truly burn.
>
> **Maitreya, kindness is the cure,**
> **in fires of kindness I am pure.**
> **Maitreya, now release the fire,**
> **that raises me forever higher.**

2. I accept a God of love

1. My soul is a vehicle created by the Conscious You for experiencing the world. The Conscious You experiences the world through imagination and free will.

> Maitreya, I am truly meek,
> your counsel wise I humbly seek,
> your vision I so want to see,
> with you in Eden I will be.
>
> **Maitreya, kindness is the cure,**
> **in fires of kindness I am pure.**
> **Maitreya, now release the fire,**
> **that raises me forever higher.**

2. It is through imagination and free will that I add to my sense of identity. What causes the Conscious You to become trapped in the material world is a limited sense of identity. That limited sense of identity is the result of an experiment with undesirable consequences.

> Maitreya, help me to return,
> to learn from you, I truly yearn,
> as oneness is all I desire
> I feel initiation's fire.
>
> **Maitreya, kindness is the cure,**
> **in fires of kindness I am pure.**
> **Maitreya, now release the fire,**
> **that raises me forever higher.**

3. The only thing that can help the Conscious You escape the prison of the material world, the only thing that can "save the soul," is to continue experimenting until I find the higher identity of the Christ mind.

> Maitreya, I hereby decide,
> from you I will no longer hide,
> expose to me the very lie
> that caused edenic self to die.

> **Maitreya, kindness is the cure,**
> **in fires of kindness I am pure.**
> **Maitreya, now release the fire,**
> **that raises me forever higher.**

4. The Conscious You must come back to a state of grace in which I accept that I am worthy in the eyes of God because I identify myself as a son or daughter of God.

> Maitreya, blessed Guru mine,
> my heart of hearts forever thine,
> I vow that I will listen well,
> so we can break the serpent's spell.

> **Maitreya, kindness is the cure,**
> **in fires of kindness I am pure.**
> **Maitreya, now release the fire,**
> **that raises me forever higher.**

5. The only way to get back to that true sense of identity is that the Conscious You must recreate my sense of identity as a Christed being. I must experiment with a higher state of consciousness.

Maitreya, help me see the lie
whereby the serpent broke the tie,
the serpent now has naught in me,
in oneness I am truly free.

**Maitreya, kindness is the cure,
in fires of kindness I am pure.
Maitreya, now release the fire,
that raises me forever higher.**

6. I am looking for a higher understanding of truth than what I have found in the serpentine lies that permeate the world.

Maitreya, truth does set me free
from falsehoods of duality,
the fruit of knowledge I let go,
so your true spirit I do know.

**Maitreya, kindness is the cure,
in fires of kindness I am pure.
Maitreya, now release the fire,
that raises me forever higher.**

7. There is indeed an angry and judgmental god, as envisioned by many people on this planet. Yet the angry god is a false god created by human beings and dark forces.

Maitreya, I submit to you,
intentions pure, my heart is true,
from ego I am truly free,
as I am now all one with thee.

**Maitreya, kindness is the cure,
in fires of kindness I am pure.
Maitreya, now release the fire,
that raises me forever higher.**

8. The true God is a God of unconditional love.

> Maitreya, kindness is the key,
> all shades of kindness teach to me,
> for I am now the open door,
> the Art of Kindness to restore.

**Maitreya, kindness is the cure,
in fires of kindness I am pure.
Maitreya, now release the fire,
that raises me forever higher.**

9. God's love is unconditional, and I do not need to even ask for God's forgiveness. The moment I forsake the state of consciousness that caused me to accept an imperfect sense of identity, at that very moment I am forgiven by God.

> Maitreya, oh sweet mystery,
> immersed in your reality,
> the myst'ry school will now return,
> for this, my heart does truly burn.

**Maitreya, kindness is the cure,
in fires of kindness I am pure.
Maitreya, now release the fire,
that raises me forever higher.**

3. I forgive all

1. Even though some spiritual teachers say I could change my mind in an instant, it is not true.

> Maitreya, I am truly meek,
> your counsel wise I humbly seek,
> your vision I so want to see,
> with you in Eden I will be.

> **Maitreya, kindness is the cure,**
> **in fires of kindness I am pure.**
> **Maitreya, now release the fire,**
> **that raises me forever higher.**

2. My Conscious You is a being of energy, of spiritual energy. Over many lifetimes, the Conscious You can clothe itself in many layers of lower vibrations that form the soul.

> Maitreya, help me to return,
> to learn from you, I truly yearn,
> as oneness is all I desire
> I feel initiation's fire.

> **Maitreya, kindness is the cure,**
> **in fires of kindness I am pure.**
> **Maitreya, now release the fire,**
> **that raises me forever higher.**

3. It is those layers that give the Conscious You a mortal sense of identity. The Conscious You cannot instantly throw off the

false sense of identity because I would be left with no sense of identity.

> Maitreya, I hereby decide,
> from you I will no longer hide,
> expose to me the very lie
> that caused edenic self to die.

> **Maitreya, kindness is the cure,**
> **in fires of kindness I am pure.**
> **Maitreya, now release the fire,**
> **that raises me forever higher.**

4. The Conscious You is gradually replacing the false sense of identity with a true sense of identity. I die daily. I put off the old man and put on the new man.

> Maitreya, blessed Guru mine,
> my heart of hearts forever thine,
> I vow that I will listen well,
> so we can break the serpent's spell.

> **Maitreya, kindness is the cure,**
> **in fires of kindness I am pure.**
> **Maitreya, now release the fire,**
> **that raises me forever higher.**

5. The key to true spiritual freedom is to forgive myself, to forgive every part of life and to forgive God for anything that I think has ever been done to me.

Maitreya, help me see the lie
whereby the serpent broke the tie,
the serpent now has naught in me,
in oneness I am truly free.

**Maitreya, kindness is the cure,
in fires of kindness I am pure.
Maitreya, now release the fire,
that raises me forever higher.**

6. I forgive what has been done both in this lifetime and in other lifetimes, going all the way back to when I first descended into the material universe, and even beyond to the Garden of Eden.

Maitreya, truth does set me free
from falsehoods of duality,
the fruit of knowledge I let go,
so your true spirit I do know.

**Maitreya, kindness is the cure,
in fires of kindness I am pure.
Maitreya, now release the fire,
that raises me forever higher.**

7. The key to freedom from my current limitations is to forgive all who played a role in creating those limitations.

Maitreya, I submit to you,
intentions pure, my heart is true,
from ego I am truly free,
as I am now all one with thee.

> Maitreya, kindness is the cure,
> in fires of kindness I am pure.
> Maitreya, now release the fire,
> that raises me forever higher.

8. Those who seek revenge against other people, even those who engage in a battle against dark forces, are reinforcing the prison walls around their souls.

> Maitreya, kindness is the key,
> all shades of kindness teach to me,
> for I am now the open door,
> the Art of Kindness to restore.

> Maitreya, kindness is the cure,
> in fires of kindness I am pure.
> Maitreya, now release the fire,
> that raises me forever higher.

9. I know the truth behind the statement: "Vengeance is mine; I will repay, saith the Lord." God has created an impersonal law, the law of karma, which makes sure that no being will ever escape the consequences of its uses and misuses of God's energy.

> Maitreya, oh sweet mystery,
> immersed in your reality,
> the myst'ry school will now return,
> for this, my heart does truly burn.

> Maitreya, kindness is the cure,
> in fires of kindness I am pure.
> Maitreya, now release the fire,
> that raises me forever higher.

4. I turn the other cheek

1. I do not need to become angry at those who harm me. I do not need to seek revenge because in so doing I misqualify God's energy. Thereby, I reinforce the prison around my own soul, my own mind.

> Maitreya, I am truly meek,
> your counsel wise I humbly seek,
> your vision I so want to see,
> with you in Eden I will be.
>
> **Maitreya, kindness is the cure,**
> **in fires of kindness I am pure.**
> **Maitreya, now release the fire,**
> **that raises me forever higher.**

2. I truly forgive my enemies, I forgive those who harm me and I always turn the other cheek. When someone harms me and I turn the other cheek, I set myself free from any negative influence of their actions.

> Maitreya, help me to return,
> to learn from you, I truly yearn,
> as oneness is all I desire
> I feel initiation's fire.
>
> **Maitreya, kindness is the cure,**
> **in fires of kindness I am pure.**
> **Maitreya, now release the fire,**
> **that raises me forever higher.**

3. By turning the other cheek I avoid creating or reinforcing a negative sense of identity. I reaffirm that I am a spiritual being who is above and beyond any influence from the lower vibrations in the material world.

> Maitreya, I hereby decide,
> from you I will no longer hide,
> expose to me the very lie
> that caused edenic self to die.
>
> **Maitreya, kindness is the cure,**
> **in fires of kindness I am pure.**
> **Maitreya, now release the fire,**
> **that raises me forever higher.**

4. I will not let anything done to me in this world limit my sense of identity. I am reuniting with my Christ self and becoming a Christed being. No matter what they do to me, they cannot harm my true identity.

> Maitreya, blessed Guru mine,
> my heart of hearts forever thine,
> I vow that I will listen well,
> so we can break the serpent's spell.
>
> **Maitreya, kindness is the cure,**
> **in fires of kindness I am pure.**
> **Maitreya, now release the fire,**
> **that raises me forever higher.**

5. I am rising above all of the limitations, all of the chains, that they use to bind me. I rise above it because I know that they are simply throwing mud at the light beam of the Conscious You, and that mud has no power to cling to the true light that I AM.

> Maitreya, help me see the lie
> whereby the serpent broke the tie,
> the serpent now has naught in me,
> in oneness I am truly free.

> **Maitreya, kindness is the cure,**
> **in fires of kindness I am pure.**
> **Maitreya, now release the fire,**
> **that raises me forever higher.**

6. I accept and absorb the infinite and unconditional love of God. I am filled with the infinite power of Forgiveness' Flame, the spiritual flame of forgiveness that conquers and consumes all sin, all mistakes, all imperfections and all limitations.

> Maitreya, truth does set me free
> from falsehoods of duality,
> the fruit of knowledge I let go,
> so your true spirit I do know.

> **Maitreya, kindness is the cure,**
> **in fires of kindness I am pure.**
> **Maitreya, now release the fire,**
> **that raises me forever higher.**

7. I am free in the infinite forgiveness of God. I follow my highest love and come up higher. I am free of the shackles of mortality and sin. I accept God's forgiveness of all imperfections that I have encountered during my journey in the lower vibrations of the material world.

> Maitreya, I submit to you,
> intentions pure, my heart is true,
> from ego I am truly free,
> as I am now all one with thee.

> **Maitreya, kindness is the cure,**
> **in fires of kindness I am pure.**
> **Maitreya, now release the fire,**
> **that raises me forever higher.**

8. I am free of these imperfections because I fully accept that I am free. I fully forgive myself and accept my true identity as a spiritual being who has never been touched by anything in this world.

> Maitreya, kindness is the key,
> all shades of kindness teach to me,
> for I am now the open door,
> the Art of Kindness to restore.

> **Maitreya, kindness is the cure,**
> **in fires of kindness I am pure.**
> **Maitreya, now release the fire,**
> **that raises me forever higher.**

9. In reality, I am who I AM, namely a spiritual being. I stop thinking that I am an imperfect being. I accept my true identity as a spiritual being. I accept that I am perfect, even as my Father in heaven is perfect.

> Maitreya, oh sweet mystery,
> immersed in your reality,
> the myst'ry school will now return,
> for this, my heart does truly burn.
>
> **Maitreya, kindness is the cure,**
> **in fires of kindness I am pure.**
> **Maitreya, now release the fire,**
> **that raises me forever higher.**

Sealing

In the name of the Divine Mother, I call to Maitreya and Mother Mary for the sealing of myself and all people in the creative flow of the Divine Mother, the River of Life. I call for the multiplication of my calls by all representatives of the Divine Mother, so that we form the perfect figure-eight flow of "As Above, so below." Thus, I accept that this is fully manifest, because the mouth of the Lord, the Divine Mother that I AM, has spoken it. Amen.

15 | UNCONDITIONAL FORGIVENESS AND JOY

Excerpt from a dictation by Mother Mary, November 26, 2006.

The basic dynamic of life

My beloved hearts, if your telephone rings, would you not pick it up? When you pick up the phone, do you not listen long enough to at least find out whether the person on the other end has an important message for you or is simply trying to sell you something. If you do realize that the person at the other end has a message for you, would you not do your utmost to listen to that message and understand what it says? Surely, you will treat your telephone and the person calling with a certain measure of respect. Thus, my question to you is: "Why would you not treat life itself with the same measure of respect?"

Ah my beloved, you will say that you surely have respect for life, but I would beg to question whether that is really so. You see, life itself can be compared to a telephone. Every situation you encounter can be seen as a telephone call from life itself. Yet, there are so many situations in life where you do not pick up the phone and listen to see if that situation has an important message for you, a message that can help you transcend yourself – or some limitation – so that you can be free and be more in the River of Life.

Why you have the same problems again and again

Most people go through life with blinders on. They are only half-awake, only half-aware of what is happening. They do not realize that life is a continuous string of situations, with each situation having a message that can help them rise higher and overcome some erroneous belief, some misconception that limits them and the expression of life itself through them. So many of you have these situations happen over and over again in your life. You often cry out: "Why does this keep happening to me? Why is God doing this to me? Why are other people doing this to me? Why is destiny or fate or luck doing this to me?" But you do not take time to stand back and say: "Why am I doing this to myself?"

Every situation in life can be viewed as a telephone call, and there is a message in that call. But so often you do not bother to pick up the phone and listen to the message. Even those people who pick up the phone – who *do* consider that they might need to learn something from certain situations – so often do not truly listen for the message behind the phone call. They do not truly listen with the inner ear, trying to understand the message, trying to understand that which they cannot see with the outer mind.

They listen to the message, they evaluate, with the outer mind. Therefore, they do not see the message, they do not hear the message, for the outer mind cannot fathom that message. If your outer mind had already understood the message that life is trying to give you, then why would life bother to call you on the telephone by having you experience the same situation over and over again?

Life does not punish you

It is a complete misconception of the human consciousness and the human ego that life is trying to punish you. I can assure you that life itself – and life is created by God, so even God itself – has no desire to punish you whatsoever. It is an absolute law that once you have learned the lesson you need to learn from a specific situation, then you will not encounter that situation again.

When you encounter the same situation over and over again, it is because you have not learned the lesson. That is why life keeps calling you and presenting you with the same situation over and over again so that you have another opportunity – and another and another – to learn the lesson.

My beloved, instead of grumbling, instead of complaining that the same thing keeps happening to you over and over again, I have a very simple suggestion to you: Simply pick up the phone and listen for the message that life is trying to give. Then learn that lesson. Resolve the belief that you need to resolve in order to move up higher. I can guarantee you that – as if by magic – you will not encounter that same situation again.

Life is not very complicated. Life is really very, very simple. The underlying message behind every situation you encounter in life is simply this: "The material universe is a mirror!" The Ma-ter light will take on the forms that correspond to the contents of your consciousness. It is your state of consciousness that projects an image onto the Ma-ter light. The Ma-ter light can do nothing else but to reflect that image back to you—both the image in your conscious mind and the image in the subconscious layers of your mind, your emotional, mental and identity bodies.

Life is very simple. Life itself is the principle of growth—of becoming more, of self-transcendence. The message that life is always trying to give you is that you can become more. By seeing your limitation, by seeing the limiting belief that you have – about yourself, about the world and about God – you can transcend that limitation and come up higher and be more in God's ever-flowing River of Life.

So many people have wondered about the meaning of life, the purpose of life, the secret of life. So many people have searched for the philosopher's stone, the magic wand, some kind of shortcut that will allow them to suddenly be in a state of bliss, or a state of having what they think they need in order to be happy. Yet my beloved, the secret of life is very simple—it is self-transcendence. This does not mean that you need to attain some remote state of perfection that might seem beyond your reach. It simply means that every time you transcend yourself, you are in the flow of the River of Life. You have the potential to experience the joy, the bliss, that truly *is* that River of Life.

The message that life is trying to give you in every situation is that when you encounter a limitation, if you are willing to look inside yourself and acknowledge the belief that causes you to experience that situation as a limitation and then let go of that belief, well then you will rise above the sense of limitation and instead be in the bliss of the River of Life.

Change the way you look at the past

I hope that by giving you this discourse, I can change the way you look at your past. Your past is not out to punish you. Your past is not truly out to hold you back, although I know that it often seems like your past is holding you back or pulling you down into repeating the same old patterns over and over again in a seemingly endless cycle. The reality is that your past, and

15 | Unconditional Forgiveness and Joy

the memory of your past, is simply another expression of life's desire to see you come up higher.

Whenever you are reminded of your past, consider that this is – once again – life who is calling you on the telephone. As always, life is calling you for one purpose only, namely to show you that you can overcome yet another limitation, that you can rise above it, that you can simply let it go and join the River of Life—and then become more by transcending your old sense of self.

The situations from your past that keep hounding you are situations in which you responded to outer circumstances in such a way that you accepted a limiting belief about yourself. That belief is still in your subconscious mind, and that is why – when you are reminded of that situation in your past – you experience an uneasiness, a sense of shame or guilt or other negative feelings that cause you emotional pain. Even this pain can be seen as a reminder. It is a reminder of the fact that you have not learned your lesson, that you have not overcome the limiting belief.

Even the pain can be seen as a grace. If someone is trying to call you on the phone and give you a message that can save your life, would you not want them to turn up the volume on the phone if they could do so? Imagine that you could not hear the phone, yet someone could push a button on their own phone and turn up the volume so you could now hear it, get the call and save your life.

That is essentially what your past is doing when it is reminding you – over and over again – of the situations where you have accepted some limitation. If you will not pick up the phone the first time, then what is life going to do but call you again and increase the volume—thereby increasing the emotional pain in an attempt to finally make you pay attention. Instead of denying and refusing the pain, you say: "Okay, I have had enough of this.

I am going to look at this problem and overcome the limitation so that I can once and for all overcome that pain instead of being burdened by it over and over again for the rest of my life or even for many lifetimes."

Will you not please consider that instead of ignoring your past, or denying your past or seeking to make yourself so busy with the present or the future that you do to pay attention to your past, it would indeed be much wiser for you to simply pick up the phone and listen to the message from your past. If you would but listen to that message, you could quickly come to the realization that the situation from your past that keeps coming back over and over is a situation where you have not seen through a limiting belief and thus you have not let that belief go.

The past becomes prologue

Because you have not let go of that belief, you are constantly holding on to an imperfect belief about yourself, or about life, or about God, or about other people. Through the power of your mind, you are projecting that limiting belief onto the Ma-ter light. What can the mirror of the Ma-ter light do, except reflect back to you outer conditions that reflect your state of consciousness?

Your past becomes prologue to your present and your future. The imperfect beliefs you accepted in your past are constantly being projected upon the Ma-ter light by your subconscious mind. The Ma-ter light must take on the forms of those beliefs and send to you physical situations and circumstances that reflect those beliefs.

It is not the desire of the Ma-ter light to force you to encounter situations that cause you suffering. The Ma-ter light is the mirror so what can it do but reflect back what you send into it? The force of life itself does not want you to keep projecting the same imperfect images onto the Ma-ter light. That is why the force of life is trying to help you awaken yourself so that you can change the images you hold in your mind—and thereby change what you are projecting onto the Ma-ter light.

Yes, my beloved, life really is this simple—if only you will pay attention, if only you will pick up the phone and listen to the message. Unfortunately, I know that some of you do actually pick up the phone, but you respond the same way as when you hear a recording that is trying to sell you some product, or service, or political candidate. You immediately numb your mind to the message or you put down the phone and do not listen anymore.

It is not that your past is trying to be annoying by repeating the same message. It is simply that the mirror, the cosmic mirror, can only keep reflecting back to you the same image that you are sending out. It is not life that is the cause of your annoyance. It is the rigidity of your own mind and its unwillingness to look at its own beliefs, to evaluate whether those beliefs make sense and then to replace the beliefs that do not make sense with a higher understanding that springs from the Christ mind.

I am trying to awaken you to the absolute necessity to be willing to look beyond the outer situations from your past and look for the inner message, the inner lesson you need to learn from those situations. If you will do this honestly and openly, you will see that whenever you have a situation that causes you to suffer, it is because you are holding an imperfect belief about yourself and about life. If you will only see the imperfection of that belief and reach for the higher understanding of the Christ mind, then you can replace the limiting belief with the true realization of who you are. This will change the image you are projecting onto the Ma-ter light. With absolute certainty, this will change what the cosmic mirror reflects back to you in the form of outer circumstances. What I am telling you here is not some kind of daydream, some kind of unrealistic promise. What I am explaining to you here is the most fundamental law of the material universe. The law that was expressed in the Bible by saying that as a man sows, so will he surely reap. Of course, this applies to a woman as well.

There is an alternative to suffering

The law of God is simple. You have free will to do whatever you want. You are a co-creator with God. You are here to learn how to use your co-creative abilities to create situations for yourself that you can live with, that you can grow with. You learn in two ways. One is by listening to direction from within, from your higher self, from your I AM Presence, from your spiritual teachers. If you will not listen for that direction, or if you will not use even your reasoning mind to find direction on your own, then you must learn in the other way, which is the School of Hard Knocks whereby you see the Ma-ter light reflect back to you physical circumstances that outpicture the circumstances in your mind.

The law of God is this: You have a right to create any mental image you want. You have a right to project that mental image outside your own mind. When you do so, you will inevitably experience the physical situations that outpicture your mental image. You will experience what you project upon life. You will experience what you co-create through the power of your mind by projecting a mental image onto the Ma-ter light.

God and myself and all spiritual teachers firmly uphold your right to co-create any circumstance you want. Yet, we would like you to understand that if you co-create circumstances that cause you suffering, then you have an alternative to continuing to create the same circumstances. The only way to stop the repetitive cycle that leads to suffering is to change the cause of the outer circumstances. I know full well that throughout history people have come up with all kinds of excuses that make it seem like they are not in control of the outer circumstances, that they did not create them, that somehow God, fate, luck or other people created those circumstances. The stark reality is that *you* have co-created your own circumstances because you have formed mental images and you have projected those images onto the Ma-ter light.

The only way – the *absolutely* only way – that those outer circumstances can be changed is that you change the cause of the outer circumstances. Would you not agree that if you want to change an effect, you have to change the cause that creates that effect? What I am telling you is that the effect is your outer circumstances. The cause of that effect is the mental images you hold in your mind. The *only* way to change your outer circumstances is to change those mental images.

How can you change the mental images in your mind? Well, there is no other way but to do so consciously by seeing the mental images – seeing that they are based on the duality consciousness, on the illusions of the mind of anti-christ – and then consciously letting them go, replacing the illusions with the truth of Christ. Please take note of what I am saying. It is not a matter of somehow justifying the beliefs you have accepted in the past.

Oh my beloved, if you will look at this honestly, you will see that when so many people are confronted with a possibility that they might have an imperfect belief, they go into a defensive reaction. This defensive reaction is the default reaction of the ego, which simply will not acknowledge that it could be wrong. It goes into a reaction of trying to defend or justify its beliefs.

I hope you can see that if you keep trying to justify a past belief, you will simply build on to that belief. You will continue sending mental images into the cosmic mirror that are based on that original belief. Of course, what can the cosmic mirror do but send back to you the same kind of circumstances that you have created all along? My beloved, will you please realize that if you keep doing the same thing and expect different results, then you are trapped in the basic insanity of the human ego. You must step away from the old patterns and be willing to openly acknowledge that certain beliefs from your past are limiting yourself. It is not in your own best interest to uphold those beliefs. On the contrary, it is in your own best interest to simply let them go.

You are more than your past

The key realization here is the teaching that the core of your identity is the conscious self, the Conscious You. The Conscious You is a spark of God's own Being. It is infinitely more than your past, than any circumstance or any belief from your past. Your conscious self has the God-given right and the God-given ability to step outside of its identification with your past. You can do so at any moment, including right now.

I ask you to acknowledge that there is a force in this world that is very determined to keep you trapped in your identification with the past so that you do not think you can let go of the past. You might even fear that if you let go of the past, you lose your very identity. This force is comprised of your personal ego, the egos of other people and the entire dark force, the force of anti-christ, what Jesus called the prince of this world. The prince of this world will constantly come to you. He will come to see if he can make you attached to the past so that you are not willing to simply let it go, to let the imperfect beliefs go, by acknowledging that you are more than any imperfect belief.

Do you truly hear what I am saying here? You have the God-given right and the ability to let go of any imperfect belief from the past. How can you do this? By being willing to look at the belief, acknowledge that it is unreal, that it springs from the mind of anti-christ. Then, you can acknowledge that you are more than the belief. The belief is simply like an old worn-out coat that you took on sometime in the past. You can take that coat off at any time and throw it into the fire and let it be burned so that it is consumed and is no more.

You can take off the old sense of identity, based on that belief, and throw it into the spiritual fires of the violet flame and the Flame of Forgiveness, and you can simply let it go. The Flame of Forgiveness, what we have called the violet flame or the Flame of Mercy, is simply the cosmic eraser that allows you to take the old worn-out sense of identity that you have built and throw it into the fire. Your God is truly a consuming fire that can consume all imperfect sense of self that you might have built in any past lifetime. You have an alternative to repeating these old patterns. The alternative is to take off the overcoat of your imperfect sense of identity and throw it into the bonfire of God where it will be consumed and you will then be free as if that identity had never existed.

The master key to letting go

What is the master key to doing this? What is the master key to letting go of an imperfect sense of identity? It is the willingness to forgive. In order to be free of your past, you must forgive and you must forgive unconditionally. Your ego has tricked you into thinking that in order for you to forgive, certain conditions must be fulfilled. For example, many people believe that in order to forgive someone who has hurt them, then that person must somehow be punished first. Only when the person has been sufficiently punished, can you forgive that person. Some people might believe that only if the other person has *truly* changed, can you forgive that person. This, of course, is a belief that will be like a double-edged sword where one edge of the sword is pointing to yourself and therefore able to give you a nasty wound. What you do unto others is what you have already done to yourself. This is the reason Jesus told you to do unto others as you want them to do to you. The deeper meaning is that you can only do unto others what you have already done to yourself, both good and bad.

If you think that other people must live up to certain conditions before they can be forgiven, then you also think that *you* must live up to certain conditions before you can be forgiven. Your ego is very clever at defining such conditions and defining them in such a way that no one can live up to them, including yourself. That is how your ego keeps you trapped in the cycle of never wanting to forgive others and never wanting to forgive yourself. Your ego essentially makes you believe that because you have made certain mistakes in the past, you are unforgivable, you are unredeemable, you can never rise above that past and be free of it.

The last thing your ego wants you to realize is that you have the God-given right and the power to simply walk away from the imperfections of your past. Your ego does not want you to realize that you can do this. It does not want you to realize that you can do this by openly acknowledging the imperfect beliefs that caused you to encounter those physical situations that gave you so much pain. Will you not please realize that the master key to rising above your past is to forgive—but not to forgive in a human way that is based on outer conditions. No, the master key to rising above your past is to forgive *unconditionally*.

When you have not forgiven another person, you are in reality holding on to the old situation. That means you are holding on – whether you are aware of this or not – to the pain created in the situation when the other person hurt you. The pain pulls on your conscious attention and pulls you into remembering that situation. Whenever you think about the situation, you reinforce the original hurt, the original pain and the original anger against the other person. Thereby, you tie yourself to your past and you actually reinforce the past.

By not forgiving the other person, you are harming yourself because you are holding on to the imperfect images and feelings, and you are projecting them onto the Ma-ter light. The Ma-ter light must reason that you want to experience situations where other people hurt you. What is the Ma-ter light going to give you? Well, it has no other option than to give you future situations where other people hurt you. It truly believes that this is what you want to experience, based on the fact that you are projecting a mental and emotional image into the cosmic mirror of other people hurting you.

Non-forgiveness hurts yourself

Can you finally see here that when you do not forgive other people, you are in reality hurting yourself? What is the excuse you use for not forgiving others? It is that they do not live up to the outer conditions that your ego has defined. It seems as if – as long as other people do not live up to those outer conditions – you cannot let go of the situation, you cannot forgive and rise above it.

Do you not see that this is the very same psychology that caused you to be hurt in the original situation? What happened in the original situation was that somebody else did something to *you*. But it was not what they did to you that caused you to be hurt. It was the imperfect beliefs that you hold about yourself and life that caused you to respond to that situation in a way that hurt yourself.

What really caused the hurt in that original situation was that you had a belief that turned you into a passive victim. You thought that when other people did certain things to you, you could only respond with negative feelings that caused you to be hurt. It was *this* belief that turned you into a victim in the original situation.

Even today you are holding on to the belief that you are a victim by thinking that only when the other person lives up to certain conditions, can you forgive that person and let go of the situation. By not forgiving, you are actually perpetuating the original situation. You are projecting the beliefs and the feelings from that situation into the cosmic mirror, thereby inevitably setting yourself up to reap what you have sown. You have projected an imperfect mental image into the mirror and thereby inevitably set in motion a chain reaction that will eventually return to you physical situations that reflect your mental image.

What can break this situation? There is only one thing that can break it, and that is that you pick up the telephone and listen long enough to realize that what life is trying to teach you is that it is your own beliefs that cause you to be hurt. Only by changing your own beliefs, can you break the cycle of experiencing physical situations that put you in a situation – in your own mind – where you think that your only potential response is to respond as a victim and feel hurt.

Take back your power to choose a response

The only thing that can change the equation is that you change the way you look at the equation, the way you look at life, the way you look at yourself. You must take back your power to respond to situations based on a choice you make today – now – instead of a choice you made in the past. In the past, you chose to accept an imperfect belief about yourself. As long as you allow that belief to remain in your subconscious mind, you cannot make a choice as to how you will respond to the situations you will experience in the present. The choice was already made in the past, and you can only repeat the same old pattern over and over again.

What can break the situation is that you become aware of what is happening, and therefore you decide to go back and look at the original belief and dismiss it as being unreal. When you have dismissed the belief, then the next time you experience a similar situation, you will not have that baggage weighing you down. Your mind will be able to say: "But you know, I don't have to respond to this situation by feeling hurt, by feeling afraid, by feeling ashamed, by coming down on myself and thinking I am a bad person because someone else treats me as if I was a bad person."

Instead, you can realize that what the other person does to you is a reflection of that person's state of consciousness. It is not because the other person has an imperfect image of *you*, although this might seem to be so based on the person's outer mind and actions. In reality, the person has an imperfect image of him or herself, and the person is projecting that image upon you. But you do not have to accept the other person's image of you. You have a God-given right to live your life based on the images in your own mind. You can *choose* to respond to the other person freely—when you do not accept the other person's images or any other limiting beliefs from your own past.

What is the key to letting go of these imperfect images that you accepted in the past or that other people have accepted? What is the key to not being affected by the imperfect beliefs of other people or the imperfect beliefs of your own past self? It is to forgive—to forgive by being completely non-attached to what is projected at you from other people or from your own mind. It is to accept the absolute power to unconditionally forgive yourself or other people and to simply let go of all sense of hurt, all sense of pain.

Perpetual forgiveness

I know that once you have become caught in this downward spiral of hurt and pain, it can seem as if there is no way out. I have indeed risen above the human condition and so have many other ascended beings. I must tell you that most people on earth are caught in an illusion. The reality proven by so many ascended beings is that you can indeed rise above the downward spirals from the past. You can do so not by transforming the past, not by controlling the past or controlling other people. You can do so only by transforming the way you *look at* the past so you are willing to let go of the belief that you have been holding on to up until now.

It is not a matter of finding some magic wand that can set you free from the past. The magic wand is your conscious awareness and your willingness to simply let go, to let go of the pain, to let go of the hurt, to let go of the belief that you need to respond to certain situations in a negative way, to let go of the entire tendency to think that in certain situations you can only respond with negative feelings. Once you truly enter into the spirit of forgiveness – and allow the spirit of forgiveness to enter into your lower being – you will be in a state of perpetual forgiveness. You have already forgiven yourself and other people before they have done anything to you.

When they do something to you – for truly you cannot control the actions of others – they are already forgiven. When you know that *they* are already forgiven, you also know that *you* can stay free of any negative reaction, no matter what other people do to you. You can follow the most profound advice given by Jesus, namely that you resist not evil, but when a person smites you on one cheek, you will turn to him the other also.

Turning the other cheek can be done only when you are in a state of perpetual and unconditional forgiveness. When some person does something to you, you do not go into a negative reaction. You stay in peace, you stay in love, you stay in forgiveness. You simply turn the other cheek so that you can give the other person another opportunity to see his or her own evil, his or her own imperfections.

Helping others see their illusions

What happens when a person hurts you and you respond negatively and seek to hurt the other person? Do you not validate the other person's belief that you are a bad person? Was it not such a belief that in most cases caused other people to hurt you in the first place, namely that they believe you have done something wrong and you deserve to be punished or hurt?

When you allow yourself to be hurt and respond back by trying to hurt them or defend yourself, then you only reinforce the other person's belief. You not only reinforce the belief in the mind of the other person, but you reinforce it in your own mind. After all, it was only because you have an imperfect belief about yourself that you allowed the other person's actions to hurt you.

When you turn the other cheek, you break the spiral. When you respond with love when someone else hurts you, you are challenging the other person's belief that you are a bad person or that you deserve to be punished. You are showing the other person that you are a person who can respond with love. Thereby, the other person is forced to reconsider his or her own actions and his or her own image of you. This can often help people step out of their own illusions so that they see that they are trapped in imperfect beliefs about themselves and about life. They receive an opportunity to overcome those beliefs.

Yes, my beloved, I know full well that there are persons with whom you can turn the other cheek and they will hurt you again. But you see, when you turn the other cheek in perfect love and forgiveness – in unconditional forgiveness – and another person still hurts you, then that second act of hurting you becomes the person's judgment. That judgment will release a reaction from life itself that will cause that person to experience an accelerated return of what it is sending into the cosmic mirror. That accelerated return will either cause the person to wake up or will ultimately cause the person to be judged to the point where the person will not be allowed to reincarnate on earth until it has changed its consciousness.

What Jesus was really saying was that if people would adopt his advice of turning the other cheek and not resisting evil, then they would allow the law of God to work in full measure. By doing this, the law of God will be able to remove evil from the earth at an accelerated rate. When you allow other people to hurt you while you are turning the other cheek, then God can step in and remove those people from the earth. Thereby, you will quickly have a situation where the most evil people – the most selfish, self-centered, egotistical people – will be removed from the earth. Therefore, humankind as a whole will simply rise up to a higher level and overcome certain states of consciousness that you today see outplayed over and over again in a seemingly endless spiral of people hurting each other and seeking revenge for hurt—thereby creating a new hurt that gives the other people an excuse for seeking revenge.

Breaking the cycle of revenge

This has been going on over and over again on this planet, especially in the Middle East where the cycle of revenge and revenge for revenge goes on and on. This downward spiral will not be broken until someone decides that they have had enough. They will not perpetuate the cycle, and therefore they will do something completely different instead of responding to hurt with pain and revenge and a desire to punish. They will respond with love and unconditional forgiveness.

Ah my beloved, can you also see that by doing this, you will set yourself free from any ties to the people who have hurt you? When you think about it, does it make any sense whatsoever that when a person has hurt you, you will want to keep yourself tied to that person? Unless you are a masochist – which I trust most of you are not – why would you want to come back and invite another person to hurt you again? If someone hurts you, your logical response should be that you simply want to be free of that person and never encounter them again. If you go into the cycle of being hurt and wanting the other person to be punished, you tie yourself to that person.

The very desire to punish another person means that you are not willing to turn away from that person until you have seen the other person be punished. You will automatically keep yourself tied to that person until you feel that the person has been punished sufficiently, and that might not happen in this lifetime or even in many lifetimes. This is how people in the Middle East have created these ties with each other so that the same souls keep reincarnating over and over again. I have told you before that it is not a matter of the outer race or religion, for people will switch places so that many of the people who are now incarnated as Jews were in their past lives incarnated as Germans who perpetrated the Holocaust or as Arabs who persecuted the Jews. Many of the people who are now Arabs were in past lives Jews.

It is these people's unwillingness to forgive unconditionally that keeps them repeating these cycles. There is indeed an entire consciousness in the Arab world that believes that Jews cannot be forgiven. There is a consciousness in the Jewish community that believes that Arabs or Germans or Christians cannot be forgiven. When a person is born into a certain culture, the challenge for that person is to rise above the cultural belief and to forgive unconditionally, to forgive regardless of the cultural belief. The person must realize that he or she is more than the cultural belief, more than race, more than religion, more than political affiliation, more than national affiliation or any other outer label. When you forgive regardless of outer labels, you also set yourself free from these labels. That is how you can rise and transcend yourself and rejoin the River of Life whereby you experience that bliss of constant self-transcendence.

Mother Mary's tool for overcoming the past

My beloved, I could go on with this discourse forever by citing examples of how people hurt themselves by not forgiving. But if what I have said so far is not enough to make you think and look at your past in a different way, then what is the point of going on?

I will return to my opening theme, and I will say: "This dictation is a telephone call from your cosmic Mother. Please pick up the phone and listen to my message!" If you feel that you have not understood the fullness of my message by reading or listening once, then I ask you to listen again. I am willing to repeat my message as many times as it takes for you to understand my point.

Try me. Ask me for my inner direction. Ask me to show you the message behind the outer situations you encounter. Ask me, and I will show you—if you will but pick up the phone and listen. I bid you peace, and I bid you a joyful Christmas season.

My beloved, is not the Christmas Spirit itself the very Spirit of Forgiveness, the very Spirit that awakens people to the possibility of being reborn, of starting life afresh, of starting a new day? Is not the life of Christ, the birth of Christ, another telephone call from life, seeking to awaken humankind to the possibility of rising above the past and rising into the new day of the kingdom of God? I seal you in the Flame of Unconditional Forgiveness. When your forgiveness is unconditional, your joy will be full.

16 | INVOCATION FOR HEARING THE INNER MESSAGE

In the name I AM THAT I AM, Jesus Christ, I call to all representatives of the Divine Mother, especially Portia and Mother Mary, to help me free my conscious mind from the ego and the lower mind so I can hear the inner message from my Christ self and spiritual teachers. I call for you to help me overcome all illusions that stand in the way of my healing, especially…

[Make personal calls.]

1. I listen for the inner message

1. Every situation I encounter is a telephone call from life itself. I will pick up the phone and listen to see if that situation has an important message for me, a message that can help me transcend myself or some limitation so that I can be free and be more in the River of Life.

O Portia, in your own retreat,
with Mother's Love you do me greet.
As all my tests I now complete,
old patterns I no more repeat.

O Portia, opportunity,
I am beyond duality.
I focus now internally,
with you I grow eternally.

2. I no longer go through life with blinders on. I approach each situation as having a message that can help me rise higher and overcome some erroneous belief, some misconception that limits me and the expression of life itself through me.

O Portia, Justice is your name,
upholding Cosmic Honor Flame,
No longer will I play the game,
of seeking to remain the same.

O Portia, opportunity,
I am beyond duality.
I focus now internally,
with you I grow eternally.

3. Instead of asking: "Why does this keep happening to me? Why is God doing this to me?" I will ask: "Why am I doing this to myself?"

O Portia, in the cosmic flow,
one with you, I ever grow.
I am the chalice here below,
of cosmic justice you bestow.

**O Portia, opportunity,
I am beyond duality.
I focus now internally,
with you I grow eternally.**

4. I listen with the inner ear. I understand the message, I understand that which I cannot see with the outer mind. I see what my outer mind does not see.

> O Portia, cosmic balance bring,
> eternal hope, my heart does sing.
> Protected by your Mother's wing,
> I feel at one with everything.

**O Portia, opportunity,
I am beyond duality.
I focus now internally,
with you I grow eternally.**

5. I see how I evaluate with the outer mind. The outer mind cannot fathom the message. If my outer mind had already understood the message, then why would I experience the same situation over and over again?

> O Portia, bring the Mother Light,
> to set all free from darkest night.
> Your Love Flame shines forever bright,
> with Saint Germain now hold me tight.

**O Portia, opportunity,
I am beyond duality.
I focus now internally,
with you I grow eternally.**

6. I am transcending the misconception of the human consciousness and the ego that life is trying to punish me. Life and God have no desire to punish me.

> O Portia, in your mastery,
> I feel transforming chemistry.
> In your light of reality,
> I find the golden alchemy.

> **O Portia, opportunity,**
> **I am beyond duality.**
> **I focus now internally,**
> **with you I grow eternally.**

7. It is an absolute law that once I have learned the lesson I need to learn from a specific situation, then I will not encounter that situation again.

> O Portia, in the cosmic stream,
> I am awake from human dream.
> Removing now the ego's beam,
> I earn my place on cosmic team.

> **O Portia, opportunity,**
> **I am beyond duality.**
> **I focus now internally,**
> **with you I grow eternally.**

8. When I encounter the same situation over and over again, it is because I have not learned the lesson. Life presents me with the same situation again so that I have another opportunity to learn the lesson.

16 | Invocation for Hearing the Inner Message

O Portia, you come from afar,
you are a cosmic avatar.
So infinite your repertoire,
you are for earth a guiding star.

**O Portia, opportunity,
I am beyond duality.
I focus now internally,
with you I grow eternally.**

9. Instead of grumbling, instead of complaining that the same thing keeps happening to me over and over again, I will pick up the phone and learn the lesson. I am resolving the belief that I need to resolve, and I am moving up higher.

O Portia, I am confident,
I am a cosmic instrument.
I came to earth from heaven sent,
to help bring forward her ascent.

**O Portia, opportunity,
I am beyond duality.
I focus now internally,
with you I grow eternally.**

2. I transcend my past

1. Life is not complicated because the material universe is a mirror. The Ma-ter light will take on the forms that correspond to the contents of my consciousness.

> O Portia, in your own retreat,
> with Mother's Love you do me greet.
> As all my tests I now complete,
> old patterns I no more repeat.
>
> **O Portia, opportunity,**
> **I am beyond duality.**
> **I focus now internally,**
> **with you I grow eternally.**

2. It is my state of consciousness that projects an image onto the Ma-ter light. The Ma-ter light can only reflect that image back to me, both the image in my conscious mind and the image in the subconscious mind, my emotional, mental and identity bodies.

> O Portia, Justice is your name,
> upholding Cosmic Honor Flame,
> No longer will I play the game,
> of seeking to remain the same.
>
> **O Portia, opportunity,**
> **I am beyond duality.**
> **I focus now internally,**
> **with you I grow eternally.**

3. Life itself is the principle of growth—of becoming more, of self-transcendence. The message that life is always trying to give me is that I can become more.

> O Portia, in the cosmic flow,
> one with you, I ever grow.
> I am the chalice here below,
> of cosmic justice you bestow.

16 | Invocation for Hearing the Inner Message

**O Portia, opportunity,
I am beyond duality.
I focus now internally,
with you I grow eternally.**

4. I am seeing my limitation, I am seeing the limiting belief that I have about myself, about the world and about God. I am transcending that limitation and coming up higher. I am more in God's ever-flowing River of Life.

> O Portia, cosmic balance bring,
> eternal hope, my heart does sing.
> Protected by your Mother's wing,
> I feel at one with everything.

**O Portia, opportunity,
I am beyond duality.
I focus now internally,
with you I grow eternally.**

5. I stop searching for the philosopher's stone, the magic wand, some kind of shortcut that will allow me to suddenly be in a state of bliss, or a state of having what I think I need in order to be happy.

> O Portia, bring the Mother Light,
> to set all free from darkest night.
> Your Love Flame shines forever bright,
> with Saint Germain now hold me tight.

**O Portia, opportunity,
I am beyond duality.
I focus now internally,
with you I grow eternally.**

6. Life is self-transcendence. I do not need to attain perfection. I am seeking to transcend myself, I am in the flow of the River of Life. I am experiencing the joy, the bliss, that truly is that River of Life.

> O Portia, in your mastery,
> I feel transforming chemistry.
> In your light of reality,
> I find the golden alchemy.

**O Portia, opportunity,
I am beyond duality.
I focus now internally,
with you I grow eternally.**

7. Every time I encounter a limitation, I look inside myself and acknowledge the belief that causes me to experience that situation as a limitation. I let go of that belief, and I rise above the sense of limitation. I am in the bliss of the River of Life.

> O Portia, in the cosmic stream,
> I am awake from human dream.
> Removing now the ego's beam,
> I earn my place on cosmic team.

**O Portia, opportunity,
I am beyond duality.
I focus now internally,
with you I grow eternally.**

8. I am changing the way I look at my past. I am free of the sense that my past is out to punish me or is seeking to hold me back in an endless cycle of suffering.

O Portia, you come from afar,
you are a cosmic avatar.
So infinite your repertoire,
you are for earth a guiding star.

**O Portia, opportunity,
I am beyond duality.
I focus now internally,
with you I grow eternally.**

9. My past, and the memory of my past, is simply another expression of life's desire to see me come up higher. Whenever I am reminded of my past, I consider that this is life calling me on the telephone.

O Portia, I am confident,
I am a cosmic instrument.
I came to earth from heaven sent,
to help bring forward her ascent.

**O Portia, opportunity,
I am beyond duality.
I focus now internally,
with you I grow eternally.**

3. I see my limiting beliefs

1. Life is calling to show me that I can overcome yet another limitation. I am rising above it, I am simply letting it go and joining the River of Life. I am becoming more by transcending my old sense of self.

> O Portia, in your own retreat,
> with Mother's Love you do me greet.
> As all my tests I now complete,
> old patterns I no more repeat.
>
> **O Portia, opportunity,**
> **I am beyond duality.**
> **I focus now internally,**
> **with you I grow eternally.**

2. The situations from my past that keep hounding me are situations in which I responded to outer circumstances in such a way that I accepted a limiting belief about myself.

> O Portia, Justice is your name,
> upholding Cosmic Honor Flame,
> No longer will I play the game,
> of seeking to remain the same.
>
> **O Portia, opportunity,**
> **I am beyond duality.**
> **I focus now internally,**
> **with you I grow eternally.**

3. My subconscious belief is the reason I experience uneasiness, a sense of shame or guilt or other negative feelings that cause me emotional pain.

> O Portia, in the cosmic flow,
> one with you, I ever grow.
> I am the chalice here below,
> of cosmic justice you bestow.
>
> **O Portia, opportunity,**
> **I am beyond duality.**
> **I focus now internally,**
> **with you I grow eternally.**

4. Even the pain can be seen as a reminder. It is a reminder of the fact that I have not learned my lesson, that I have not overcome the limiting belief.

> O Portia, cosmic balance bring,
> eternal hope, my heart does sing.
> Protected by your Mother's wing,
> I feel at one with everything.
>
> **O Portia, opportunity,**
> **I am beyond duality.**
> **I focus now internally,**
> **with you I grow eternally.**

5. Life must continue to remind me of the situations where I have accepted some limitation. I am picking up the phone the first time so that life does not have to increase the emotional pain in an attempt to make me pay attention.

> O Portia, bring the Mother Light,
> to set all free from darkest night.
> Your Love Flame shines forever bright,
> with Saint Germain now hold me tight.
>
> **O Portia, opportunity,**
> **I am beyond duality.**
> **I focus now internally,**
> **with you I grow eternally.**

6. I have had enough of this limitation. I am going to look at this problem and overcome the limitation so that I can once and for all overcome that pain instead of being burdened by it over and over again for the rest of my life or even for many lifetimes.

> O Portia, in your mastery,
> I feel transforming chemistry.
> In your light of reality,
> I find the golden alchemy.
>
> **O Portia, opportunity,**
> **I am beyond duality.**
> **I focus now internally,**
> **with you I grow eternally.**

7. I stop ignoring or denying my past or seeking to make myself so busy with the present or the future that I do to pay attention to my past. I am learning the lesson from my past.

> O Portia, in the cosmic stream,
> I am awake from human dream.
> Removing now the ego's beam,
> I earn my place on cosmic team.

16 | *Invocation for Hearing the Inner Message*

> **O Portia, opportunity,**
> **I am beyond duality.**
> **I focus now internally,**
> **with you I grow eternally.**

8. The situation from my past that keeps coming back over and over is a situation where I have not seen through a limiting belief and thus I have not let that belief go.

> O Portia, you come from afar,
> you are a cosmic avatar.
> So infinite your repertoire,
> you are for earth a guiding star.

> **O Portia, opportunity,**
> **I am beyond duality.**
> **I focus now internally,**
> **with you I grow eternally.**

9. I will no longer use the power of my mind to project a limiting belief onto the Ma-ter light. The mirror of the Ma-ter light can only reflect back to me outer conditions that reflect my state of consciousness.

> O Portia, I am confident,
> I am a cosmic instrument.
> I came to earth from heaven sent,
> to help bring forward her ascent.

> **O Portia, opportunity,**
> **I am beyond duality.**
> **I focus now internally,**
> **with you I grow eternally.**

4. I will not numb my mind

1. My past becomes prologue to my present and my future. The imperfect beliefs I accepted in my past are constantly being projected upon the Ma-ter light by my subconscious mind. The Ma-ter light must take on the forms of those beliefs and send me physical situations and circumstances that reflect those beliefs.

> O Portia, in your own retreat,
> with Mother's Love you do me greet.
> As all my tests I now complete,
> old patterns I no more repeat.
>
> **O Portia, opportunity,**
> **I am beyond duality.**
> **I focus now internally,**
> **with you I grow eternally.**

2. It is not the desire of the Ma-ter light to force me to encounter situations that cause me suffering. The Ma-ter light is the mirror so what can it do but reflect back what I send into it?

> O Portia, Justice is your name,
> upholding Cosmic Honor Flame,
> No longer will I play the game,
> of seeking to remain the same.
>
> **O Portia, opportunity,**
> **I am beyond duality.**
> **I focus now internally,**
> **with you I grow eternally.**

16 | Invocation for Hearing the Inner Message

3. The force of life itself does not want me to keep projecting the same imperfect images onto the Ma-ter light. The force of life is trying to help me awaken myself so that I can change the images I hold in my mind—and thereby change what I am projecting onto the Ma-ter light.

> O Portia, in the cosmic flow,
> one with you, I ever grow.
> I am the chalice here below,
> of cosmic justice you bestow.
>
> **O Portia, opportunity,**
> **I am beyond duality.**
> **I focus now internally,**
> **with you I grow eternally.**

4. I will listen for the message and I will no longer numb myself or feel annoyed at life.

> O Portia, cosmic balance bring,
> eternal hope, my heart does sing.
> Protected by your Mother's wing,
> I feel at one with everything.
>
> **O Portia, opportunity,**
> **I am beyond duality.**
> **I focus now internally,**
> **with you I grow eternally.**

5. It is not life that is the cause of my annoyance. It is the rigidity of my own mind and its unwillingness to look at my own beliefs, to evaluate whether those beliefs make sense. I am replacing the

beliefs that do not make sense with a higher understanding that springs from the Christ mind.

> O Portia, bring the Mother Light,
> to set all free from darkest night.
> Your Love Flame shines forever bright,
> with Saint Germain now hold me tight.

> **O Portia, opportunity,**
> **I am beyond duality.**
> **I focus now internally,**
> **with you I grow eternally.**

6. I am awakening to the absolute necessity to look beyond the outer situations from my past and look for the inner lesson I need to learn from those situations. I do this honestly and openly.

> O Portia, in your mastery,
> I feel transforming chemistry.
> In your light of reality,
> I find the golden alchemy.

> **O Portia, opportunity,**
> **I am beyond duality.**
> **I focus now internally,**
> **with you I grow eternally.**

7. Whenever I have a situation that causes me to suffer, it is because I am holding an imperfect belief about myself and about life. I see the imperfection of that belief and I reach for the higher understanding of the Christ mind.

O Portia, in the cosmic stream,
I am awake from human dream.
Removing now the ego's beam,
I earn my place on cosmic team.

**O Portia, opportunity,
I am beyond duality.
I focus now internally,
with you I grow eternally.**

8. I am replacing the limiting belief with the true realization of who I am. I am changing the image I am projecting onto the Ma-ter light. With absolute certainty, this will change what the cosmic mirror reflects back to me in the form of outer circumstances.

O Portia, you come from afar,
you are a cosmic avatar.
So infinite your repertoire,
you are for earth a guiding star.

**O Portia, opportunity,
I am beyond duality.
I focus now internally,
with you I grow eternally.**

9. This is not a daydream or an unrealistic promise. It is the most fundamental law of the material universe. I am completely changing what I am projecting into the cosmic mirror.

O Portia, I am confident,
I am a cosmic instrument.
I came to earth from heaven sent,
to help bring forward her ascent.

**O Portia, opportunity,
I am beyond duality.
I focus now internally,
with you I grow eternally.**

Sealing

In the name of the Divine Mother, I call to Portia and Mother Mary for the sealing of myself and all people in the creative flow of the Divine Mother, the River of Life. I call for the multiplication of my calls by all representatives of the Divine Mother, so that we form the perfect figure-eight flow of "As Above, so below." Thus, I accept that this is fully manifest, because the mouth of the Lord, the Divine Mother that I AM, has spoken it. Amen.

17 | INVOCATION FOR LETTING THE PAST GO

In the name I AM THAT I AM, Jesus Christ, I call to all representatives of the Divine Mother, especially the Goddess of Liberty and Mother Mary, to help me truly and finally let go of my past. I call for you to help me overcome all illusions that stand in the way of my healing, especially…

[Make personal calls.]

1. I am learning through inner direction

1. The law of God is simple. I have free will to do whatever I want. I am a co-creator with God. I am here to learn how to use my co-creative abilities to create situations for myself that I can live with, that I can grow with.

> O Liberty now set me free
> from devil's curse of poverty.
> I blame not Mother for my lack,
> O Blessed Mother, take me back.

> **O Cosmic Mother Liberty,
> conduct Abundance Symphony.
> My highest service I now see,
> abundance is now real for me.**

2. I learn in two ways. One is by listening to direction from within, from my I AM Presence, from my spiritual teachers.

> O Liberty, from distant shore,
> I come with longing to be More.
> I see abundance is a flow,
> abundance consciousness I grow.

> **O Cosmic Mother Liberty,
> conduct Abundance Symphony.
> My highest service I now see,
> abundance is now real for me.**

3. If I do not listen for direction, I must learn through the School of Hard Knocks, whereby I see the Ma-ter light reflect back to me physical circumstances that outpicture the circumstances in my mind.

> O Liberty, expose the lie,
> that limitations can me tie.
> The Ma-ter light is not my foe,
> true opulence it does bestow.

> **O Cosmic Mother Liberty,
> conduct Abundance Symphony.
> My highest service I now see,
> abundance is now real for me.**

4. I have a right to create any mental image I want. I have a right to project that mental image outside my own mind. When I do so, I will inevitably experience the physical situations that out-picture my mental image.

> O Liberty, expose the plot,
> projected by the fallen lot.
> O Cosmic Mother, I now see,
> that Mother's not my enemy.
>
> **O Cosmic Mother Liberty,**
> **conduct Abundance Symphony.**
> **My highest service I now see,**
> **abundance is now real for me.**

5. I will experience what I project upon life. I will experience what I co-create through the power of my mind by projecting a mental image onto the Ma-ter light.

> O Liberty, with opened eyes,
> I now reject the devil's lies.
> I now embrace the Mother realm,
> for I see Father at the helm.
>
> **O Cosmic Mother Liberty,**
> **conduct Abundance Symphony.**
> **My highest service I now see,**
> **abundance is now real for me.**

6. If I co-create circumstances that cause me suffering, I have an alternative to continuing to create the same circumstances.

> O Liberty, a chalice pure,
> my lower bodies are for sure.
> Release through me your symphony,
> your gift of Cosmic Liberty.
>
> **O Cosmic Mother Liberty,**
> **conduct Abundance Symphony.**
> **My highest service I now see,**
> **abundance is now real for me.**

7. The only way to stop the repetitive cycle that leads to suffering is to change the cause of the outer circumstances.

> O Liberty, the open door,
> I am for Symphony of More.
> In chakras mine light you release,
> the flow of love shall never cease.
>
> **O Cosmic Mother Liberty,**
> **conduct Abundance Symphony.**
> **My highest service I now see,**
> **abundance is now real for me.**

8. I see through the excuses that make it seem like I am not in control of the outer circumstances, that I did not create them, that somehow God, fate, luck or other people created those circumstances.

> O Liberty, release the flow,
> of opulence that you bestow.
> For I am willing to receive,
> the Golden Fleece that you now weave.

**O Cosmic Mother Liberty,
conduct Abundance Symphony.
My highest service I now see,
abundance is now real for me.**

9. I hereby accept the stark reality that I have co-created my own circumstances because I have formed mental images and I have projected those images onto the Ma-ter light.

> O Liberty, release the cure,
> to free the tired and the poor.
> The huddled masses are set free,
> by loving Song of Liberty.

**O Cosmic Mother Liberty,
conduct Abundance Symphony.
My highest service I now see,
abundance is now real for me.**

2. I let go of limiting beliefs

1. The absolutely only way that my outer circumstances can be changed is that I change the cause of the outer circumstances.

> O Liberty now set me free
> from devil's curse of poverty.
> I blame not Mother for my lack,
> O Blessed Mother, take me back.

**O Cosmic Mother Liberty,
conduct Abundance Symphony.
My highest service I now see,
abundance is now real for me.**

2. The effect is my outer circumstances. The cause of that effect is the mental images I hold in my mind. The only way to change my outer circumstances is to change those mental images.

O Liberty, from distant shore,
I come with longing to be More.
I see abundance is a flow,
abundance consciousness I grow.

**O Cosmic Mother Liberty,
conduct Abundance Symphony.
My highest service I now see,
abundance is now real for me.**

3. The only way to change the mental images in my mind is by consciously seeing the mental images, seeing that they are based on the duality consciousness, on the illusions of the mind of anti-christ, and then consciously letting them go, replacing the illusions with the truth of Christ.

O Liberty, expose the lie,
that limitations can me tie.
The Ma-ter light is not my foe,
true opulence it does bestow.

17 | Invocation for Letting the Past Go

> **O Cosmic Mother Liberty,**
> **conduct Abundance Symphony.**
> **My highest service I now see,**
> **abundance is now real for me.**

4. It is not a matter of somehow justifying the beliefs I have accepted in the past.

> O Liberty, expose the plot,
> projected by the fallen lot.
> O Cosmic Mother, I now see,
> that Mother's not my enemy.

> **O Cosmic Mother Liberty,**
> **conduct Abundance Symphony.**
> **My highest service I now see,**
> **abundance is now real for me.**

5. I am transcending the tendency to go into a defensive reaction. A defensive reaction is the default reaction of the ego, which simply will not acknowledge that I could be wrong. The ego goes into a reaction of trying to defend or justify my beliefs.

> O Liberty, with opened eyes,
> I now reject the devil's lies.
> I now embrace the Mother realm,
> for I see Father at the helm.

> **O Cosmic Mother Liberty,**
> **conduct Abundance Symphony.**
> **My highest service I now see,**
> **abundance is now real for me.**

6. If I keep trying to justify a past belief, I will simply build on to that belief. I will continue sending mental images into the cosmic mirror that are based on that original belief.

> O Liberty, a chalice pure,
> my lower bodies are for sure.
> Release through me your symphony,
> your gift of Cosmic Liberty.
>
> **O Cosmic Mother Liberty,**
> **conduct Abundance Symphony.**
> **My highest service I now see,**
> **abundance is now real for me.**

7. If I keep doing the same thing and expect different results, then I am trapped in the basic insanity of the human ego.

> O Liberty, the open door,
> I am for Symphony of More.
> In chakras mine light you release,
> the flow of love shall never cease.
>
> **O Cosmic Mother Liberty,**
> **conduct Abundance Symphony.**
> **My highest service I now see,**
> **abundance is now real for me.**

8. I am stepping away from the old patterns. I am willing to openly acknowledge that certain beliefs from my past are limiting me.

> O Liberty, release the flow,
> of opulence that you bestow.
> For I am willing to receive,
> the Golden Fleece that you now weave.
>
> **O Cosmic Mother Liberty,**
> **conduct Abundance Symphony.**
> **My highest service I now see,**
> **abundance is now real for me.**

9. It is not in my own best interest to uphold my limiting beliefs. It is in my own best interest to let them go.

> O Liberty, release the cure,
> to free the tired and the poor.
> The huddled masses are set free,
> by loving Song of Liberty.
>
> **O Cosmic Mother Liberty,**
> **conduct Abundance Symphony.**
> **My highest service I now see,**
> **abundance is now real for me.**

3. I am more than my beliefs

1. My Conscious You is a spark of God's own Being. It is infinitely more than my past, than any circumstance or any belief from my past.

O Liberty now set me free
from devil's curse of poverty.
I blame not Mother for my lack,
O Blessed Mother, take me back.

**O Cosmic Mother Liberty,
conduct Abundance Symphony.
My highest service I now see,
abundance is now real for me.**

2. My conscious self has the God-given right and the God-given ability to step outside of my identification with my past. I can do so at any moment, including right now.

O Liberty, from distant shore,
I come with longing to be More.
I see abundance is a flow,
abundance consciousness I grow.

**O Cosmic Mother Liberty,
conduct Abundance Symphony.
My highest service I now see,
abundance is now real for me.**

3. There is a force in this world that is very determined to keep me trapped in my identification with the past. I know I can let go of the past. I know that by letting go of the past I will *not* lose my identity.

O Liberty, expose the lie,
that limitations can me tie.
The Ma-ter light is not my foe,
true opulence it does bestow.

> **O Cosmic Mother Liberty,**
> **conduct Abundance Symphony.**
> **My highest service I now see,**
> **abundance is now real for me.**

4. This force is comprised of my personal ego, the egos of other people and the entire dark force, the force of anti-christ, what Jesus called the prince of this world.

> O Liberty, expose the plot,
> projected by the fallen lot.
> O Cosmic Mother, I now see,
> that Mother's not my enemy.

> **O Cosmic Mother Liberty,**
> **conduct Abundance Symphony.**
> **My highest service I now see,**
> **abundance is now real for me.**

5. The prince of this world will constantly come to me. He will come to see if he can make me attached to the past. I am willing to let the imperfect beliefs go. I acknowledge that I am more than any imperfect belief.

> O Liberty, with opened eyes,
> I now reject the devil's lies.
> I now embrace the Mother realm,
> for I see Father at the helm.

> **O Cosmic Mother Liberty,**
> **conduct Abundance Symphony.**
> **My highest service I now see,**
> **abundance is now real for me.**

6. I have the God-given right and the ability to let go of any imperfect belief from the past.

> O Liberty, a chalice pure,
> my lower bodies are for sure.
> Release through me your symphony,
> your gift of Cosmic Liberty.

> **O Cosmic Mother Liberty,**
> **conduct Abundance Symphony.**
> **My highest service I now see,**
> **abundance is now real for me.**

7. I am willing to look at the belief, acknowledge that it is unreal, that it springs from the mind of anti-christ. I also acknowledge that I am more than the belief. It is simply an old worn-out coat that I took on sometime in the past.

> O Liberty, the open door,
> I am for Symphony of More.
> In chakras mine light you release,
> the flow of love shall never cease.

> **O Cosmic Mother Liberty,**
> **conduct Abundance Symphony.**
> **My highest service I now see,**
> **abundance is now real for me.**

8. I am taking off the old sense of identity and throwing it into the spiritual fires of the violet flame and the Flame of Forgiveness. I am simply letting it go.

17 | Invocation for Letting the Past Go

O Liberty, release the flow,
of opulence that you bestow.
For I am willing to receive,
the Golden Fleece that you now weave.

**O Cosmic Mother Liberty,
conduct Abundance Symphony.
My highest service I now see,
abundance is now real for me.**

9. My God is truly a consuming fire that can consume all imperfect sense of self that I might have built in any past lifetime.

O Liberty, release the cure,
to free the tired and the poor.
The huddled masses are set free,
by loving Song of Liberty.

**O Cosmic Mother Liberty,
conduct Abundance Symphony.
My highest service I now see,
abundance is now real for me.**

4. I let my past go

1. I have an alternative to repeating old patterns. I am taking off the overcoat of my imperfect sense of identity and throwing it into the bonfire of God where it is consumed. I am as free as if that identity had never existed.

> O Liberty now set me free
> from devil's curse of poverty.
> I blame not Mother for my lack,
> O Blessed Mother, take me back.
>
> **O Cosmic Mother Liberty,**
> **conduct Abundance Symphony.**
> **My highest service I now see,**
> **abundance is now real for me.**

2. The master key to letting go of an imperfect sense of identity is the willingness to forgive. In order to be free of my past, I forgive and I forgive unconditionally.

> O Liberty, from distant shore,
> I come with longing to be More.
> I see abundance is a flow,
> abundance consciousness I grow.
>
> **O Cosmic Mother Liberty,**
> **conduct Abundance Symphony.**
> **My highest service I now see,**
> **abundance is now real for me.**

3. My ego has tricked me into thinking that in order for me to forgive, certain conditions must be fulfilled. In order to forgive someone who has hurt me, that person must be punished or must change.

> O Liberty, expose the lie,
> that limitations can me tie.
> The Ma-ter light is not my foe,
> true opulence it does bestow.

17 | Invocation for Letting the Past Go

**O Cosmic Mother Liberty,
conduct Abundance Symphony.
My highest service I now see,
abundance is now real for me.**

4. What I do unto others is what I have already done to myself at subconscious levels. I can only do unto others what I have already done to myself, both good and bad.

O Liberty, expose the plot,
projected by the fallen lot.
O Cosmic Mother, I now see,
that Mother's not my enemy.

**O Cosmic Mother Liberty,
conduct Abundance Symphony.
My highest service I now see,
abundance is now real for me.**

5. If I think that other people must live up to certain conditions before they can be forgiven, then I also think that *I* must live up to certain conditions before I can be forgiven.

O Liberty, with opened eyes,
I now reject the devil's lies.
I now embrace the Mother realm,
for I see Father at the helm.

**O Cosmic Mother Liberty,
conduct Abundance Symphony.
My highest service I now see,
abundance is now real for me.**

6. My ego is very clever at defining such conditions and defining them in such a way that no one can live up to them, including myself. That is how my ego keeps me trapped in the cycle of never wanting to forgive others and never wanting to forgive myself.

> O Liberty, a chalice pure,
> my lower bodies are for sure.
> Release through me your symphony,
> your gift of Cosmic Liberty.
>
> **O Cosmic Mother Liberty,**
> **conduct Abundance Symphony.**
> **My highest service I now see,**
> **abundance is now real for me.**

7. My ego makes me believe that because I have made certain mistakes in the past, I am unforgivable, I am unredeemable. I am rising above the past and I am free of it.

> O Liberty, the open door,
> I am for Symphony of More.
> In chakras mine light you release,
> the flow of love shall never cease.
>
> **O Cosmic Mother Liberty,**
> **conduct Abundance Symphony.**
> **My highest service I now see,**
> **abundance is now real for me.**

8. The last thing my ego wants me to realize is that I have the God-given right and the power to simply walk away from the imperfections of my past by acknowledging my imperfect beliefs.

O Liberty, release the flow,
of opulence that you bestow.
For I am willing to receive,
the Golden Fleece that you now weave.

**O Cosmic Mother Liberty,
conduct Abundance Symphony.
My highest service I now see,
abundance is now real for me.**

9. I hereby accept that the master key to rising above my past is to forgive—but not to forgive in a human way that is based on outer conditions. The master key to rising above my past is to forgive unconditionally. I do forgive with no conditions.

O Liberty, release the cure,
to free the tired and the poor.
The huddled masses are set free,
by loving Song of Liberty.

**O Cosmic Mother Liberty,
conduct Abundance Symphony.
My highest service I now see,
abundance is now real for me.**

Sealing

In the name of the Divine Mother, I call to Liberty and Mother Mary for the sealing of myself and all people in the creative flow of the Divine Mother, the River of Life. I call for the multiplication of my calls by all representatives of the Divine Mother, so that we form the perfect figure-eight flow of "As Above, so below." Thus, I accept that this is fully manifest, because the mouth of the Lord, the Divine Mother that I AM, has spoken it. Amen.

18 | INVOKING FREEDOM FROM EMOTIONAL PAIN

In the name I AM THAT I AM, Jesus Christ, I call to all representatives of the Divine Mother, especially Venus and Mother Mary, to help me transcend all emotional pain that makes it impossible for me to look at my past and forgive. I call for you to help me overcome all illusions that stand in the way of my healing, especially…

[Make personal calls.]

1. I see the real cause of my pain

1. When I have not forgiven another person, I am holding on to the old situation. That means I am holding on to the pain created in the situation when the other person hurt me.

> O Venus, show me how to serve,
> your cosmic beauty I observe.
> What love from Venus you now bring,
> our planets do in tandem sing.
>
> **O Venus, service so divine,
> you are for earth a cosmic sign.
> Your selfless service is now mine,
> a life in service I define.**

2. The pain pulls on my conscious attention and pulls me into remembering the situation. Whenever I think about the situation, I reinforce the original pain. Thereby, I tie myself to my past and I reinforce the pain.

> O Venus, your love is the key,
> the hardened hearts on earth are free.
> Embracing future bright and bold,
> our planet's story is retold.
>
> **O Venus, service so divine,
> you are for earth a cosmic sign.
> Your selfless service is now mine,
> a life in service I define.**

3. By not forgiving the other person, I am harming myself because I am holding on to the imperfect images and feelings, and I am projecting them onto the Ma-ter light.

> O Venus, loving Mother mine,
> my heart your love does now refine.
> I am the open door for love,
> descending like a Holy Dove.

**O Venus, service so divine,
you are for earth a cosmic sign.
Your selfless service is now mine,
a life in service I define.**

4. The Ma-ter light reasons that I want to experience situations where other people hurt me. It has no other option than to give me future situations where other people cause me pain.

O Venus, play the secret note,
that is for hatred antidote.
All poisoned hearts you gently heal,
as love's true story you reveal.

**O Venus, service so divine,
you are for earth a cosmic sign.
Your selfless service is now mine,
a life in service I define.**

5. The excuse I use for not forgiving others is that they do not live up to the outer conditions that my ego has defined.

O Venus, love fills every need,
for truly, love is God's first seed.
O let it blossom, let it grow,
sweep earth into your loving flow.

**O Venus, service so divine,
you are for earth a cosmic sign.
Your selfless service is now mine,
a life in service I define.**

6. My ego makes me think that as long as other people do not live up to my conditions, I cannot let go of the situation, I cannot forgive and rise above it. This is the very same psychology that caused me to be hurt in the original situation.

> O Venus, music of the spheres,
> heard by those who God reveres.
> Our voices now as one we raise,
> singing in adoring praise.

> **O Venus, service so divine,**
> **you are for earth a cosmic sign.**
> **Your selfless service is now mine,**
> **a life in service I define.**

7. In the original situation somebody else did something to me. But it was not what they did to me that caused me to be hurt. It was the imperfect beliefs that I hold about myself and life that caused me to respond to that situation in a way that hurt myself.

> O Venus, we are joining ranks,
> Sanat Kumara we give thanks.
> Our planet has received new life,
> to lift her out of war and strife.

> **O Venus, service so divine,**
> **you are for earth a cosmic sign.**
> **Your selfless service is now mine,**
> **a life in service I define.**

8. What really caused the hurt was that I had a belief that turned me into a passive victim. I thought that when other people did certain things to me, I could only respond with negative feelings

that caused me to be hurt. It was this belief that turned me into a victim.

> O Venus, your sweet melody,
> consumes veil of duality.
> Absorbed in tones of Cosmic Love,
> all conflict we now rise above.
>
> **O Venus, service so divine,**
> **you are for earth a cosmic sign.**
> **Your selfless service is now mine,**
> **a life in service I define.**

9. Even today I am holding on to the belief that I am a victim by thinking that only when the other person lives up to certain conditions, can I forgive that person and let go of the situation. By not forgiving, I am perpetuating the original situation.

> O Venus, shining Morning Star,
> a cosmic herald, that you are.
> The earth set free by sacred sound,
> our planet is now heaven-bound.
>
> **O Venus, service so divine,**
> **you are for earth a cosmic sign.**
> **Your selfless service is now mine,**
> **a life in service I define.**

2. I let go of my pain

1. Only by changing my own beliefs can I break the cycle of experiencing physical situations where I think that my only potential response is to be a victim and feel hurt.

> O Venus, show me how to serve,
> your cosmic beauty I observe.
> What love from Venus you now bring,
> our planets do in tandem sing.
>
> **O Venus, service so divine,**
> **you are for earth a cosmic sign.**
> **Your selfless service is now mine,**
> **a life in service I define.**

2. The only thing that can change the equation is that I change the way I look at the equation, the way I look at life, the way I look at myself.

> O Venus, your love is the key,
> the hardened hearts on earth are free.
> Embracing future bright and bold,
> our planet's story is retold.
>
> **O Venus, service so divine,**
> **you are for earth a cosmic sign.**
> **Your selfless service is now mine,**
> **a life in service I define.**

18 | Invoking Freedom from Emotional Pain

3. I hereby take back my power to respond to situations based on a choice I make today, instead of a choice I made in the past.

> O Venus, loving Mother mine,
> my heart your love does now refine.
> I am the open door for love,
> descending like a Holy Dove.
>
> **O Venus, service so divine,**
> **you are for earth a cosmic sign.**
> **Your selfless service is now mine,**
> **a life in service I define.**

4. I am willing to go back and look at the original belief and dismiss it as being unreal. I am dismissing the belief, and I am free to respond to situations without having that baggage weighing me down.

> O Venus, play the secret note,
> that is for hatred antidote.
> All poisoned hearts you gently heal,
> as love's true story you reveal.
>
> **O Venus, service so divine,**
> **you are for earth a cosmic sign.**
> **Your selfless service is now mine,**
> **a life in service I define.**

5. I don't have to respond to this situation by feeling hurt, by feeling afraid, by feeling ashamed, by coming down on myself and thinking I am a bad person because someone else treats me as if I was a bad person.

O Venus, love fills every need,
for truly, love is God's first seed.
O let it blossom, let it grow,
sweep earth into your loving flow.

O Venus, service so divine,
you are for earth a cosmic sign.
Your selfless service is now mine,
a life in service I define.

6. What another person does to me is a reflection of that person's state of consciousness. The person has an imperfect image of him- or herself, and the person is projecting that image upon me.

O Venus, music of the spheres,
heard by those who God reveres.
Our voices now as one we raise,
singing in adoring praise.

O Venus, service so divine,
you are for earth a cosmic sign.
Your selfless service is now mine,
a life in service I define.

7. I do not have to accept another person's image of me. I have a God-given right to live my life based on the images in my own mind. I choose to respond to the other person freely.

O Venus, we are joining ranks,
Sanat Kumara we give thanks.
Our planet has received new life,
to lift her out of war and strife.

> **O Venus, service so divine,**
> **you are for earth a cosmic sign.**
> **Your selfless service is now mine,**
> **a life in service I define.**

8. The key to being free from the imperfect beliefs of other people or the imperfect beliefs of my own past self is to forgive. I forgive by being completely non-attached to what is projected at me from other people or from my outer mind.

> O Venus, your sweet melody,
> consumes veil of duality.
> Absorbed in tones of Cosmic Love,
> all conflict we now rise above.
>
> **O Venus, service so divine,**
> **you are for earth a cosmic sign.**
> **Your selfless service is now mine,**
> **a life in service I define.**

9. I have the absolute power to unconditionally forgive myself or other people. I simply let go of all sense of hurt, all sense of pain.

> O Venus, shining Morning Star,
> a cosmic herald, that you are.
> The earth set free by sacred sound,
> our planet is now heaven-bound.
>
> **O Venus, service so divine,**
> **you are for earth a cosmic sign.**
> **Your selfless service is now mine,**
> **a life in service I define.**

3. I stop downward spirals

1. I am rising above the downward spirals from the past. I am no longer seeking to transform the past, control the past or control other people. I am transforming the way I look at the past. I am letting go of the belief I have been holding on to.

> O Venus, show me how to serve,
> your cosmic beauty I observe.
> What love from Venus you now bring,
> our planets do in tandem sing.
>
> **O Venus, service so divine,**
> **you are for earth a cosmic sign.**
> **Your selfless service is now mine,**
> **a life in service I define.**

2. The magic wand is my conscious awareness and my willingness to simply let go. I hereby let go of the pain, I let go of the hurt, I let go of the belief that I need to respond to certain situations in a negative way. I let go of the belief that in certain situations I can only respond with negative feelings.

> O Venus, your love is the key,
> the hardened hearts on earth are free.
> Embracing future bright and bold,
> our planet's story is retold.
>
> **O Venus, service so divine,**
> **you are for earth a cosmic sign.**
> **Your selfless service is now mine,**
> **a life in service I define.**

3. I choose to enter into the spirit of forgiveness. I allow the Spirit of Forgiveness to enter my lower being. I accept that I am in a state of perpetual forgiveness. I have already forgiven myself and other people before they have done anything to me.

> O Venus, loving Mother mine,
> my heart your love does now refine.
> I am the open door for love,
> descending like a Holy Dove.
>
> **O Venus, service so divine,**
> **you are for earth a cosmic sign.**
> **Your selfless service is now mine,**
> **a life in service I define.**

4. When I know that others are already forgiven, I also know that I can stay free of any negative reaction, no matter what other people do to me. I am following the advice of Jesus and I am turning the other cheek.

> O Venus, play the secret note,
> that is for hatred antidote.
> All poisoned hearts you gently heal,
> as love's true story you reveal.
>
> **O Venus, service so divine,**
> **you are for earth a cosmic sign.**
> **Your selfless service is now mine,**
> **a life in service I define.**

5. From a state of perpetual and unconditional forgiveness, I am turning the other cheek. I am giving the other person another opportunity to see his or her imperfections.

O Venus, love fills every need,
for truly, love is God's first seed.
O let it blossom, let it grow,
sweep earth into your loving flow.

**O Venus, service so divine,
you are for earth a cosmic sign.
Your selfless service is now mine,
a life in service I define.**

6. If a person hurts me and I respond by trying to hurt the other person or defend myself, then I only reinforce the other person's belief. I not only reinforce the belief in the mind of the other person, but I reinforce it in my own mind.

O Venus, music of the spheres,
heard by those who God reveres.
Our voices now as one we raise,
singing in adoring praise.

**O Venus, service so divine,
you are for earth a cosmic sign.
Your selfless service is now mine,
a life in service I define.**

7. When I turn the other cheek, I break the spiral. When I respond with love when someone else hurts me, I am challenging the other person's belief that I am a bad person. I am showing the other person that I am a person who can respond with love.

> O Venus, we are joining ranks,
> Sanat Kumara we give thanks.
> Our planet has received new life,
> to lift her out of war and strife.
>
> **O Venus, service so divine,**
> **you are for earth a cosmic sign.**
> **Your selfless service is now mine,**
> **a life in service I define.**

8. When I turn the other cheek in unconditional forgiveness, and another person still hurts me, then that second act of hurting me becomes the person's judgment.

> O Venus, your sweet melody,
> consumes veil of duality.
> Absorbed in tones of Cosmic Love,
> all conflict we now rise above.
>
> **O Venus, service so divine,**
> **you are for earth a cosmic sign.**
> **Your selfless service is now mine,**
> **a life in service I define.**

9. I accept Jesus' teaching that by turning the other cheek and not resisting evil, I allow the law of God to work in full measure. By doing this, the law of God will be able to remove evil from the earth at an accelerated rate.

> O Venus, shining Morning Star,
> a cosmic herald, that you are.
> The earth set free by sacred sound,
> our planet is now heaven-bound.

**O Venus, service so divine,
you are for earth a cosmic sign.
Your selfless service is now mine,
a life in service I define.**

4. I am an instrument for the judgment

1. When I allow other people to hurt me while I am turning the other cheek, then God can step in and remove those people from the earth. Thereby, the most selfish, self-centered, egotistical people will be removed from the earth.

> O Venus, show me how to serve,
> your cosmic beauty I observe.
> What love from Venus you now bring,
> our planets do in tandem sing.

> **O Venus, service so divine,
> you are for earth a cosmic sign.
> Your selfless service is now mine,
> a life in service I define.**

2. I am the instrument for helping humankind rise to a higher level and overcome certain states of consciousness that are outplayed over and over again in a seemingly endless spiral.

> O Venus, your love is the key,
> the hardened hearts on earth are free.
> Embracing future bright and bold,
> our planet's story is retold.

**O Venus, service so divine,
you are for earth a cosmic sign.
Your selfless service is now mine,
a life in service I define.**

3. I have had enough of this downward spiral. I will not perpetuate the cycle, and therefore I will do something completely different. Instead of responding to hurt with pain and revenge and a desire to punish, I am responding with love and unconditional forgiveness.

O Venus, loving Mother mine,
my heart your love does now refine.
I am the open door for love,
descending like a Holy Dove.

**O Venus, service so divine,
you are for earth a cosmic sign.
Your selfless service is now mine,
a life in service I define.**

4. By doing this, I will set myself free from any ties to the people who have hurt me. I do not want to keep myself tied to the people who have hurt me. I am free of those people once and for all.

O Venus, play the secret note,
that is for hatred antidote.
All poisoned hearts you gently heal,
as love's true story you reveal.

**O Venus, service so divine,
you are for earth a cosmic sign.
Your selfless service is now mine,
a life in service I define.**

5. The desire to punish another person means that I am not willing to turn away from that person until I have seen the other person be punished. I am rising above this and I am forgiving unconditionally.

O Venus, love fills every need,
for truly, love is God's first seed.
O let it blossom, let it grow,
sweep earth into your loving flow.

**O Venus, service so divine,
you are for earth a cosmic sign.
Your selfless service is now mine,
a life in service I define.**

6. I am rising above my cultural beliefs and forgiving unconditionally, forgiving regardless of the cultural belief. I am more than the cultural belief. I forgive regardless of outer labels, and I set myself free from these labels.

O Venus, music of the spheres,
heard by those who God reveres.
Our voices now as one we raise,
singing in adoring praise.

18 | Invoking Freedom from Emotional Pain

> **O Venus, service so divine,**
> **you are for earth a cosmic sign.**
> **Your selfless service is now mine,**
> **a life in service I define.**

7. I hear the inner message and I am transcending my limitations and rejoining the River of Life. I am experiencing the bliss of constant self-transcendence.

> O Venus, we are joining ranks,
> Sanat Kumara we give thanks.
> Our planet has received new life,
> to lift her out of war and strife.

> **O Venus, service so divine,**
> **you are for earth a cosmic sign.**
> **Your selfless service is now mine,**
> **a life in service I define.**

8. I hereby ask for the inner direction of my Christ self and ascended teachers. Show me the message behind the outer situations I encounter.

> O Venus, your sweet melody,
> consumes veil of duality.
> Absorbed in tones of Cosmic Love,
> all conflict we now rise above.

> **O Venus, service so divine,**
> **you are for earth a cosmic sign.**
> **Your selfless service is now mine,**
> **a life in service I define.**

9. I am being reborn, I am starting a new day. I am being reborn in Christ and rising above the past. I am rising into the new day of the kingdom of God. I am opening myself to and I am absorbing the Flame of Unconditional Forgiveness. My forgiveness is unconditional, and my joy is indeed full.

> O Venus, shining Morning Star,
> a cosmic herald, that you are.
> The earth set free by sacred sound,
> our planet is now heaven-bound.
>
> **O Venus, service so divine,**
> **you are for earth a cosmic sign.**
> **Your selfless service is now mine,**
> **a life in service I define.**

Sealing

In the name of the Divine Mother, I call to Venus and Mother Mary for the sealing of myself and all people in the creative flow of the Divine Mother, the River of Life. I call for the multiplication of my calls by all representatives of the Divine Mother, so that we form the perfect figure-eight flow of "As Above, so below." Thus, I accept that this is fully manifest, because the mouth of the Lord, the Divine Mother that I AM, has spoken it. Amen.

19 | THE POWER OF UNCONDITIONAL ACCEPTANCE

A dictation by Mother Mary, May 18, 2007.

My beloved hearts, there truly is no greater joy for your spiritual mother than to experience her children sharing their heart flames in an environment where everyone is accepted for their uniqueness. If there was one message that I would want to get across to all humankind, it is precisely this: In heaven everyone is unconditionally accepted for who they are. In heaven we see only the uniqueness of your individuality in God, the individuality with which you were created, and the individuality that you yourself have co-created in oneness with the Christ flame in your heart.

This unconditional acceptance could literally solve all of the world's problems and remove all of the world's conflicts—if, of course, it could be accepted unconditionally by the people of the world. Here, precisely, is the problem, for so many people in the world have been conditioned to think that there must always be conditions.

Conditions keep you outside the kingdom

It is precisely the conditions that prevent you from experiencing the kingdom that is within you. You think that you are separated from that inner kingdom, and what is separating you? You might very well think that it is some outer condition, such as your sins, your karma or your psychology, but these outer conditions are nothing but symbols. They are symbols for the fact that in your own mind, in your own being, you have come to accept conditions. You have come to believe in the lie, the serpentine lie, that in order to come back to God, you have to fulfill certain conditions.

What was it that separated you from God in the first place? *It was conditions!* You began to believe that you needed to fulfill certain conditions in this world in order to be worthy to enter the kingdom of God, which you had now come to see as being outside of, separate from, yourself. There is a mountain in Ireland that primarily is climbed by Catholics who do this as a penance. They have come to accept the basic belief that in order to be saved, they have to fulfill certain conditions in this world. The more painful those conditions are, the more they think they are paying back their sins.

Why did Jesus say that unless you become as little children, ye shall in no wise enter the kingdom? Do little children have conditions? No! They love unconditionally, and they accept love unconditionally. They do not have the adult sophistication of the mind and the intellect to even come up with these conditions. But they learn quickly by observing the adults around them, from their parents to their teachers, to their ministers in church.

They quickly learn that in order to receive love or whatever else they need, they need to live up to certain conditions. This makes them susceptible to believing in a religion that says that if you put yourself through pain by walking up a very steep mountain with lose rocks, perhaps even doing it barefoot, then somehow through that pain of yours, the God in heaven is satisfied and will now forgive your sins and let you into his kingdom. The reality is that God will let you into his kingdom any time you let go of the conditions that you think keep you outside that kingdom.

The more pain people put themselves through, the more distance they create in their minds between themselves and the kingdom of God. They will not truly contemplate and accept the momentous statement made by Jesus that the kingdom of God is within you. Did he not say: "The kingdom of God comes not with observation?" Is walking barefoot up a mountain not observing some outer rule, some outer concept, of what it takes to enter the kingdom of God?

God accepts you for who you are

Your Creator, your God, accepts you right now unconditionally for who you are. There are two meanings to this statement. It should be obvious, given the knowledge that you have, that you were created out of a greater spiritual being who came out of an even greater spiritual being, and that chain of being reaches all the way back to the Creator.

Perhaps you do not fully internalize and accept this teaching. You can understand it – at least intellectually – and therefore you can understand that when you were created out of the Creator's own Being, surely God the Creator accepts itself. Certainly, God the Creator accepts that part of its own Being that is imparted to you. You should be able to understand and accept that God can have unconditional acceptance for that part of your Being that truly is an individualization of the Creator. I desire to give you an even deeper teaching, which I know will require you to stretch the mind and the heart and to watch your emotions and see the inner reaction. I ask you, as I am speaking these words, to watch your reaction, your thoughts, your feelings—the conditions that come up in you. I must tell you that many of you might look at yourselves today and say: "I can understand that God accepts my God Flame, my I AM Presence, my divine individuality, but surely I have fallen into a lower state of consciousness. I have created an ego. I have accepted conditions. I may have psychological issues. I may have done certain things in my life. How could God accept this? How could God accept the outer personality, the outer sense of identity that I have created in this world?"

The reality is that God accepts you for who you are right this moment. God's acceptance of you is unconditional. Watch your reactions. Watch how your ego will struggle with this statement and come up with reasons for why this cannot be so. "If God accepts me for who I am right now, then why do I have to go through this arduous path of penance and forgiveness of sin and being saved by some external savior?"

The truth is that the path *you* have to go through is the path that *you* have created through the conditions that you have accepted. Depending on what kind and how many conditions you have accepted, there is a path for each one of you to follow. Here is the essential key that so few people have understood. The path that you have to follow in order to qualify for your freedom is *not* fulfilling the outer conditions that you have come to accept. *The path is to let go of those conditions!* You need to come to see that they are unreal, that they are illusions, that they are dualistic illusions created by the serpentine mind, by the fallen state of consciousness, by the consciousness of separation and duality.

Many of you have already realized this. You have experienced in your own lives that you had to go through a period of searching, or depression, or outer difficulties. Eventually, you came to a point where you surrendered, you let go and said: "I don't need this belief anymore. I don't need this vicarious atonement. I don't need to feel like a sinner."

This is the essential characteristic of thinking that in order to be saved you have to fulfill an outer condition. You strive all of your life to be a good Catholic, or a good Muslim, or a good Hindu, or a good New Age person, or whatever you think is the outer path. The alternative is to realize that the real path, the inner path, is to let go of the conditions that are inside of *you*. Trying to fulfill outer conditions only takes your attention away from the kingdom of God that is within you, making you think that you have to enter some external kingdom, that you need an external savior or an external church, or that you need to fulfill some external conditions.

Do whatever it takes to let go of your conditions

Sometimes it is indeed necessary for you to ascend a physical mountain in order to realize that you did not need to ascend the mountain because you can find it all inside yourself. There is nothing wrong with ascending the mountain in order to come to that realization. Yet there is nothing wrong with going halfway or not going at all. Whatever you have to do on the outer in order to be able to surrender the outer is fully acceptable.

I wish to impart to you – and I wish I could inspire you to impart to the world – that the essence of the spiritual path, the essence of salvation, is precisely to overcome the inner condition that makes you think you have to fulfill an outer condition. When you realize *that* – when you fully realize it – then you can let go of the outer conditions. You can be reborn of the Spirit.

Did not Jesus say to Nicodemus (John 3:5) that in order to enter the kingdom, a man must be born of water and he must be born of Spirit? Following an outer path is the process of being born of water. When you come to the point of realizing what I have just explained – that it is not the *outer* conditions, but it is letting go of the *inner* conditions – you can experience the total surrender – the unconditional surrender – that brings about the rebirth of the Spirit. Thereby, you can suddenly accept who you are, and when you accept who you are right now, then you can let go of what is unreal instead of holding on to it.

Do you understand the very subtle psychological mechanism that comes into play when you accept the serpentine lie that in order to enter God's kingdom, you have to be acceptable to God? The lie also says that what determines whether you are acceptable to God is whether you fulfill certain outer conditions defined in this world by some institution or teacher or even by your own ego. When you believe that in order to be saved, you have to fulfill these outer conditions, the psychological mechanism that comes into play is that you cannot fully accept that you have these conditions. You cannot, as Jesus has said, take ownership of them.

When you cannot take ownership of them, you cannot surrender them. You cannot look at them squarely and say: "But this is unreal. I no longer need to carry this with me. I no longer need to accept this condition or to accept the belief that caused me to accept whatever illusion I have carried around for a long time."

When you think the path is about fulfilling outer conditions, it becomes impossible for you to look at your own imperfections, to look at your human condition and say: "This is unreal, this has to go." Instead, you do what so many people in the world do: They ignore the beam in their own eye. Either they focus all attention on the splinter in the eye of another or they focus on the outer path. They say that if only I give so many Hail Marys and light so many candles or walk up a mountain barefoot and put myself through this or that pain, then God will have to accept me, even though I have not let go of the conditions that keep me – in my own mind – outside the inner kingdom.

When you come to the realization that God accepts you for who you are right now, then you can say: "If God can accept me even though I might look at myself as being an imperfect human being, then certainly I can accept myself." The reason you should be able to accept yourself is precisely this: God has given you free will. God has given you the right to enter this world and to create a certain world view based on whatever conditions you have chosen to accept. God has set up the universe as a mirror, to mirror that view back to you so that you can create for yourself any experience you desire.

You must choose to let go of your conditions

Do you see that God gave you free will? God has given you the right to create the experience that you are having right now because you have free will. God accepts that you have a right to create your present experience. When you realize what the path is all about, you realize that you can let go of the experience you have right now at any moment. Your path will take on a new meaning when you realize that your present experience is unreal and: "I have had enough of that experience. I don't want it anymore. I don't need it anymore." Your life will change because you suddenly realize that all of the outer conditions are unreal, and they cannot keep you outside the kingdom—unless you allow them to do so by continuing to accept them.

This is precisely what the world wants you to do. The world wants you to continue to accept these conditions that you have come to believe and that the world still believes. Your family, your friends, your society, the world at large, your priests, all want you to accept the conditions that they accept. If you do not, you disturb them in their belief that they could not change themselves, that they don't have to take responsibility for their own lives and their own salvation. They can just wait for Jesus to appear in the sky or wait for some miraculous apparition by Mother Mary or wait for Saint Patrick to come back in some chariot of fire to lift up the people.

This is why there has always been idolatry of the saints and the sages who have stood out from the crowd. By elevating us, it gives people's egos an excuse for saying: "*They* were special so *I* cannot do what they did." If you will honestly look at my life as Mother Mary, what was so spectacular that I did in that lifetime? I gave birth to a child, but have not many women done so? Surely, he was at times a difficult child, but certainly other children have been a challenge to their parents. Some of you would probably admit that *you* challenged your parents in many ways. Some of you feel that your children have been a great challenge, so why was I so different?

If there was one thing that I would want the world to learn from my lifetime as Mary, it was that what was special about me was my willingness to surrender—to surrender everything, to flow with the inner prompting that came from my higher Being. Ah, you say, but did I not have an angel appear to me and tell me what to do? How do you know how that apparition took place? I can assure you that it was not the version that Hollywood has come up with in their ever-accelerating quest to do better than the latest movie and to have more special effects or more violence.

It is the idolatry of the world that wants to create these conditions. Your ego is born of conditions. Your ego seriously and truly believes that it could not survive without conditions. This is true because the moment you let go of your conditions, your ego will have no hold over you. Neither your ego nor the prince of the world will have anything in you. Your ego does not want you to surrender because the more conditions you have, the more your ego has control over you and the more comfortable your ego feels.

There are many people in the world who have become so identified with their egos that they are so comfortable in having created this very neat little box for themselves. They feel they have everything under control and their lives are so ritualized, and every morning they get up and they do the exact same thing. They go to work and they come home and they watch the same shows on TV and everything is ritualized and regimented. Yet if they were thrown into a new situation, an unexpected situation, they would disintegrate, they would not be able to handle it.

You see in your own lives that you have been willing to come away from your comfortability, to find the spiritual path in whatever form and allow it to change your life. The only true difference between those of us who have ascended and those who have not ascended is that we were willing to surrender – gradually – all of our conditions. We were willing to die daily, as Paul said, to have some of our conditions die every day. We kept doing this over and over and over again until there suddenly was nothing more to surrender because we truly had been willing to lose our lives for the sake of following Christ.

The essence of the spiritual path is surrender

Certainly, it was a big surrender for me to break off my very comfortable and regimented monastic lifestyle to suddenly go back into the world and have a child. It was, again, a big adjustment to realize that we had to take that child out of Israel and flee to Egypt. There were many other adjustments as Jesus grew up and as he gained a clearer vision of his mission, and I gained a clearer vision. Joseph's death was a big adjustment for me, left with many children. It was an adjustment when Jesus left home at an early age to go on his spiritual pilgrimage and when he came back. Certainly, my beloved, it was an adjustment when I stood in front of the cross, watching him struggle and finally watching him give up the ghost, giving up the last of his conditions. This inspired me to give up the conditions I had about how my son's life and mission should unfold. As Jesus has explained, he had certain illusions until the very end on the cross. I too had certain illusions about how his spiritual mission should unfold. I even had certain illusions that I held on to after that until the end of my embodiment when I finally let go of them all.

I simply tell you this: You have already surrendered much to be where you are right now. You have surrendered much, my beloved. Is it so difficult to accept that the path is about one thing: surrender, letting go of conditions? Once you accept this, it becomes so much easier to surrender the conditions. You realize that the more you surrender, the more free you feel inside. You build a momentum, and once you get beyond a certain point, you realize that surrender is not loss, surrender is not sacrifice, surrender is not the Via Dolorosa. *Surrender is joy. Surrender is freedom.* The more you let go of, the more free you are.

This is my gift to you, the gift of surrender. Should you need help surrendering or gaining a clear vision of what to surrender – seeing the illusion so you can let it go – then apply to my heart. Give an invocation if you feel you need to. Or simply ask me and then listen for my answer. Listen both within and without. I will find a way to give you the answer you seek. If you cannot hear me in your heart, I will send you a book or a person who will tell you.

The beauty of a spiritual community is that when you come together, you can help each other see things that you could not see in yourself. The more unconditional acceptance you can have in your community, the more you can help each other and the faster you can grow both individually and collectively. We have no greater desire than to see a spiritual movement, a spiritual community, that will manifest what very few communities have manifested throughout the ages, namely an environment where everyone is unconditionally accepted for who they are. This does not mean that this is a community where anything goes and where the ego and the people who are caught in a serpentine consciousness of wanting control and power can control the community. It means an environment where everyone can feel accepted.

If you can create such an environment, you have the greatest protection possible against those who seek to destroy or control. They will not be able to handle an environment where they are accepted. They want you to reject them, my beloved, because it confirms their essential illusion that they are separated from you and separated from God. This is the illusion they need in order to maintain their need to feel that they are better than others. They have not yet tired of playing the dualistic game.

My beloved, I leave you with the unconditional acceptance of a Mother's heart. I commend you for your willingness to share your heart flames. I ask you to ponder how to unconditionally accept each other. Do not forget to look in the mirror and work on unconditionally accepting yourself. I seal you in the unconditional acceptance of my Mother's heart, which truly can hold all people on this beautiful planet. Be at peace in my love.

20 | INVOKING THE POWER OF UNCONDITIONAL ACCEPTANCE

In the name I AM THAT I AM, Jesus Christ, I call to all representatives of the Divine Mother, especially Omega and Mother Mary, to help me accept myself as unconditionally as God accepts me. I call for you to help me overcome all illusions that stand in the way of my healing, especially…

[Make personal calls.]

1. I accept that God accepts me

1. It is only my conditions that prevent me from experiencing the kingdom that is within me.

> Omega, I now meditate,
> upon your throne in cosmic gate.
> I'm born out of the figure-eight,
> that Alpha and you co-create.

**O Song of Life, you vitalize,
all hearts you truly synchronize.
O Sacred Sound, you alchemize,
turn earth into a paradise.**

2. What separated me from God in the first place was conditions. I began to believe that I needed to fulfill certain conditions in this world in order to be worthy to enter the kingdom of God, which I had come to see as being outside myself.

> Omega, in your sacred space,
> my cosmic parents I embrace.
> I see that it is such a grace,
> that I take part in cosmic race.

**O Song of Life, you vitalize,
all hearts you truly synchronize.
O Sacred Sound, you alchemize,
turn earth into a paradise.**

3. My ego is programmed to think that in order to receive love, I need to live up to certain conditions. I am transcending any religion that says I must fulfill conditions in order to be worthy of God's love.

> Omega in the Central Sun,
> you show me life is cosmic fun.
> And thus a victory is won,
> my homeward journey has begun.

**O Song of Life, you vitalize,
all hearts you truly synchronize.
O Sacred Sound, you alchemize,
turn earth into a paradise.**

4. God will let me into the kingdom any time I let go of the conditions that I think keep me outside that kingdom.

Omega, femininity
is doorway to infinity.
With you I have affinity,
to know my own divinity.

**O Song of Life, you vitalize,
all hearts you truly synchronize.
O Sacred Sound, you alchemize,
turn earth into a paradise.**

5. The more pain I put myself through in order to buy my way into God's kingdom, the more distance I create in my mind between myself and God.

Omega, in your cosmic flow,
my plan divine I clearly know.
My heart is now a lamp aglow,
as love on all I do bestow.

**O Song of Life, you vitalize,
all hearts you truly synchronize.
O Sacred Sound, you alchemize,
turn earth into a paradise.**

6. I am experiencing that my Creator, my God, accepts me right now unconditionally for who I am.

> Omega, cosmic Mother Flame,
> this is the light from which I came.
> As I take part in cosmic game,
> Christ victory I do proclaim.
>
> **O Song of Life, you vitalize,**
> **all hearts you truly synchronize.**
> **O Sacred Sound, you alchemize,**
> **turn earth into a paradise.**

7. I was created out of a greater spiritual being who came out of an even greater spiritual being, and that chain of being reaches all the way to the Creator.

> Omega, I now comprehend,
> why I did to earth descend.
> And thus I fully do intend,
> to help this planet to ascend.
>
> **O Song of Life, you vitalize,**
> **all hearts you truly synchronize.**
> **O Sacred Sound, you alchemize,**
> **turn earth into a paradise.**

8. Because I was created out of the Creator's own Being, surely God the Creator accepts itself.

Omega, I do now aspire,
to join the ranks of cosmic choir.
My heart burns with a Christic fire,
that is this planet's sanctifier.

**O Song of Life, you vitalize,
all hearts you truly synchronize.
O Sacred Sound, you alchemize,
turn earth into a paradise.**

9. God the Creator accepts that part of its own Being that is imparted to me. God has unconditional acceptance for the part of my Being that truly is an individualization of the Creator.

Omega, my heart is ablaze,
my life is in an upward phase.
Come teach me now the secret phrase,
so that I can this planet raise.

**O Song of Life, you vitalize,
all hearts you truly synchronize.
O Sacred Sound, you alchemize,
turn earth into a paradise.**

2. I accept that I define my own path

1. Despite the fact that I have created an ego, that I have accepted conditions, that I have psychological issues and that I have done certain things in my life, God accepts me for who I am right this moment. God's acceptance of me is unconditional.

Omega, I now meditate,
upon your throne in cosmic gate.
I'm born out of the figure-eight,
that Alpha and you co-create.

**O Song of Life, you vitalize,
all hearts you truly synchronize.
O Sacred Sound, you alchemize,
turn earth into a paradise.**

2. The path I have to go through in order to return home is the path that I have created through the conditions that I have accepted.

Omega, in your sacred space,
my cosmic parents I embrace.
I see that it is such a grace,
that I take part in cosmic race.

**O Song of Life, you vitalize,
all hearts you truly synchronize.
O Sacred Sound, you alchemize,
turn earth into a paradise.**

3. The path I have to follow in order to qualify for my freedom is *not* fulfilling the outer conditions that I have come to accept. The path is to let go of those conditions!

Omega in the Central Sun,
you show me life is cosmic fun.
And thus a victory is won,
my homeward journey has begun.

**O Song of Life, you vitalize,
all hearts you truly synchronize.
O Sacred Sound, you alchemize,
turn earth into a paradise.**

4. My conditions are unreal, they are illusions, they are dualistic illusions created by the serpentine mind, by the fallen state of consciousness, by the consciousness of separation and duality.

Omega, femininity
is doorway to infinity.
With you I have affinity,
to know my own divinity.

**O Song of Life, you vitalize,
all hearts you truly synchronize.
O Sacred Sound, you alchemize,
turn earth into a paradise.**

5. I am at the point of surrender. I let go and say: "I don't need this belief anymore. I don't need this vicarious atonement. I don't need to feel like a sinner."

Omega, in your cosmic flow,
my plan divine I clearly know.
My heart is now a lamp aglow,
as love on all I do bestow.

**O Song of Life, you vitalize,
all hearts you truly synchronize.
O Sacred Sound, you alchemize,
turn earth into a paradise.**

6. I am transcending the approach that I have to live a good life according to a system on earth. The real path, the inner path, is to let go of the conditions that are inside of me.

> Omega, cosmic Mother Flame,
> this is the light from which I came.
> As I take part in cosmic game,
> Christ victory I do proclaim.

> **O Song of Life, you vitalize,**
> **all hearts you truly synchronize.**
> **O Sacred Sound, you alchemize,**
> **turn earth into a paradise.**

7. Trying to fulfill outer conditions only takes my attention away from the kingdom of God that is within me. I need no external kingdom. I need no external savior. I need no external church. I no *not* need to fulfill external conditions.

> Omega, I now comprehend,
> why I did to earth descend.
> And thus I fully do intend,
> to help this planet to ascend.

> **O Song of Life, you vitalize,**
> **all hearts you truly synchronize.**
> **O Sacred Sound, you alchemize,**
> **turn earth into a paradise.**

8. The real purpose for fulfilling outer conditions is to come to the point where I realize I do not need to fulfill those conditions. I am finding everything inside myself.

Omega, I do now aspire,
to join the ranks of cosmic choir.
My heart burns with a Christic fire,
that is this planet's sanctifier.

**O Song of Life, you vitalize,
all hearts you truly synchronize.
O Sacred Sound, you alchemize,
turn earth into a paradise.**

9. The essence of the spiritual path is to overcome the inner condition that makes me think I have to fulfill an outer condition. I am letting go of the outer conditions and I am being reborn of the Spirit.

Omega, my heart is ablaze,
my life is in an upward phase.
Come teach me now the secret phrase,
so that I can this planet raise.

**O Song of Life, you vitalize,
all hearts you truly synchronize.
O Sacred Sound, you alchemize,
turn earth into a paradise.**

3. I want a higher life experience

1. I understand Jesus' statement that in order to enter the kingdom, I must be born of water and I must be born of Spirit. Following an outer path is the process of being born of water, and being born of Spirit is the inner path.

Omega, I now meditate,
upon your throne in cosmic gate.
I'm born out of the figure-eight,
that Alpha and you co-create.

**O Song of Life, you vitalize,
all hearts you truly synchronize.
O Sacred Sound, you alchemize,
turn earth into a paradise.**

2. I am experiencing the total surrender – the unconditional surrender – that brings about the rebirth of the Spirit.

Omega, in your sacred space,
my cosmic parents I embrace.
I see that it is such a grace,
that I take part in cosmic race.

**O Song of Life, you vitalize,
all hearts you truly synchronize.
O Sacred Sound, you alchemize,
turn earth into a paradise.**

3. I accept who I am and I let go of what is unreal instead of holding on to it.

Omega in the Central Sun,
you show me life is cosmic fun.
And thus a victory is won,
my homeward journey has begun.

**O Song of Life, you vitalize,
all hearts you truly synchronize.
O Sacred Sound, you alchemize,
turn earth into a paradise.**

4. When I believe that in order to be saved, I have to fulfill outer conditions, the psychological mechanism that comes into play is that I cannot fully accept that I have these conditions. I cannot take ownership of them.

Omega, femininity
is doorway to infinity.
With you I have affinity,
to know my own divinity.

**O Song of Life, you vitalize,
all hearts you truly synchronize.
O Sacred Sound, you alchemize,
turn earth into a paradise.**

5. When I cannot take ownership of my conditions, I cannot surrender them. I now look at them and say: "This is unreal. I no longer need to carry this with me. I no longer need to accept this condition or to accept the belief that caused me to accept whatever illusion I have carried around for a long time."

Omega, in your cosmic flow,
my plan divine I clearly know.
My heart is now a lamp aglow,
as love on all I do bestow.

> **O Song of Life, you vitalize,**
> **all hearts you truly synchronize.**
> **O Sacred Sound, you alchemize,**
> **turn earth into a paradise.**

6. I look at my human condition and say: "This is unreal, this has to go." I will no longer ignore the beam in my own eye. I dismiss the illusion that if I put myself through this or that pain, then God will have to accept me. I am letting go of the conditions in my mind that keep me outside the inner kingdom.

> Omega, cosmic Mother Flame,
> this is the light from which I came.
> As I take part in cosmic game,
> Christ victory I do proclaim.

> **O Song of Life, you vitalize,**
> **all hearts you truly synchronize.**
> **O Sacred Sound, you alchemize,**
> **turn earth into a paradise.**

7. God accepts me for who I am right now. If God can accept me even though I might look at myself as being an imperfect human being, then certainly I can accept myself.

> Omega, I now comprehend,
> why I did to earth descend.
> And thus I fully do intend,
> to help this planet to ascend.

**O Song of Life, you vitalize,
all hearts you truly synchronize.
O Sacred Sound, you alchemize,
turn earth into a paradise.**

8. God has given me the right to create the experience that I am having right now because I have free will. God accepts that I have a right to create my present experience.

> Omega, I do now aspire,
> to join the ranks of cosmic choir.
> My heart burns with a Christic fire,
> that is this planet's sanctifier.

**O Song of Life, you vitalize,
all hearts you truly synchronize.
O Sacred Sound, you alchemize,
turn earth into a paradise.**

9. I can let go of the experience I have at any moment. I realize that my present experience is unreal and I say: "I have had enough of that experience. I don't want it anymore. I don't need it anymore."

> Omega, my heart is ablaze,
> my life is in an upward phase.
> Come teach me now the secret phrase,
> so that I can this planet raise.

**O Song of Life, you vitalize,
all hearts you truly synchronize.
O Sacred Sound, you alchemize,
turn earth into a paradise.**

4. I choose growth over comfortability

1. All of the outer conditions are unreal, and they cannot keep me outside the kingdom—unless I allow them to do so by continuing to accept them.

> Omega, I now meditate,
> upon your throne in cosmic gate.
> I'm born out of the figure-eight,
> that Alpha and you co-create.
>
> **O Song of Life, you vitalize,**
> **all hearts you truly synchronize.**
> **O Sacred Sound, you alchemize,**
> **turn earth into a paradise.**

2. The world wants me to continue to accept the conditions that I have come to believe and that the world still believes. My family, friends, society and the world at large want me to accept the conditions that they accept.

> Omega, in your sacred space,
> my cosmic parents I embrace.
> I see that it is such a grace,
> that I take part in cosmic race.
>
> **O Song of Life, you vitalize,**
> **all hearts you truly synchronize.**
> **O Sacred Sound, you alchemize,**
> **turn earth into a paradise.**

3. Other people do not want me to disturb them in their belief that they could not change themselves, that they don't have to take responsibility for their own lives and their own salvation.

> Omega in the Central Sun,
> you show me life is cosmic fun.
> And thus a victory is won,
> my homeward journey has begun.

> **O Song of Life, you vitalize,**
> **all hearts you truly synchronize.**
> **O Sacred Sound, you alchemize,**
> **turn earth into a paradise.**

4. I am transcending the idolatry of the saints and the sages who have stood out from the crowd. I accept that I can indeed do what they did.

> Omega, femininity
> is doorway to infinity.
> With you I have affinity,
> to know my own divinity.

> **O Song of Life, you vitalize,**
> **all hearts you truly synchronize.**
> **O Sacred Sound, you alchemize,**
> **turn earth into a paradise.**

5. What was special about Jesus and Mother Mary was their willingness to surrender everything, to flow with the inner prompting that came from their higher Beings.

Omega, in your cosmic flow,
my plan divine I clearly know.
My heart is now a lamp aglow,
as love on all I do bestow.

**O Song of Life, you vitalize,
all hearts you truly synchronize.
O Sacred Sound, you alchemize,
turn earth into a paradise.**

6. My ego is born of conditions. My ego believes that it could not survive without conditions. I am letting go of my conditions, and my ego has no hold over me and neither does the prince of this world.

Omega, cosmic Mother Flame,
this is the light from which I came.
As I take part in cosmic game,
Christ victory I do proclaim.

**O Song of Life, you vitalize,
all hearts you truly synchronize.
O Sacred Sound, you alchemize,
turn earth into a paradise.**

7. My ego does not want me to surrender because the more conditions I have, the more my ego has control over me and the more comfortable my ego feels.

Omega, I now comprehend,
why I did to earth descend.
And thus I fully do intend,
to help this planet to ascend.

**O Song of Life, you vitalize,
all hearts you truly synchronize.
O Sacred Sound, you alchemize,
turn earth into a paradise.**

8. I am letting go of the boxes that my ego has created and in which it feels like everything is under its control, including me.

Omega, I do now aspire,
to join the ranks of cosmic choir.
My heart burns with a Christic fire,
that is this planet's sanctifier.

**O Song of Life, you vitalize,
all hearts you truly synchronize.
O Sacred Sound, you alchemize,
turn earth into a paradise.**

9. I am coming away from my comfortability. I am walking the spiritual path and allowing it to change my life. I am gradually surrendering all of my conditions.

Omega, my heart is ablaze,
my life is in an upward phase.
Come teach me now the secret phrase,
so that I can this planet raise.

**O Song of Life, you vitalize,
all hearts you truly synchronize.
O Sacred Sound, you alchemize,
turn earth into a paradise.**

5. I continue to surrender

1. I die daily, I have some of my conditions die every day.

> Omega, I now meditate,
> upon your throne in cosmic gate.
> I'm born out of the figure-eight,
> that Alpha and you co-create.
>
> **O Song of Life, you vitalize,**
> **all hearts you truly synchronize.**
> **O Sacred Sound, you alchemize,**
> **turn earth into a paradise.**

2. The path is all about surrender. I continue to surrender until there is nothing more to surrender. I am willing to lose my life for the sake of following Christ.

> Omega, in your sacred space,
> my cosmic parents I embrace.
> I see that it is such a grace,
> that I take part in cosmic race.
>
> **O Song of Life, you vitalize,**
> **all hearts you truly synchronize.**
> **O Sacred Sound, you alchemize,**
> **turn earth into a paradise.**

3. I am at the point where it is easier to surrender the conditions because I am experiencing that the more I surrender, the more free I feel inside.

Omega in the Central Sun,
you show me life is cosmic fun.
And thus a victory is won,
my homeward journey has begun.

**O Song of Life, you vitalize,
all hearts you truly synchronize.
O Sacred Sound, you alchemize,
turn earth into a paradise.**

4. I am building a momentum, and I am realizing that surrender is not loss, surrender is not sacrifice, surrender is not the Via Dolorosa. Surrender is joy. Surrender is freedom. The more I let go of, the more free I am.

Omega, femininity
is doorway to infinity.
With you I have affinity,
to know my own divinity.

**O Song of Life, you vitalize,
all hearts you truly synchronize.
O Sacred Sound, you alchemize,
turn earth into a paradise.**

5. I accept Mother Omega's gift of surrender. I apply to your heart to help me surrender. Help me gain a clear vision of what to surrender. Help me see the illusion so I can let it go, for I am willing to lose all illusions in order to be one with you.

Omega, in your cosmic flow,
my plan divine I clearly know.
My heart is now a lamp aglow,
as love on all I do bestow.

**O Song of Life, you vitalize,
all hearts you truly synchronize.
O Sacred Sound, you alchemize,
turn earth into a paradise.**

6. Mother Omega, I ask you to show me what to surrender, and I will listen for your answer from within and without.

Omega, cosmic Mother Flame,
this is the light from which I came.
As I take part in cosmic game,
Christ victory I do proclaim.

**O Song of Life, you vitalize,
all hearts you truly synchronize.
O Sacred Sound, you alchemize,
turn earth into a paradise.**

7. Mother Omega, I receive the unconditional acceptance of your Mother's heart.

Omega, I now comprehend,
why I did to earth descend.
And thus I fully do intend,
to help this planet to ascend.

**O Song of Life, you vitalize,
all hearts you truly synchronize.
O Sacred Sound, you alchemize,
turn earth into a paradise.**

8. I am looking in the mirror, and I am unconditionally accepting myself. I am unconditionally accepting others.

Omega, I do now aspire,
to join the ranks of cosmic choir.
My heart burns with a Christic fire,
that is this planet's sanctifier.

**O Song of Life, you vitalize,
all hearts you truly synchronize.
O Sacred Sound, you alchemize,
turn earth into a paradise.**

9. Mother Omega, seal me in the unconditional acceptance of your Mother's heart. I am at peace in your love.

Omega, my heart is ablaze,
my life is in an upward phase.
Come teach me now the secret phrase,
so that I can this planet raise.

**O Song of Life, you vitalize,
all hearts you truly synchronize.
O Sacred Sound, you alchemize,
turn earth into a paradise.**

Sealing

In the name of the Divine Mother, I call to Omega and Mother Mary for the sealing of myself and all people in the creative flow of the Divine Mother, the River of Life. I call for the multiplication of my calls by all representatives of the Divine Mother, so that we form the perfect figure-eight flow of "As Above, so below." Thus, I accept that this is fully manifest, because the mouth of the Lord, the Divine Mother that I AM, has spoken it. Amen.

21 | HOW TO RISE ABOVE THE PAST

Excerpt from a dictation by Gautama Buddha, May 20, 2007.

When you cannot fix the past – when you cannot change it – how can you be free of it? You can be free in only one way—by letting it go! You can be free of the past, not by holding on to the anger and hatred against another group of people, not by seeking to compensate for the wrong that was done to your people in the past by committing a greater wrong by destroying those who have wronged you before.

You can be free of the past only through forgiveness, but only through the special type of forgiveness that is unconditional forgiveness. Even though the world has a hard time understanding unconditional forgiveness, if you will think about this, you will realize that there is no other form of forgiveness but unconditional forgiveness. As long as there are conditions, you have not truly forgiven, have you, my beloved? Nay, you have not.

You have in fact created a very subtle sense of logic, which gives your ego an excuse for not forgiving other people. You have in your mind set up conditions that say that only if they live up to those conditions, are they worthy of your forgiveness. Your forgiveness is now no longer determined by *you* making the choice to forgive; it will be determined by the choices *they* make.

What have you done with this subtle reasoning? You have given away your own power over your own destiny. You have put your destiny in the hands of other people. Who are the people in whose hands you have put your destiny? Are they not the very people that you see as having wronged you in the past? What sense does it make that you would allow them to control your future by letting your forgiveness be conditioned upon their response or non-response?

Do you see that this makes no sense whatsoever? If someone has wronged you, why would you want to in any way be dependent upon them? Would you not want to be free of those who have wronged you so they can no longer control you. How can you be free from other people? Well, you can only be free through total and unconditional forgiveness.

When you forgive other people, you are not setting *them* free; you are setting *yourself* free. If they are not willing to come up higher and forgive you, then they will be left in their old state of consciousness. You will transcend that dualistic state of consciousness and rise higher. As we have said, the universe is a mirror. It will inevitably reflect back to you conditions that reflect your higher state of consciousness. Those who were your enemies and not willing to forgive will receive back conditions that reflect *their* state of consciousness. They will still have an enemy, but it will not be you, for you are now free to rise above the dualistic struggle.

When you look at this continent of Europe, you will see that there are places where entire groups of people are so focused on the past that it is literally consuming their present and overpowering their vision of the future. They do not have the ability or even the courage to envision a better future, a golden future. How shall there ever be a better future, as long as people are so focused on the past that the past becomes prologue and sets the pattern for continuing the dualistic struggle that has been going on for centuries?

For things to change, there must be some who will come to the realization that they want to be free and that they cannot be free by seeking to change the past, by seeking to right the wrongs of the past. They can be free only by *forgiving* the wrongs of the past, by leaving them behind and rising above the old state of consciousness, the old view of other people, the old view of themselves, and the old feelings of anger, hatred, fear, or the sense of being threatened.

It is the sense of struggle that creates the struggle. It is *your* consciousness that sets the stage for what you experience in the physical. If you seek to change outer conditions before you change your consciousness, you are, as the old saying goes, putting the cart before the horse and you will get nowhere.

Understanding the office of Lord of the World

What I shall anchor on this continent is my momentum of unconditional forgiveness. I, Gautama Buddha, do indeed hold the office that is titled "Lord of the World." How did I ascend to become worthy of that office? We have explained that you have an I AM Presence and that there is light flowing from your I AM Presence into your lower being. It is this light that sustains you – even sustains the physical body – and you could not survive without it.

The light from your I AM Presence does indeed flow through the Office of the Lord of the World. It flows through my I AM Presence, my heart. This means, my beloved, that as the Lord of the World, I literally hold in my heart the life of every human being embodying on this planet. If I were to do so, I could snuff out the life, the life-force, in any human being—even groups of people or even the entire human race.

How can one become worthy to hold that office? One can do so only when one has overcome all tendency towards anger, or hatred, or animosity. If there was the slightest aspect of such human emotions, it would be entirely possible that I would look down upon the earth and become annoyed by certain human beings who would not learn their lessons. Thus, in that anger, I might snuff out the flame in their hearts.

This would be a violation of the Law of Free Will. God has mandated that people have opportunity for a certain time. If I were to arbitrarily decide that someone should have taken away their opportunity, I would violate that law. Certainly, as Lord of the World, I cannot be in violation of the laws that I am entrusted to uphold. I can only be worthy of this office by embodying the Flame of Unconditional Forgiveness, whereby I forgive people even before they have committed a wrong. It is truly unconditional forgiveness when there is no wrong that human beings on earth could commit that could disturb me in any way and cause me to leave the Flame of Peace that I am and that I hold for the earth.

In order to ascend to this office, I have indeed built a considerable momentum of unconditional forgiveness. The special dispensation that I hereby bring to this continent is that I will anchor that momentum on the continent of Europe [You can take advantage of this dispensation no matter where you live]. I will offer a vast multiplication factor for anyone who desires to practice unconditional forgiveness in their personal lives, and anyone who desires to become an example for others, and even speak out about the necessity of unconditional forgiveness, giving forth the teachings I have given in this release and that we have given in other dictations. As the Lord of the World, I am indeed looking for the faithful servants who will be faithful over a few things so that I can make them ruler over many things. Not in the sense that you have physical power over other people, but in the sense that I can multiply your momentum of unconditional forgiveness so that you can become shining examples for others.

An opportunity to let go of non-forgiveness

Do not forget to look in the mirror and practice unconditional forgiveness towards yourself. Many of you find it easier to forgive others than to forgive yourself. But unconditional forgiveness is unconditional, meaning that it is not dependent upon any conditions on earth. In order to forgive your neighbor unconditionally, you must be willing to look beyond his or her imperfections, and so you must do with yourself.

If forgiveness is unconditional, what conditions could you possibly have to fulfill in order to be worthy of that unconditional forgiveness? Do you not see the logic of this? You do not need to *become* worthy of unconditional forgiveness. You *are* worthy of it right now.

As the sealing of this release, I offer you the opportunity to take all non-forgiveness of yourself, all sense of being imperfect, of not being good enough, of having made this or that mistake. I give you the opportunity that I will take all of it as you perform the following meditation:

1. Envision how you gather the imperfections from all corners of your forcefield, all corners of your aura. You draw them together, and you might envision them as black threads that are interwoven with the fabric of your

being. Visualize how you pull them out of your being as so many black threads.

2. You pull them together and you pull them tighter and tighter towards your heart. In the light of your heart, you begin to see them. You pull them together in a ball.

3. Visualize how you cram together that ball, making it tighter and tighter, as if it was a roll of yarn or string that at first is somewhat unruly, but as you keep pulling it together, it becomes more and more compact until it is so small that you can hold it in both of your hands.

4. Envision that you hold that ball of yarn of non-forgiveness in your hands, and you throw it into the burning furnace of my heart chakra. My heart burns with a light so bright that it will instantly consume any imperfection on earth. Be not concerned about my ability to be able to consume and transmute this substance. Am I not the Lord of the World? Truly, there is nothing you can have that could be so bad that I could not consume it.

5. Take it now and throw it into my heart chakra and see how it is consumed instantly upon touching the fire of my fiery love for you.

6. Now accept that you are free of this non-forgiveness.

7. Accept that you are worthy of the unconditional forgiveness.

8. Accept that I, Gautama Buddha, the Lord of the World, has forgiven you unconditionally and completely.

As Jesus said: "Thy sins be forgiven thee. Now go and sin no more." Do not go back into the old momentums and recreate the non-forgiveness of yourself—even if you continue to make certain mistakes. When you make the mistake, seek honestly to learn from it but then forgive yourself rather than holding on to it.

The very fact that you are open to these teachings – the new teachings of the Christ and Buddha for the Aquarian Age – demonstrates that you have the potential to be one of the forerunners for the Golden Age. How can you fulfill that mission if you hold on to non-forgiveness of yourself? How can you demonstrate forgiveness to others if you do not practice it towards yourself? Forgive yourself, and let go of the conditions that your ego and the forces of this world are using in order to trick you into thinking that you are not worthy of forgiveness. They might even trick you into believing the age-old lie of the serpentine mind that once you have made a certain mistake, you are doomed forever and can never be redeemed.

I tell you, the reality is that God has no other desire than to see you rise above all imperfections on earth and become the God-free being you were created to be. You can rise only when you accept unconditional forgiveness. What I have said applies on a continental scale, it applies on an individual scale. You cannot right the wrongs of the past. You can only learn from them and then let them go by unconditionally forgiving yourself.

My beloved, I have said my peace, and I seal you in the Flame of Unconditional Forgiveness. Allow yourself to feel the Presence of the Buddha where you are.

When everything is the Buddha nature, then *you* are the Buddha nature. You are already the Buddha—if you could only accept it and accept it unconditionally. When you *are* already the Buddha, how could there be conditions that you have to fulfill before you *become* the Buddha? Ponder the eternal truth that the ego and the intellect can never fathom: You cannot *become* the Buddha. You can only *be* the Buddha.

22 | INVOKING FREEDOM FROM THE PAST

In the name I AM THAT I AM, Jesus Christ, I call to all representatives of the Divine Mother, especially Gautama Buddha and Mother Mary, to help me attain the non-attachment of the Buddha and be free from my past. I call for you to help me overcome all illusions that stand in the way of my healing, especially…

[Make personal calls.]

1. I will not let others control me

1. I cannot fix the past. I cannot change it. I can be free of the past in only one way—by letting it go!

> Gautama, show my mental state
> that does give rise to love and hate,
> your exposé I do endure,
> so my perception will be pure.

> Gautama, Flame of Cosmic Peace,
> unruly thoughts do hereby cease,
> we radiate from you and me
> the peace to still Samsara's Sea.

2. I can be free of the past not by holding on to the anger and hatred, not by seeking to compensate for the wrong that was done in the past by committing a greater wrong, not by destroying those who have wronged me before.

> Gautama, in your Flame of Peace,
> the struggling self I now release,
> the Buddha Nature I now see,
> it is the core of you and me.

> **Gautama, Flame of Cosmic Peace,
> unruly thoughts do hereby cease,
> we radiate from you and me
> the peace to still Samsara's Sea.**

3. I am free of the past only through forgiveness, but only through the special type of forgiveness that is unconditional forgiveness.

> Gautama, I am one with thee,
> Mara's demons do now flee,
> your Presence like a soothing balm,
> my mind and senses ever calm.

> **Gautama, Flame of Cosmic Peace,
> unruly thoughts do hereby cease,
> we radiate from you and me
> the peace to still Samsara's Sea.**

22 | Invoking Freedom from the Past

4. There is no other form of forgiveness but unconditional forgiveness. As long as there are conditions, I have not truly forgiven.

> Gautama, I now take the vow,
> to live in the eternal now,
> with you I do transcend all time,
> to live in present so sublime.

> **Gautama, Flame of Cosmic Peace,**
> **unruly thoughts do hereby cease,**
> **we radiate from you and me**
> **the peace to still Samsara's Sea.**

5. I am transcending the ego's subtle sense of logic, which gives me an excuse for not forgiving other people. I am transcending the conditions that say that only if others live up to those conditions, are they worthy of my forgiveness.

> Gautama, I have no desire,
> to nothing earthly I aspire,
> in non-attachment I now rest,
> passing Mara's subtle test.

> **Gautama, Flame of Cosmic Peace,**
> **unruly thoughts do hereby cease,**
> **we radiate from you and me**
> **the peace to still Samsara's Sea.**

6. I am transcending the catch-22 where my forgiveness is not determined by me making the choice to forgive; it is determined by the choices others make. I take back my power to forgive.

> Gautama, I melt into you,
> my mind is one, no longer two,
> immersed in your resplendent glow,
> Nirvana is all that I know.
>
> **Gautama, Flame of Cosmic Peace,
> unruly thoughts do hereby cease,
> we radiate from you and me
> the peace to still Samsara's Sea.**

7. I am transcending the illusion that causes me to give away my power over my destiny by putting it in the hands of other people.

> Gautama, in your timeless space,
> I am immersed in Cosmic Grace,
> I know the God beyond all form,
> to world I will no more conform.
>
> **Gautama, Flame of Cosmic Peace,
> unruly thoughts do hereby cease,
> we radiate from you and me
> the peace to still Samsara's Sea.**

8. The people in whose hands I have put my destiny are the very people that I see as having wronged me in the past. I will not allow them to control my future by letting my forgiveness be conditioned upon their response or non-response.

> Gautama, I am now awake,
> I clearly see what is at stake,
> and thus I claim my sacred right
> to be on earth the Buddhic Light.

> Gautama, Flame of Cosmic Peace,
> unruly thoughts do hereby cease,
> we radiate from you and me
> the peace to still Samsara's Sea.

9. I do not want to in any way be dependent upon those who have hurt me. I am free of those who have wronged me, and they can no longer control me.

> Gautama, with your thunderbolt,
> we give the earth a mighty jolt,
> I know that some will understand,
> and join the Buddha's timeless band.

> Gautama, Flame of Cosmic Peace,
> unruly thoughts do hereby cease,
> we radiate from you and me
> the peace to still Samsara's Sea.

2. I am free from other people

1. I can be free of other people only through total and unconditional forgiveness.

> Gautama, show my mental state
> that does give rise to love and hate,
> your exposé I do endure,
> so my perception will be pure.

**Gautama, Flame of Cosmic Peace,
unruly thoughts do hereby cease,
we radiate from you and me
the peace to still Samsara's Sea.**

2. When I forgive other people, I am not setting *them* free; I am setting *myself* free.

Gautama, in your Flame of Peace,
the struggling self I now release,
the Buddha Nature I now see,
it is the core of you and me.

**Gautama, Flame of Cosmic Peace,
unruly thoughts do hereby cease,
we radiate from you and me
the peace to still Samsara's Sea.**

3. If others are not willing to come up higher and forgive me, they will be left in their old state of consciousness. I am transcending that dualistic state of consciousness and rising higher.

Gautama, I am one with thee,
Mara's demons do now flee,
your Presence like a soothing balm,
my mind and senses ever calm.

**Gautama, Flame of Cosmic Peace,
unruly thoughts do hereby cease,
we radiate from you and me
the peace to still Samsara's Sea.**

4. The universe is a mirror and will reflect back to me conditions that reflect my higher state of consciousness. Those who are not willing to forgive, will receive back conditions that reflect *their* state of consciousness. They will still have an enemy, but it will not be me, for I am now free and I rise above the dualistic struggle.

> Gautama, I now take the vow,
> to live in the eternal now,
> with you I do transcend all time,
> to live in present so sublime.

> **Gautama, Flame of Cosmic Peace,**
> **unruly thoughts do hereby cease,**
> **we radiate from you and me**
> **the peace to still Samsara's Sea.**

5. I am transcending the ego's trap of being so focused on the past that it is consuming my present and overpowering my vision of the future. I have the ability and the courage to envision a better future, a golden future.

> Gautama, I have no desire,
> to nothing earthly I aspire,
> in non-attachment I now rest,
> passing Mara's subtle test.

> **Gautama, Flame of Cosmic Peace,**
> **unruly thoughts do hereby cease,**
> **we radiate from you and me**
> **the peace to still Samsara's Sea.**

6. I am transcending the ego's trap of being so focused on the past that the past becomes prologue and sets the pattern for continuing the dualistic struggle that has been going on for centuries.

> Gautama, I melt into you,
> my mind is one, no longer two,
> immersed in your resplendent glow,
> Nirvana is all that I know.

> **Gautama, Flame of Cosmic Peace,**
> **unruly thoughts do hereby cease,**
> **we radiate from you and me**
> **the peace to still Samsara's Sea.**

7. I cannot be free by seeking to change the past, by seeking to right the wrongs of the past. I am free because I am forgiving the wrongs of the past, I am leaving them behind and rising above the old state of consciousness. I surrender the old view of other people, the old view of myself, and the old feelings of anger, hatred, fear, or the sense of being threatened.

> Gautama, in your timeless space,
> I am immersed in Cosmic Grace,
> I know the God beyond all form,
> to world I will no more conform.

> **Gautama, Flame of Cosmic Peace,**
> **unruly thoughts do hereby cease,**
> **we radiate from you and me**
> **the peace to still Samsara's Sea.**

8. It is the sense of struggle that creates the struggle. It is my consciousness that sets the stage for what I experience in the physical.

> Gautama, I am now awake,
> I clearly see what is at stake,
> and thus I claim my sacred right
> to be on earth the Buddhic Light.

> **Gautama, Flame of Cosmic Peace,**
> **unruly thoughts do hereby cease,**
> **we radiate from you and me**
> **the peace to still Samsara's Sea.**

9. I am transcending the ego's trap of seeking to change outer conditions before I change my consciousness. I see this is putting the cart before the horse and I will get nowhere.

> Gautama, with your thunderbolt,
> we give the earth a mighty jolt,
> I know that some will understand,
> and join the Buddha's timeless band.

> **Gautama, Flame of Cosmic Peace,**
> **unruly thoughts do hereby cease,**
> **we radiate from you and me**
> **the peace to still Samsara's Sea.**

3. I am an example of forgiveness

1. I am tied in to Gautama Buddha's momentum of unconditional forgiveness.

Gautama, show my mental state
that does give rise to love and hate,
your exposé I do endure,
so my perception will be pure.

**Gautama, Flame of Cosmic Peace,
unruly thoughts do hereby cease,
we radiate from you and me
the peace to still Samsara's Sea.**

2. I am surrendering the ego's tendency towards anger, hatred or animosity.

Gautama, in your Flame of Peace,
the struggling self I now release,
the Buddha Nature I now see,
it is the core of you and me.

**Gautama, Flame of Cosmic Peace,
unruly thoughts do hereby cease,
we radiate from you and me
the peace to still Samsara's Sea.**

3. I accept the Law of Free Will. God has mandated that people have opportunity for a certain time, and I have no opinion or judgment about how others exercise their God-given opportunity.

Gautama, I am one with thee,
Mara's demons do now flee,
your Presence like a soothing balm,
my mind and senses ever calm.

22 | Invoking Freedom from the Past

**Gautama, Flame of Cosmic Peace,
unruly thoughts do hereby cease,
we radiate from you and me
the peace to still Samsara's Sea.**

4. I am embodying the Flame of Unconditional Forgiveness. I am forgiving people even before they have committed a wrong.

Gautama, I now take the vow,
to live in the eternal now,
with you I do transcend all time,
to live in present so sublime.

**Gautama, Flame of Cosmic Peace,
unruly thoughts do hereby cease,
we radiate from you and me
the peace to still Samsara's Sea.**

5. There is no wrong that human beings on earth could commit that could disturb me in any way and cause me to leave the Flame of Peace that I am holding for the earth.

Gautama, I have no desire,
to nothing earthly I aspire,
in non-attachment I now rest,
passing Mara's subtle test.

**Gautama, Flame of Cosmic Peace,
unruly thoughts do hereby cease,
we radiate from you and me
the peace to still Samsara's Sea.**

6. I am taking advantage of Gautama Buddha's momentum of unconditional forgiveness. I accept the multiplication factor, and I am practicing unconditional forgiveness in my personal life.

> Gautama, I melt into you,
> my mind is one, no longer two,
> immersed in your resplendent glow,
> Nirvana is all that I know.
>
> **Gautama, Flame of Cosmic Peace,**
> **unruly thoughts do hereby cease,**
> **we radiate from you and me**
> **the peace to still Samsara's Sea.**

7. I am an example for others, and I am speaking out about the necessity of unconditional forgiveness.

> Gautama, in your timeless space,
> I am immersed in Cosmic Grace,
> I know the God beyond all form,
> to world I will no more conform.
>
> **Gautama, Flame of Cosmic Peace,**
> **unruly thoughts do hereby cease,**
> **we radiate from you and me**
> **the peace to still Samsara's Sea.**

8. I am Gautama's faithful servant. He is multiplying my momentum of unconditional forgiveness and I am becoming a shining example for others.

Gautama, I am now awake,
I clearly see what is at stake,
and thus I claim my sacred right
to be on earth the Buddhic Light.

**Gautama, Flame of Cosmic Peace,
unruly thoughts do hereby cease,
we radiate from you and me
the peace to still Samsara's Sea.**

9. I am looking in the mirror and practicing unconditional forgiveness towards myself. I am forgiving others and I am forgiving myself.

Gautama, with your thunderbolt,
we give the earth a mighty jolt,
I know that some will understand,
and join the Buddha's timeless band.

**Gautama, Flame of Cosmic Peace,
unruly thoughts do hereby cease,
we radiate from you and me
the peace to still Samsara's Sea.**

4. I give my non-forgiveness to Gautama

1. Unconditional forgiveness is unconditional, meaning that it is not dependent upon any conditions on earth. I am looking beyond the imperfections of both other people and myself.

Gautama, show my mental state
that does give rise to love and hate,
your exposé I do endure,
so my perception will be pure.

**Gautama, Flame of Cosmic Peace,
unruly thoughts do hereby cease,
we radiate from you and me
the peace to still Samsara's Sea.**

2. Since forgiveness is unconditional, what conditions could I possibly have to fulfill in order to be worthy of it?

Gautama, in your Flame of Peace,
the struggling self I now release,
the Buddha Nature I now see,
it is the core of you and me.

**Gautama, Flame of Cosmic Peace,
unruly thoughts do hereby cease,
we radiate from you and me
the peace to still Samsara's Sea.**

3. I do not need to become worthy of unconditional forgiveness. I am worthy of it right now.

Gautama, I am one with thee,
Mara's demons do now flee,
your Presence like a soothing balm,
my mind and senses ever calm.

> **Gautama, Flame of Cosmic Peace,**
> **unruly thoughts do hereby cease,**
> **we radiate from you and me**
> **the peace to still Samsara's Sea.**

4. I am willing to let Gautama take all non-forgiveness of myself, all sense of being imperfect, of not being good enough, of having made this or that mistake.

> Gautama, I now take the vow,
> to live in the eternal now,
> with you I do transcend all time,
> to live in present so sublime.

> **Gautama, Flame of Cosmic Peace,**
> **unruly thoughts do hereby cease,**
> **we radiate from you and me**
> **the peace to still Samsara's Sea.**

5. I now gather the imperfections from all corners of my forcefield, all corners of my aura. I draw them together as black threads that are interwoven with the fabric of my being. I pull them out of my being.

> Gautama, I have no desire,
> to nothing earthly I aspire,
> in non-attachment I now rest,
> passing Mara's subtle test.

> **Gautama, Flame of Cosmic Peace,**
> **unruly thoughts do hereby cease,**
> **we radiate from you and me**
> **the peace to still Samsara's Sea.**

6. I pull them together and I pull them tighter and tighter towards my heart. In the light of my heart, I begin to see them. I pull them together in a ball.

> Gautama, I melt into you,
> my mind is one, no longer two,
> immersed in your resplendent glow,
> Nirvana is all that I know.
>
> **Gautama, Flame of Cosmic Peace,**
> **unruly thoughts do hereby cease,**
> **we radiate from you and me**
> **the peace to still Samsara's Sea.**

7. I cram together that ball, making it tighter and tighter, and it becomes more and more compact until it is so small that I can hold it in both of my hands.

> Gautama, in your timeless space,
> I am immersed in Cosmic Grace,
> I know the God beyond all form,
> to world I will no more conform.
>
> **Gautama, Flame of Cosmic Peace,**
> **unruly thoughts do hereby cease,**
> **we radiate from you and me**
> **the peace to still Samsara's Sea.**

8. I hold the ball of yarn of non-forgiveness in my hands, and I throw it into the burning furnace of Gautama's heart chakra. Gautama's heart burns with a light so bright that it will instantly consume any imperfection on earth.

22 | Invoking Freedom from the Past

> Gautama, I am now awake,
> I clearly see what is at stake,
> and thus I claim my sacred right
> to be on earth the Buddhic Light.
>
> **Gautama, Flame of Cosmic Peace,**
> **unruly thoughts do hereby cease,**
> **we radiate from you and me**
> **the peace to still Samsara's Sea.**

9. I take it now and throw it into Gautama's heart chakra. I see how it is consumed instantly upon touching the fire of his fiery love for me.

> Gautama, with your thunderbolt,
> we give the earth a mighty jolt,
> I know that some will understand,
> and join the Buddha's timeless band.
>
> **Gautama, Flame of Cosmic Peace,**
> **unruly thoughts do hereby cease,**
> **we radiate from you and me**
> **the peace to still Samsara's Sea.**

5. I accept that I am the Buddha

1. I now accept that I am free of all non-forgiveness. I accept that I am worthy of Gautama's unconditional forgiveness.

> Gautama, show my mental state
> that does give rise to love and hate,
> your exposé I do endure,
> so my perception will be pure.
>
> **Gautama, Flame of Cosmic Peace,**
> **unruly thoughts do hereby cease,**
> **we radiate from you and me**
> **the peace to still Samsara's Sea.**

2. I accept that Gautama Buddha, the Lord of the World, has forgiven me unconditionally and completely.

> Gautama, in your Flame of Peace,
> the struggling self I now release,
> the Buddha Nature I now see,
> it is the core of you and me.
>
> **Gautama, Flame of Cosmic Peace,**
> **unruly thoughts do hereby cease,**
> **we radiate from you and me**
> **the peace to still Samsara's Sea.**

3. I will not go back into the old momentums and recreate the non-forgiveness of myself. When I make a mistake, I seek honestly to learn from it but then forgive myself rather than holding on to it.

> Gautama, I am one with thee,
> Mara's demons do now flee,
> your Presence like a soothing balm,
> my mind and senses ever calm.

> **Gautama, Flame of Cosmic Peace,
> unruly thoughts do hereby cease,
> we radiate from you and me
> the peace to still Samsara's Sea.**

4. I am one of the forerunners for the Golden Age. How can I fulfill that mission if I hold on to non-forgiveness of myself? How can I demonstrate forgiveness to others if I do not practice it towards myself?

> Gautama, I now take the vow,
> to live in the eternal now,
> with you I do transcend all time,
> to live in present so sublime.

> **Gautama, Flame of Cosmic Peace,
> unruly thoughts do hereby cease,
> we radiate from you and me
> the peace to still Samsara's Sea.**

5. I am forgiving myself. I am letting go of the conditions that my ego and the forces of this world are using in order to trick me into thinking that I am not worthy of forgiveness. I am letting go of the serpentine lie that once I have made a certain mistake, I am doomed forever and can never be redeemed.

> Gautama, I have no desire,
> to nothing earthly I aspire,
> in non-attachment I now rest,
> passing Mara's subtle test.

> **Gautama, Flame of Cosmic Peace,**
> **unruly thoughts do hereby cease,**
> **we radiate from you and me**
> **the peace to still Samsara's Sea.**

6. God has no other desire than to see me rise above all imperfections on earth and become the God-free being I am created to be. I can rise only when I accept unconditional forgiveness.

> Gautama, I melt into you,
> my mind is one, no longer two,
> immersed in your resplendent glow,
> Nirvana is all that I know.

> **Gautama, Flame of Cosmic Peace,**
> **unruly thoughts do hereby cease,**
> **we radiate from you and me**
> **the peace to still Samsara's Sea.**

7. I cannot right the wrongs of the past. I can only learn from them and then let them go by unconditionally forgiving myself.

> Gautama, in your timeless space,
> I am immersed in Cosmic Grace,
> I know the God beyond all form,
> to world I will no more conform.

> **Gautama, Flame of Cosmic Peace,**
> **unruly thoughts do hereby cease,**
> **we radiate from you and me**
> **the peace to still Samsara's Sea.**

8. I am feeling the Peace and the Presence of the Buddha where I am. Since *everything* is the Buddha nature, then *I* am the Buddha nature. I am already the Buddha and I accept it unconditionally.

> Gautama, I am now awake,
> I clearly see what is at stake,
> and thus I claim my sacred right
> to be on earth the Buddhic Light.

> **Gautama, Flame of Cosmic Peace,**
> **unruly thoughts do hereby cease,**
> **we radiate from you and me**
> **the peace to still Samsara's Sea.**

9. I am already the Buddha. There can be no conditions that I have to fulfill before I become the Buddha. I cannot *become* the Buddha. I can only *be* the Buddha—and *I AM*.

> Gautama, with your thunderbolt,
> we give the earth a mighty jolt,
> I know that some will understand,
> and join the Buddha's timeless band.

> **Gautama, Flame of Cosmic Peace,**
> **unruly thoughts do hereby cease,**
> **we radiate from you and me**
> **the peace to still Samsara's Sea.**

Sealing

In the name of the Divine Mother, I call to Gautama and Mother Mary for the sealing of myself and all people in the creative flow of the Divine Mother, the River of Life. I call for the multiplication of my calls by all representatives of the Divine Mother, so that we form the perfect figure-eight flow of "As Above, so below." Thus, I accept that this is fully manifest, because the mouth of the Lord, the Divine Mother that I AM, has spoken it. Amen.

About the Author

Kim Michaels is an accomplished writer and author. He has conducted spiritual conferences and workshops in 14 countries, has counseled hundreds of spiritual students and has done numerous radio shows on spiritual topics. Kim has been on the spiritual path since 1976. He has studied a wide variety of spiritual teachings and practiced many techniques for raising consciousness. Since 2002 he has served as a messenger for Jesus and other ascended masters. He has brought forth extensive teachings about the mystical path, many of them available for free on his websites: *www.askrealjesus.com, www.ascendedmasteranswers.com, www.ascendedmasterlight.com* and *www.transcendencetoolbox.com*. For personal information, visit Kim at *www.KimMichaels.info*.

Transcendence Toolbooks, vol 1

Flowing with the River of Life Exercise Book

This book is the companion to "Flowing With the River of Life" and contains four unique invocations based on the teachings by the Maha Chohan. The invocations are designed to help you accomplish the following:

- Rise above the death consciousness,
- Attain freedom from aggressive spirits seeking to influence you,
- Expose the spirit in your own being that is holding you back right now,
- Help you let go of spirits in your own being.

This book also contains abbreviated teachings on the death consciousness and how you create and transcend spirits.

Part two of the book contains all of the decrees you use in the seven-month vigil to the spiritual rays. This vigil is designed to help you become familiar with the creative energies of the seven rays and thus unlock your creative potential. You will also find short descriptions of the pure qualities and the perversions of each ray.

Transcendence Toolbooks, vol 2

The Song of Life Healing Matrix

Every day we experience situations where we are exposed to uncertainties, mental or emotional disturbances, positive or negative stress. Everything we go through leaves a mark on our personal story. Some are uplifting positive memories, others are painful to a degree that we suppress them in order to escape the trauma. Each detail of our personal story reveals part of who we are and what blocks our growth. In these spheres of our personal stories we hide our deepest beliefs, concepts, feelings and thoughts that all affect the way we look at life, each other and ourselves. This often generates diseases in our mental, emotional or physical bodies.

The Song of Life Healing Matrix provides you with the unique tools to bring to light the deepest details of your of own song of life. This highly effective tool contains the teachings from eight representatives of the Divine Mother–the ascended masters who represent the Divine Feminine for planet earth. They address the blocks to your personal healing and introduce a highly effective tool for sound healing in the form of the Song Life. The eight invocations that you can easily learn, allow you to call forth the following types of healing:

- The transformation of your sense of identity so you realize you are a spiritual being in a human body.

- The clearing of your mental body from all blocking illusions and destructive thought patterns.
- The healing of emotional wounds and the release of the accumulated negative feelings that reinforce self-destructive reactionary patterns.
- The healing of the organs and systems in your physical body from any disease.
- The healing of all lack of balance that prevents you from manifesting your goals in life.
- The healing of all sense of lack that block the manifestation of a spiritually and materially abundant life.
- The healing of all blocks to your acceptance of unconditional love and the flow of love through your being.
- The healing of the denial of your true identity as a co-creator with God and the fact that we are all are part of the Divine Feminine.

www.ingramcontent.com/pod-product-compliance
Lightning Source LLC
Chambersburg PA
CBHW031419150426
43191CB00006B/330